ON THE FRINGE

ON THE FRINGE

Living in the Realms of Hitler and Stalin

Katherine Harrison

Book Guild Publishing
Sussex, England

SUFFOLK COUNTY COUNCIL	
07046626	
Bertrams	29.01.08
327.41	£17.99
159078	

First published in Great Britain in 2007 by
The Book Guild Ltd
Pavilion View
19 New Road
Brighton, BN1 1UF

Copyright © Katherine Harrison 2007

The right of Katherine Harrison to be identified as the author of this work has been asserted by her in accordance with the Copyright, Designs and Patents Act 1988.

All rights reserved. No part of this publication may be reproduced, transmitted, or stored in a retrieval system, in any form or by any means, without permission in writing from the publisher, nor be otherwise circulated in any form of binding or cover other than that in which it is published and without a similar condition being imposed on the subsequent purchaser.

Typesetting in Times by
YHT Ltd, Middlesex

Printed in Great Britain by
Athenaeum Press Ltd, Gateshead

A catalogue record for this book is available from
The British Library.

ISBN 978 1 84624 156 7

Contents

Preface: On the Fringe: Living in the Realms of Hitler and Stalin — xi

I   Berlin, 1937–1939   1

II   Moscow, 1947–1949   43

III   Back to Moscow, 1965–1968   115

Index   275

Foreword

The kick-start to writing these memoirs was given to me by the Globetrotters of Horsham U3A (University of the Third Age), a group I had belonged to when living in the Horsham district. During my first summer here in Hampshire I received a letter from the Globetrotters asking me if I would write something for them on Countries of Ice and Snow. My answer was: '*Countries of Ice and Snow* is a vast spectrum and quite beyond me, but I could write about *Cities of Ice and Snow* with Leningrad and Moscow in mind' and so I began to scribble. I found it an enjoyable occupation which kept my mind active rather than stagnating in this retirement home.

Acknowledgements

First and foremost I must acknowledge the enormous debt I owe to my mother for having kept all my letters, which I wrote on a regular weekly basis during my time in Russia—without them this book could not have been written.

I would also like to acknowledge the encouragement I received from both close and wider circles of my family to write these memoirs. I would like to single out my two daughters-in-law, Jenny and Janet, the former for beautifully typed indexes and further short pieces at the behest of her husband John, and to Janet for doing some very helpful research for me on the internet.

An enormous fund of gratitude goes to my son John for the many hours he spent with me checking through the edited manuscripts and pointing out paragraphs where I repeated myself, a process which entailed some quite difficult readjustments and a certain amount of juggling the manuscripts to get them into their right order.

I am also very grateful to Brian Fall and Simon Hemans, who not only corrected me when my memory was faulty but who also supplied information that I had no written record of and could not remember accurately.

Many thanks also to Theresa Bowie for typing my manuscripts so efficiently and returning them so promptly.

Preface

On The Fringe: Living in the Realms of Hitler and Stalin

The twentieth century saw various dictators emerge around the globe. At least two of these will go down in history for their impact on the world stage. They were Hitler and Stalin.

I focus in this book on the momentous middle decades of the twentieth century when I lived in the realms of these two men, Hitler's Germany from 1937 to 1939 and Stalin's Russia, first from 1947 to 1949 when he was alive, and subsequently from 1965 to 1968, when Stalin's legacy of Communism was still the dominant factor.

Having divested myself of house and home and retired to where I am looked after and my daily needs catered for, I have discovered leisure and the time to reflect on these three periods of my life.

I dedicate the book to my grandchildren, who live in such a different world from that of my generation, with the great sociological changes which have taken place together with the tremendous scientific and technological developments. It is not surprising that they have little awareness of what these mid-decades meant to the generation affected.

My husband was private secretary to Sir Nevile Henderson, the British ambassador in Berlin during the two years up to the outbreak of the Second World War in September 1939. In Moscow, during our first stint (1947–1949) he was the

PREFACE

Minister at the British embassy and in charge of our mission when the ambassador was on leave. In our second period (1965–1968) he was the ambassador.

In all three cases, he was at the very hub of official relations between Great Britain and Germany in the run-up years to the war, and then between Great Britain and the Soviet Union, in both his assignments to Moscow at significant periods of the Cold War.

As his wife, I was on the fringe of it all. Hence the title of my book.

As the daughter of a diplomat, then married to a diplomat, from babyhood my home has been in many countries: Stockholm, Peking, Munich, Tangiers, Teheran (twice), Rome, Tokyo, Berlin, Brussels, Moscow (twice) and also Rio de Janeiro. From time to time I had a home in England. All these locations have contributed their quota of education, interest, happiness and enjoyment, but also, at times, of stress, strain and unhappiness.

I thus have a large gallery of memoirs, with many different rooms each relating to a different country. I call it the Clive Harrison gallery, since I was born a Clive and married a Harrison.

Two of the rooms of my gallery are larger than the others, with a partition down the middle separating the two periods of my life spent in these countries. They are Iran and Russia. In this book I compare the two sections of the Russian room, and link them with the single room of Germany. Hitler and Stalin may have been deadly enemies, but they were both paranoid, ruthless dictators. I was in a position, albeit on the sidelines, to witness in their own countries some of the effects of their rule on daily life.

For the first two years after the end of the Second World War, we were lucky enough to find ourselves in Brussels. Belgium had been liberated by British troops, and as Britishers we lived in an aura of boundless popularity. It was

PREFACE

'lovely'! Although there had been fierce fighting in the Ardennes at the end of the war and of course in 1940 when the Germans invaded Belgium, the towns had luckily been spared bombing and there were no large areas of urban destruction. The Belgians were quick to rehabilitate themselves. Plenty of good food gradually became available, the black market was thriving. No longer dominated by the Germans, the Belgians were in a state of near euphoria.

From here we were transferred to Moscow, where we arrived on 15 October 1947 with our two younger sons, the eldest John having joined a prep school in Sussex in 1946.

No greater contrast with Brussels could be imagined. Yes, the Russians had booted the Germans out of their country, but at what tremendous cost. Towns bombed and devastated, the countryside ravaged, millions of their citizens killed, but what next? The terrors of the 1930s now returned for the second time.

Stalin was the all-powerful dictator who dominated each and everyone's lives. One could not help but be strongly reminded of Hitler and the terror he exerted over a large, highly intelligent and artistic section of the German population—the Jews—and woe betide anyone who lent them a helping hand in their plight.

My two years in Berlin up to the outbreak of the war had given me first-hand experience of this terror and of sheer brutality. The loud, excitable ranting voice of Hitler each time one turned on the radio did not help to allay feelings of alarm and apprehension. Stalin's terror was more subtle and individually angled. It happened behind the scenes at night. A knock on the door by the KGB, and someone would be apprehended and carted off. Family would have no news until weeks or months later, when they would learn that the luckless person carted off had been shot or sent to a hard labour Gulag camp in far north-eastern Siberia. Volga Germans working in Moscow would suddenly be picked up and

PREFACE

deported and dumped in Siberia to get on with life there as best they could beside their fellow ethnic compatriots already there.

Although Stalin died in 1952 and his special brand of terror gradually came to an end, imprisonment in a concentration camp within Soviet Russia in the succeeding years or incarceration in a mental hospital was often the lot of critics or dissidents of Soviet rule, but exile to a Gulag in Siberia was still the lot of a number of Soviet citizens and the creed of Communism continued for several more decades.

I

Berlin 1937–1939

Berlin 1937: Setting the Scene	2
Berlin 1938: A Little Potted History	8
Kristal Nacht (The Night of Breaking Glass)	12
November and December 1938	15
January to June 1939	16
Aftermath of the Occupation of Prague and Czechoslovakia	17
Summer 1939: Leaving Berlin	19
Postscript 1: Back in England	22
Postscript 2: Berlin Post-War	23
Happy Recollections of Berlin	24
July 1938: Holiday (Austrian Alps)	25
Dalmatian Holiday	26
Happy Weekends	32
The End of the Second World War and the Three Conferences (mainly Yalta and Aftermath)	35

Berlin 1937: Setting the Scene

I arrived in Berlin in the middle of September, 1937. I was young, enthusiastic and had a two-month-old baby son; I was delighted to come to Berlin, and so was my husband. We were both relatively fluent German speakers: I had been for one term to school in Munich when aged 10, having been intensively taught German for the previous five months. Thereafter I had kept up with the language, and when aged 18 had spent five months with a German family in Heidelberg, where I followed courses at the university. My husband had equally studied German at Cambridge and at various German universities and we both had German friends.

My old Swiss nanny, who had brought me up from babyhood as I had been born in Bern, accompanied me and my baby to Berlin. My husband had preceded me there by two weeks and had finalised renting a flat and engaging a cook and a maid. The flat and these servants had been found for us by my cousin Catherine Steel, whose husband Kit was second secretary at the Embassy. Our first secretary and head of chancery, Ivan Kirkpatrick, and his wife Violet, were also well known to me, as Ivan had been in Rome as secretary when my father was there as Minister to the Vatican for the Holy Year of 1933. As the Steels were on leave that September they very kindly offered us their flat for our initial two weeks until their return—and a very busy two weeks they were. Our big luggage from England did include certain important items of furniture, as well as crockery, glass tableware, linen and blankets, but all the rest of necessities for starting up a home had to be bought locally. We just managed to vacate the Steels' lovely and comfortable flat for a pretty chaotic existence in our own flat just 24 hours before the Steels' return—but we soon got everything bought, unpacked and sorted out. We soon felt settled in this our own home with our own bits and pieces around us, including all the lovely wedding presents given to us the previous year in Tokyo. It was all very exciting.

Our second-floor flat was well situated on the sunny side of the Kurfürsten Strasse, an easy walk with pram to the Tiergarten, a large park which incorporates the zoo. The Polish embassy was a little way down the street on the opposite side of the road. One disadvantage was that our immediate neighbour on our left was the headquarters of the Hitlerjugend and club. It could be very noisy at times. Above the bow window of the flat below us was a verandah leading out of our drawing room and enclosed by a low parapet wall on top of which we attached flower boxes in the spring. There was room for two garden chairs and a low table large enough to support the baby's carrycot. Weather permitting, and until he outgrew his carrycot, baby John would have his two hours' morning nap out on the verandah. When sitting on this verandah we could only see the flowers on the parapet, the branches of the trees lining the Kurfürsten Strasse and the sky above. It was perfect. Our elderly Jewish landlord and his wife occupied the ground floor and our own Commercial Counsellor from our embassy lived on the first floor. The back stairs, with room at the bottom for our baby's pram, led into a small courtyard. Here there was a garage for our car and I well remember how tricky it was manoeuvring the car in and out onto the street.

A young Swiss nanny trained in baby care had joined us at the Steels' flat during our second week there. She had been recruited for us by my own elderly Swiss nanny. My thought in asking her to find someone in Bern rather than my engaging someone in England was that a Bernese person would be fluent in German and this would make life easier for her, so Hanni Braun came into our life and brought up all three of my sons. We kept in touch with her all of her long life.

We soon became absorbed into embassy life and we also met young diplomats from the German Foreign Office. These had mostly studied English at Oxford and knew England well and had friends there. We made special friends with one family who had a young baby like ourselves. As the months passed by they would ogle each other sharing a playpen together. On these social encounters, politics were never discussed or even alluded to—it was too sensitive a subject. We always felt that members of the German Foreign Office were by and large not at all in sympathy with the current trend of affairs.

It was not possible to live in Berlin in 1937 without being aware of the general, rather tense, atmosphere around one. We had hardly settled down in our flat when the yearly Nazi rally in Nüremberg took place. I switched on the radio and heard the raucous tones of Hitler's voice. He was ranting away at his bewitched audience standing shoulder to shoulder on the floor below him. I switched off.

I had been aware of the Nazis ever since, as a 10-year-old, I had watched several columns of men in brown shirts with red armbands with a curious misshapen black cross on a white background around their arms march down the Prinz Regenten Strasse in Munich (a copy of the Champs Elysée of Paris). It so happened that my father had a special assignment in Munich that year and we had a house in the Kaulbach Strasse, parallel to the Prinz Regenten Strasse, with a garden running down to it. Suddenly, one day around midday, our garden was invaded by policemen and soldiers with rifles. They had come over the fence and through the shrubs. I ran out to see what they were doing. '*Zurück, zurück*' (back, back), shouted one of these men. I ran to an upstairs window to watch. Then these columns of brown-shirted men marched past. Presently we heard a few desultory shots in the distance. Policemen and soldiers disappeared. The Putsch of 1923 was over. It had been led by a chap called Hitler, who ended up in jail, but not for long. Ten years later he had become 'Reichskanzler' Chancellor of Germany—the top dog. Four years on, here he was in Berlin, his ambition to gather all German-speaking people into one realm, '*Ein Volk, ein Reich*'.

Seven years after the Munich Putsch, I was studying German in Heidelberg and living with the family of a war widow. Her husband, an academic attached to the university, had been killed in the war, leaving her with four young children. She had an agreeable house on the hillside opposite the great ruins of the castle on top of a great bluff above the river Necker.

Her second son, now aged 18, was working hard for his 'abitur'—the equivalent to the French baccalaureate. He was an enthusiastic member of the Hitler Youth and a hero worshipper of Hitler. During our evening suppers he was wont to expatiate on 'National Socialism' and on how wonderful Hitler, the founder of this movement, was.

'Enough, Till,' his mother would say to interrupt the flow, and she would change the subject. A great friend of hers lived in Frankfurt and one day she came to visit her here in Heidelberg. That evening at supper, Till suddenly exclaimed, 'I wish, Mutti, you would cease being friends with Frau D.'

'Why on earth, how so?' asked his mother, very taken aback by her son's remark.

'Well, she's a Jewess, a member of an alien race, and Hitler says we don't want Jews in our country—we must keep our German race pure; the Jews sully it.'

'Don't talk such rubbish, what arrant nonsense,' retorted Till's mother angrily. She was obviously very put out, too, that her son should make such remarks to her in front of foreigners. Besides myself, there was another English girl studying German. Till's older sister Lilly, an art history student at the university, together with a much older friend of the family, all formed part of the Burger family. An embarrassed and rather stunned silence followed this interchange between mother and son, but Lilly rescued us by making some joke or other.

At the time I think I did feel a certain unease and a feeling of surprise. We all liked Till, he was a nice cheerful lad, tall, good-looking and friendly. I forgot the incident, but seven years later in Berlin it came vividly back to mind.

My next encounter with Nazism was four years later in July 1934. I was on holiday with Italian friends in a Dolomite village thirty minutes' drive from Bolzano, the little town on the Italian side of the Brenner pass which links Austria and Italy. Suddenly, on the 25th, there was a great commotion and apprehension in our hotel when the announcement came over the radio that Dolfuss, the Austrian Chancellor, had been murdered in Vienna by a posse of young Austrian Nazis. Ever since Hitler had taken over the reins of power he had not ceased to proclaim his mantra that the Austrian people should be united with the German people. 'We are all one people and should be living together in one realm,' he stated. Undoubtedly there was much sympathy with the notion in Austria, particularly amongst the younger element who could not but admire the benefits that had accrued to the German nation from the social and economic measures instituted by Hitler. In spite of efforts by successive governments, Austria remained in the post-1914 war doldrums, with massive unemployment, and there was a good deal of unrest in the country, but there was also strong opposition to the idea of unity with Germany.

Herr von Schuschnigg immediately stepped into Dolfuss' shoes. He outlawed the Nazi party and hundreds of them fled across the frontier into Germany.

That autumn I sailed across the oceans to faraway Japan and forgot all about Nazis and Germany. But two years later I became aware of them again. In the spring of 1936 the newly reconstituted German army, a small but highly trained and disciplined force, marched into the Rhineland, which was administered by a consortium of wartime allies under a clause of the Versailles Peace Treaty of 1918. The reaction of the

BERLIN 1937: SETTING THE SCENE

French and British at this flagrant violation of a clause of this treaty was lots of words and angry protests but nothing more. The entire German nation, including the Rhinelanders, were jubilant and Hitler's stock rose ever higher.

My father was deeply worried over these developments and I remember him saying, 'That man (Hitler) is a fanatic and fanatics are dangerous.'

Well, here we were now in Berlin, in the autumn of 1937, in the fanatic's den three years after the murder of Dolfuss.

No particular incidents to trouble the mind unduly occurred during that autumn. As winter advanced it got ever colder, with much snow and an arctic wind. It was the precursor of a freezing decade. We had no open fireplace with glowing coals and crackling logs before which we could warm our hands and our bodies. Our radiators seemed totally inadequate and a single-bar electric fire made scant difference. Evenings at home would find me wrapped in a rug. But we were quite happy with our lot, our baby was a joy and my husband found his work enthralling. As well, as being dogsbody in chancery, he was private secretary to our ambassador, Sir Nevile Henderson.

As newcomers, our social life was still rather restricted, but we had a sufficient amount of it and it was particularly helpful to me having close friends within our own embassy circle.

Berlin had plenty to offer in the way of culture: museums, picture galleries, concerts, excellent light operas, and, of course, grand opera as well. We became acquainted with Wagner's *Lohengrin* and *Tannhauser*—but all this was in the traditional vein of culture. However, one afternoon we thought we would visit an exhibition of modern German painting. It had opened two days previously. When we arrived at the gallery we found it was closed. We learned this had been on Hitler's express orders. He declared that the pictures were unseemly and degenerate (*'Entartete' kunst*) and no further exhibitions of this type of work would be allowed. So, not surprisingly, painters and sculptors made their way to Paris, the art Mecca of the world since the mid-nineteenth century.

Heidelberg days had alerted me to Hitler's paranoid attitude towards all Jews and now in Berlin every time he spoke to the nation, anti-Jewish tirades invariably formed part of his speech. German Jews saw the way the wind was blowing and many musicians, doctors, scientists and academics in all disciplines upped sticks and emigrated to the USA. Many also came to England. This exodus took place in the early thirties. By the time we arrived it was extremely difficult for them to obtain visas, but, unable to travel themselves, they were still able to send their children out of the country, and many of these came to make their homes with British families. Tragically, few of them ever saw their parents again.

Anti-Jewish feeling was not, however, confined to Hitler and his Nazi followers in Germany. Ghettos, where Jews were forced to live, were widespread throughout eastern Europe, and terrible pogroms did take place in Russia and in Poland from time to time during the nineteenth century and on into the twentieth century up to the outbreak of war in 1914. But in countries where ghettos no longer existed, Jews tended to live together in their own communities. This was very much so in Italy—in Rome and some other cities there are entirely Jewish quarters.

Berlin, 1938: A Little Potted History

The year 1938 is important in the annals of history. In Berlin it was a year of ever-increasing crises, culminating in the controversial agreement signed in Munich at the end of September between Germany, Britain, France and Italy. Much has been published on the events of 1938 and on this

BERLIN, 1938: A LITTLE POTTED HISTORY

agreement. After a brief outline of the circumstances, I will give an account of the effects of these events on myself.

This was also the year of the notorious 'Kristal Nacht' on 9 November, so called because of the smashing of shop windows, and the windows of flats and houses owned by Jews. It was the start of the violent anti-Jewish campaign, leading ultimately to the horrors of Auschwitz. For me, it was the absolute nadir of stress experienced that year.

Finally, 1938 marked the watershed between two very different eras. The Munich agreement was the prelude to the war which broke out a year later on 3 September. At the end of the war in 1945, the political map of the entire world was re-drawn in various stages. At the same time, great sociological changes took place, together with fantastic scientific and technological developments. All these changes have revolutionised the life of all of us.

Hitler achieved two of his cherished ambitions in the course of this year, leading to the crises mentioned above. The first crisis was the Anschluss (incorporation) of Austria into Germany on 10 March. On 29 September, the second and third crises centred on the added incorporation of the Sudeten lands, situated within the post-1918 Versailles Treaty boundaries of Czechoslovakia, when the Munich agreement was signed. The inhabitants of this region were all German.

Before Hitler achieved full power in Germany, he had been making speeches about the unhappy lot of 'our brothers and sisters across the border in Austria,' saying 'they should be united with us—we are all of the same Germanic stock.' Each year, emphasis on this particular theme was continually repeated, with a great crescendo from January 1938. Austrians were fairly evenly divided on the issue of union. The government led by Herr Schushnigg wanted Austria to remain independent—and he did have much support. Hitler, however, became even more insistent. Suddenly, on the spur of the moment, Schushnigg called for a referendum on the issue with a bare week's notice. This so infuriated Hitler that he immediately ordered his troops to cross the frontier and overrun the whole country—and so the Anschluss was proclaimed.

As in 1936 when Hitler's army marched into the Rhineland, those in the western world were stunned by this very sudden development. There was nothing they could do but accept the situation. Hitler was triumphant. There was great jubilation in Berlin and throughout Germany and also in Austria, save amongst those who had opposed union, and of course the members of the large Jewish community mostly centred in Vienna were very alarmed. Many arrests were made and Nazis who had fled to Germany after the murder of Dolfuss now returned and took revenge on their opponents. The Austrian and the Sudeten problems were quite different from each other. The first had not involved any other country and the Austrians were all of German stock, whereas the second was of major concern to the Czech nation with their separate language and culture. The Sudeten lands formed an important economic part of Czechoslovakia. Moreover, the Czechs had other minorities living within their borders. These were Polish and Hungarian, each of these communities contiguous with their own countries just across their common frontiers.

Deeply concerned, the British and the French (who had a tripartite agreement with Czechoslovakia and Romania that they would mutually help each other if either of them were attacked) jointly proposed to Beneš, the Czech president, that these three regions should be granted autonomy within the Czechoslovakian state which should then transform itself into a federation on the model of Switzerland with its three linguistically separate regions. The British and French ambassadors then sought an interview with Hitler to inform him of this approach to solving the problem. Reluctantly, Hitler agreed but added that these changes should take place immediately.

BERLIN, 1938: A LITTLE POTTED HISTORY

Unfortunately Beneš demurred. This infuriated Hitler and Henlein, the leader of the Sudeten Germans, and from now on not a day passed without impassioned and strident speeches by both these men being addressed to the Sudeten people. Not unnaturally, this incited unrest which led to a number of incidents, including the loss of life.

Gradually it all built up to a crisis point. In May, rumour had it that German troops were on the frontiers of the Sudeten lands and were ready to invade the region. The Czechs immediately ordered their army to mobilise. It was a small but efficient fighting force. The rumours, however, proved to be unfounded—there were no German troops massed on the Sudeten frontiers. Without due reflection, the Czechs proclaimed to the world that it was their prompt mobilisation which had made the Germans pull back. Hitler worked himself up into one of his furious tantrums. He declared that he and Germany had been insulted by the Czechs. 'We will teach them a lesson—autonomy within the Czech state is no longer an option, only full integration of the Sudeten lands into the German realm is acceptable from now on.' This was what was being preached ever more vociferously by both Hitler and Henlein.

A solution was sought to this intractable situation, with endless parleying in Prague during the succeeding three months, but with no positive outcome. By the beginning of September, Hitler had worked himself up into a paranoiac state of mind and declared that his army would march into Czechoslovakia on 1 October unless the Sudeten region had been ceded to Germany before this date. So the third crisis now developed, and the world was faced with a very serious situation.

Deeply concerned for peace, Neville Chamberlain flew out to Germany three times. The first time was for a private meeting with Hitler in his mountain eyrie at Berghtesgaden, then a week later there was a further meeting with advisers present on both sides at Bad Godesberg in the Rhineland, and finally, on 29 September, he went to Munich where a four-power meeting had been convened at the instigation of Mussolini, and the final Munich agreement was drawn up. It was undoubtedly Mussolini's intervention which prevented war from breaking out in 1938.

For me, the drama of 1938 meant that as each crisis reached its peak, I would gather up my babe, clamber into a carriage of the nightly 'Nord Express' and arrive in Brussels the following morning to be welcomed by my parents. It was so wonderful and convenient for me that my father was now ambassador to Belgium. For the Anschluss with Austria and the May crisis, I only remained in Brussels for three or four days before returning with babe to Berlin. For the third crisis, I remained in Brussels for nearly two weeks and witnessed the tremendous jubilation of the Belgian nation when the Munich agreement was announced, and their gratitude to Neville Chamberlain was immense.

Kristal Nacht (The Night of Breaking Glass)

After the stresses and strains of September, Berlin settled down to a peaceful and agreeable October. A twenty-minute drive would take us to a golf course situated to the west of the city about half way to the attractive lake district and on to Potsdam. We joined the club and on fine afternoons would enjoy playing nine holes between lunch and the time for my husband to return to the office. A great convenience was that one could choose either the first nine holes or the second nine, for the clubhouse was at the centre. The course was relatively easy and attractive and we enjoyed the exercise and the peace after the past two months. However, peace was rudely shattered on 9 November.

It was a cold and grey afternoon, and I needed a new pair

KRISTAL NACHT (THE NIGHT OF BREAKING GLASS)

of evening shoes. I boarded a bus in the nearby Lützow Platz which took me to the main shopping centre of the town. A 12-minute ride brought me to where the Tauntzien Strasse curves into the Kurfürstendamm. Here I alighted and walked back a short way along the Tauntzien Strasse, to a shoe shop, where I found a pair of evening shoes which suited me. I paid the bill and, feeling elated at my success, started back to the bus stop for my return journey. I had not walked for more than twenty paces when two large and noisy army trucks came down Tauntzien Strasse and pulled up against the curb just behind me. On looking around I saw a posse of uniformed men tumble out of the trucks and immediately start smashing the plate glass windows of shops, including the shop where I had just purchased my shoes. Aghast and unbelieving, I was momentarily transfixed, but when I saw the lady who had sold me my shoes roughly dragged out of the shop by her hair and screaming, I took to my heels, as did all other passers-by, and fled the scene as though pursued by a swarm of bees. I ran all the way back to our flat, taking a zigzag route—it took roughly twenty minutes. Breathless, speechless and utterly distraught, I turned the key of our door, pressing the door bell at the same time. Frieda, our nice maid, found me leaning against the inside of the door. She helped me to a chair, asking, '*Also gnädige Frau was ist los?*' (but madam what's happened?) I presume I burbled something or other, but I wanted to talk to my husband. He had told me never to ring him at the office except in an emergency—I thought this was an emergency. He listened to my tale and said, 'Calm down, darling. Get Frieda to bring you a cup of tea. I will find out what's afoot and come home.' All he was able to tell me was that Jewish premises were being attacked all over Berlin.

That evening at around 11.30, as we were getting ready for bed, we heard a commotion outside in the street. I started making my way towards the window to see what was going on when very peremptorily my husband called out, 'Stop! Don't move the curtains and attempt to peer out.' Fairly soon the rumpus quietened down.

Next day we learnt that Nazis had entered our house (in those days the street doors of houses divided into flats were left open), and they forced the lock of our landlord's flat, entered and took him away. No explanation was given to his distraught wife. A week later he was returned to his flat. Each of his ten fingers had been broken in the concentration camp of Dachau. Such brutality was quite sickening.

Afterwards, we learned that the happenings of that horrible day were in retaliation for the murder in Paris of a German diplomat by a deranged Jew. When Hitler heard of this he flew into one of his periodic rages. He summoned his two most trusted henchmen, Dr Goebels and Himmler. The former was in charge of press and propaganda and he immediately ordered the press to highlight the story with vituperative headlines and anti-Jewish articles. The latter was head of the Gestapo—the dreaded secret police—and since 1936 he was also in charge of all the police forces of the Reich. Thugs and hooligans were enrolled in these forces and Himmler found them useful for carrying out violent dirty work. The murder in Paris by a Jew was, he argued, the catalyst needed to start widespread persecution of the Jews, and so with Hitler's connivance the brutal events of Kristal Nacht took place and from then on Jews were deprived of all civil rights and forced to wear an armband with a yellow star of David woven into it. Any person of Jewish ancestry encountered on the streets not wearing an armband was immediately arrested and packed off to a concentration camp. The Jewish persecution ended with the horrors of Auschwitz.

After this horrible experience I seldom felt at complete ease living in Berlin.

November and December 1938

After the trauma of Kristal Nacht and its aftermath, the persecution of the Jews, we settled down to an uneasy winter. The Anschluss, the Czech crises and the 9 November pogrom left the resident foreign communities in Berlin full of misgiving and anxiety. Hitler's jarring, intransigent and dictatorial behaviour and his increasing monomania induced discussion as to 'what next?' and the answer pointed to Memel (now Klaypeda) and Danzig.

Memel, a Lithuanian port, and Danzig, a flourishing erstwhile Hanseatic port, and still busy and thriving, had predominantly German populations, but neither of them were contiguous with Germany. By the 1918 treaty of Versailles, Danzig had been internationalised and linked to landlocked Poland by an internationalised corridor, running through Silesia with a mixed Polish and German population.

In spite of Hitler's written assurance to Chamberlain, at the end of the Munich conference, that he had no further territorial ambitions, no one in Berlin had any trust in his word. Even Chamberlain had doubts once the euphoria had subsided after his triumphant return to London from Munich, waving a scrap of paper saying, 'Peace in our time.' Ever since 1933 when Hitler came to power, Germany had been busily expanding its armed forces with special emphasis on its air force. During this time the British government had remained blinkered to this, in spite of warnings to this effect from its embassy in Berlin. Equally blinkered were the peoples of the British Isles (save for a few voices, like that of Winston Churchill). However, Chamberlain's visits to Germany and his contacts with Hitler opened his eyes to the true situation. After Munich a complete volte-face took place. From now on, our entire nation was geared to prepare for war, the civilian population as well as the armed forces.

So 1938 moved on into 1939. We saw the new year in at a

splendid ball given by the Italian ambassador and his wife—the Attolicos. The ball ended in the early hours of the new year with the remaining guests doing the 'Lambeth Walk'. It was Signor Attolico who had urged Mussolini in September to intervene with Hitler when he was being so intractable in his negotiations with Chamberlain at Godesberg. This had led to the Munich conference and the immediate threat of war was lifted. Both Signor and Signora Attolico were Anglophiles, and though sadly our ambassador, Sir Nevile Henderson, was not in Berlin, as he was recovering from an operation in England, all our diplomatic staff were invited to the ball, the last great party before the outbreak of war.

January to June 1939

Treading the Lambeth Walk into the early hours of 1939 is both my concluding recollection of 1938 and my first recollection of 1939. Had Signor and Signora Attolico some premonition that a New Year's Eve ball might be the last party they would host at their beautiful Italian embassy? Maybe, I don't know. It was certainly my last ball for nineteen years. This next one took place at the splendid new post-war British embassy in Rio de Janeiro when we were the hosts.

My next recollection of 1939 in Berlin was that of my husband returning for lunch on a February day and announcing, 'I've just bought a house in Sussex.' Understandably, consternation on my part. 'What on earth do you mean?' I asked. It appeared that he had received a letter from his mother that morning at the office. In this she mentioned that a few days previously she had climbed up the newly installed loft ladder. She had looked out of the window facing the road with a bungalow opposite. An old lady lived in this bungalow and had a phobia of being overlooked. My mother-in-law had not herself seen the old lady but apparently the old lady had seen her. Declaring she could not remain in a house which was now overlooked, the old lady immediately put her bungalow on the market.

The letter had ended with the questioning comment, 'I wonder who will buy it?' On the spur of the moment my husband telegraphed to his mother, 'Buy the bungalow on my behalf.' He was convinced that war would break out before the end of the year, a sentiment echoed by all diplomats in Berlin and strongly reinforced by the events that took place on 15 March (ominously, the Ides of March).

During the night of 14 March, German troops invaded the two Czech provinces of Bohemia and Moravia, and on the next morning, Hitler, from the upper windows of the Hradshin Palace in Prague, announced to the Czech people that their country had now become a German Protectorate.

This coup staggered the world, not least the lightning speed with which it had been accomplished—Hitler was a great opportunist. If he perceived an opening he would without second thoughts come to an instant decision and promptly act upon it. Thus it was that a childish squabble, between two very similar Slav nations, the Czechs and the Slovaks, was astutely fuelled by clever German propaganda. This quickly reached crisis point, and the Slovaks themselves asked Hitler for support, not at all apprehending what it would lead to.

Aftermath of the Occupation of Prague and Czechoslovakia

In Germany this latest coup of Hitler's was greeted with mixed bewilderment and pride. For the younger generation it was unadulterated pride. For fifteen years Hitler had been their inspiration—he could do no wrong. The future held no dread for them, it could only be glory. But for many of those over the age of forty, there were qualms as to what this might all lead to. For the British Commonwealth it was the catalyst which fused all members into one entity. Not only the British Government but the entire British nation now had their support in the collective will of Great Britain together with the Commonwealth to resist this bully who had now become a serious menace to the peace of Europe and who knew how far beyond.

The British government agreed with the Poles: should Poland be attacked, Great Britain would come to her aid, but a signed accord to this effect only took place on 25 August.

The Steels had been told in December 1938 that they would be transferred back to London the following spring. A month after the occupation of Prague and the subjugation of the Czechs, packers and a large pantechnicon arrived to load up all the Steels' goods and chattels. However, before it was quite full, my cousin Catherine rang me up to say there would be room for one chest and my Persian rugs if we would like to send these items back to the UK. This was a wonderful opportunity to pack up my Japanese treasures, most of our silver and my lovely Persian rugs. We were for ever grateful that we were thus able to save these items. All our other possessions were lost in Berlin—bombed, in fact, by the RAF in 1945!

In June, my husband decided it was time for me and our little son to say goodbye to Berlin. So towards the end of the month, toddler, myself, Swiss nanny and as much luggage and as many bundles as possible squeezed into our valiant Ford car and my husband drove us to his mother's newly built house in Sussex. My husband had a bare three days' leave of absence from Berlin. The car was left with me and he returned to Berlin where, before our departure, he had acquired a very ancient Vauxhall car, found for him by our local garage owner, a very friendly and amusing chap with a rather wry cockney-type humour.

We never encountered any animosity towards us during our Berlin stint, in spite of Hitler turning his venom against the British after our verbal agreement with Poland and after what had become a very vituperative anti-Hitler British press. It had now become a slanging match between the journalists of Great Britain and those of Germany.

The only animosity we ever encountered then was on the occasion of a supper party following a yacht race between the Thames Yacht Club and the Wannsee Yacht Club. This race took place on the Wannsee in May 1939. Against all odds, the British team won. Of course all the Brits present were jubilant but the wife of the captain of the Wannsee team was most upset. She sat with us at a round table and she gave vent to her annoyance: '*Ganz unbillig*'—totally unfair. 'Our team worked so hard, they arrived at their boats early this morning and practised. The English team arrived a whole hour later, too late to practise. They behaved in such an amateurish fashion, typical of the British(!!)—quite unhurried—they did not deserve to win.'

Summer 1939: Leaving Berlin

For me, departure from our flat leaving 98 per cent of our possessions there and saying farewell to our devoted servants Elfrieda and Hanna was quite emotional. It was eight o'clock on a lovely summer's morning. The prospect of seeing the new house of my mother-in-law was exciting; added to which we would now be seeing our own little property, bought on the spur of the moment without us ever seeing even a photo of it!

Our journey was uneventful and the sea, on the Channel crossing, was calm and sparkling—but it was the sight of the white cliffs of Dover gleaming in the afternoon sun which gave me a real fillip.

We received a very warm welcome from my husband's mother, his two sisters and the dogs, cairn terriers, one black and one white, who yapped with excitement on recognising my husband.

It was now mid-summer and the days were long so there was plenty of time for us that same evening to view not just the new house and its grounds but also our very own little bungalow.

Before leaving Berlin, I had received a letter from my father in Brussels suggesting that I bring little John to Le Zoute for a seaside holiday from mid-July and through August. He would love playing in the sand and paddling, and sea air would be very good for me as well. A lovely idea—so a few days after his second birthday, he and I crossed the Channel once more and joined my parents at Le Zoute. Our Swiss nanny, in the meantime, had returned to Bern for a well-earned holiday. She said she would like to return to us, come what may, and look after the new baby I was expecting the following February.

The weather was sunny and hot, but at the end of a week at Le Zoute, little John fell ill with a high temperature. The doctor said that young children often found the combination of heat, sea air and sand was too much for them. We were told to keep John away from the beach for the next two weeks and thereafter only allow him down by the sea for very short spells. This was very disappointing, but luckily the villa had a shady garden in which he could play. My eldest brother and his wife came and stayed for a week, and as Peter was a scratch golfer he was invited to play golf with our ex-King Edward VIII who, with his wife Wallis, now lived in Paris but was currently on a visit to a member of the Belgian royal family.

Just like the previous year, the political crisis developed apace. For me it was a biding time—something was bound to happen soon, but what? And when? My father was, of course, in constant touch with current affairs. My husband was extremely busy in Berlin with no time for letter writing. I remember only receiving one short letter during August in

SUMMER 1939: LEAVING BERLIN

which he said that as the Polish embassy was situated in our street in Berlin, the Kurfürsten Strasse, there were now constant noisy demonstrations taking place there.

We were due to return to England at the end of the month, but suddenly, on 25 August, a telephone message from Berlin was received at the embassy in Brussels with instructions to the effect that I should take the next cross-Channel steamer immediately and return to Sussex with little John. So, by around 6 p.m. on the 27th we were back once more in the bosom of my husband's family. The following Sunday, 3 September at 12 noon, we heard Mr Chamberlain broadcast to the nation that we were now at war with Germany. Before we switched off the radio the wail of the air raid warning sirens blared forth. 'Good heavens, the German bombers are already approaching London!' exclaimed my mother-in-law. We left the radio on and within the next ten minutes the reassuring sound of the All Clear could be heard. Later in the day, the radio announced that it had been a mistake!

On Monday, 4 September, a special train left Berlin at 11 a.m. Aboard were the entire complement of the British Embassy staff. There were thirty men, seven women and two dogs, and as much luggage as they could personally carry. My husband had two suitcases, one with his personal effects, the other filled with our remaining silver and my evening dresses, including my New Year's Eve ballgown—these all carefully folded with tissue paper by Elfrieda. The suitcases had been packed earlier that last week of August. Hanna and Elfrieda departed sadly and deeply concerned on 29 August, and on Friday, 1 September, my husband locked up the flat and moved into the embassy house itself for his final three nights. I met him at 9 p.m. in the blackout at Horsham station on Thursday, 7 September. The train had been detained for twenty hours some twenty kilometres short of the Dutch frontier, until the safe arrival in Dutch territorial waters of the German mission from London. The British party arrived at the Hague at 1.30 p.m. on the Tuesday, hospitably received by the Dutch, and spent that night there. The following night was spent on board a Dutch steamer which sailed at 6 the next morning from Rotterdam, bound for Gravesend.

Only one suitcase was retrieved from the guard's van at Horsham station. The one with silver and the evening frocks had vanished and was never seen again—no doubt stolen between Victoria Station and Horsham. Well, evening frocks would have been of little use to me in the next few years, but the silver was sorely missed. It was two months since my husband and I had seen each other. What a relief to have him back safe and sound. I realise only too well how lucky I was! A sad ending to our enthusiastic arrival in Berlin two years previously.

Postscript 1: Back in England

During the first month of war the little bungalow was got ready for our occupancy. The local builder undertook repairing jobs of one kind and another and repainted the whole of the interior. He replaced the very ancient coal-burning stove with a new one of the same ilk; when lit, it served both as a cooking stove and a water heater. It was the bane of my life for the next six years; though it did heat the water efficiently, half an hour had to lapse between two baths, as the boiler was so small. In the course of the winter we invested in a small electric oven with a hotplate on top—bliss!

Swiss Nanny arrived back from Switzerland on 29 August. In the ensuing years she proved to be a tower of strength. She was an excellent needlewoman. I bought utility furniture, pots and pans, kitchen spoons and knives and yards of material which Swiss Nanny made up into curtains—two lots for every window. The inside curtain of dead black material

POSTSCRIPT 1: BACK IN ENGLAND

to fix close to the windows for the blackout which was mandatory throughout the land and woe betide you if a chink of light showed from the outside.

My husband busied himself with the garden on Sundays, his weekly so-called day of rest. Saturdays were working days at that period. That first autumn he cleared the front garden of bushes and shrubs, many of which found their way into his mother's garden. He dug over the kitchen garden and prepared it for the spring sowing. My mother-in-law bought a dozen day-old chicks. To our pleasure we found we owned a small field beyond a hedge which enclosed our back garden with its vegetable patch and in the autumn of 1940 we ourselves bought half a dozen day-old chicks and they had a movable coop which was moved around the field on a weekly basis. By the second year of the war we were self-sufficient in vegetables and plenty of lovely brown eggs. During these war years my second and third sons were born and the first years of their lives were spent in this little bungalow. Swiss Nanny remained with us throughout these years before finally returning to Switzerland in 1946. I remained in touch until her death in 2004.

Postscript 2: Berlin Post-War

In July 1945 my husband returned to Berlin as a member of the British delegation to the Potsdam conference. The RAF pilot who flew him in had been a bomber pilot and had been on two bombing missions over Berlin. He flew low over the city so that his passengers could get a good view. The following is an extract from a letter my husband wrote to me from Potsdam: 'The destruction was quite indescribable. I don't think there is an undamaged house in the whole area. The trees in the Tiergarten are just skeletons. The whole place was like those pictures of battlefields of the last war.' The delegation were able to visit Berlin on the Sunday after their arrival. He wrote 'It's an absolutely staggering sight, it will surely take decades to rebuild, even to clear.'

I had the chance of seeing Berlin for myself in the spring of 1949 when I was returning to Moscow, having dumped my boys at school in England. My cousin Catherine Steel and her husband were now back in Berlin. They now lived in a villa in the attractive lake district to the west of the city and I spent two nights with them. Catherine drove me into the city for me to view the area where we had lived. Whole areas of the city had not yet been cleared and that included the quarter where we had lived. With difficulty we climbed over a sea of boulders in the Lützow Platz and into what once had been Kurfürsten Strasse—utter destruction here.

John and his wife visited Berlin 59 years later, staying in a luxurious hotel on the Lützow Platz, and with high-rise buildings all around. The phoenix had risen, rejuvenated from its ashes.

Happy Recollections of Berlin

Before continuing my Berlin saga into 1939, I will recall enjoyable episodes of our two years in Berlin.

The gobbling up of Austria by Germany the previous month meant little to my mother-in-law who came to stay with us for ten days in April 1938. She revelled in her little grandson who had just started crawling around. Her visit gave us the occasion to visit Potsdam, the city of the Prussian Kings, with a number of palaces and museums, amongst them the ex-Kaiser's magnificent palace. I never revisited Potsdam, but my husband had occasion to do so as he formed part of the British delegation to the Potsdam conference at the end of the war.

My mother-in-law had brought with her from England the

plans of the house being built for her on land she had purchased two years previously. It was to be ready for occupancy at Easter time in 1939 and we became her first guests in June of that year. In fact, I left Berlin for good at the end of that month—just two months before war broke out.

July 1938: Holiday (Austrian Alps)

My husband was given his annual leave during July—crisis number three was as yet a little way off, and everyone hoped that negotiations with Benes would lead to an acceptable and peaceful end. So, having parked our wee son with my parents, we set off for the first real holiday of our married life (we had only enjoyed one week's honeymoon), and a wonderful holiday it was—partly amidst glorious mountains with superb scenery and walks, and swimming and sunbathing by the shores of the Adriatic on the Dalmatian coast.

Two stopovers at Nüremberg and Munich brought us to Kitzbühel in the Austrian Alps. Just beyond this favoured winter sports resort we came upon an Alpine meadow with glorious views. We pitched our little tent, regaled ourselves with provender we had bought on the way, rolled ourselves up in blankets and slept like logs until early morning—we were very tired. We packed up and motored on and came upon an inn where we ate a substantial breakfast and enjoyed a lovely walk through alpine pastures with the delicious scent of wild flowers and pine needles and the clanging of cow bells. It was a beautiful day. We then motored on over a pass with hairpin bends and along a valley to the beginning of the Gross Glockner road. We started up this but realised it was a far greater undertaking than we had bargained for so we decided to spend the night at a rather ramshackle inn at the foot of the really steep climb. Next day, another brilliantly fine day, we started up our road at 9 a.m. The road was very steep, with tight bends. We just managed to reach the top of the first part of the road, before our Ford's engine boiled—luckily not too seriously and we took a lovely walk whilst it cooled down. Our next lap was easier except for the very last part which brought us to the top of the pass, from where we had a superb view of the Gross Glockner, the highest mountain of the Austrian Alps, from which we were only separated by a large glacier. Unfortunately there was such a throng of people, chiefly German, that we dallied but a short time, and we continued on our way and over yet another pass with picturesque scenery. A short way on and we came upon a perfect camping site. It was so lovely up there we decided to remain for a second night—but the weather thought differently. Next morning, clouds had appeared, but we enjoyed our lazy morning and then walked on to the next village for lunch. On our way back we became aware that a thunderstorm was imminently catching up on us—we could hear it rumbling. We just made it to our tent where we huddled whilst the rain came sheeting down and the thunder reverberated from mountain to mountain. I was very frightened, but our little tent kept us dry. The ground, however, was so sodden that we decided to abandon camp and find more solid shelter for the night. It wasn't until 8 p.m. that we came upon a completely new rest house, timber built, with nice grounds and bathing facilities which we particularly enjoyed. A fellow guest and an excellent pianist played Viennese music after dinner, until we finally went to bed, only to be woken up by our second terrific thunderstorm.

Dalmatian Holiday

This was our last night in the Austrian Alps. Next day we were up and over another pass—the Wurzen Pass—and down a steep narrow valley flanked by rocky mountains, over the frontier and into Yugoslavia. A half hour later and we had our first puncture—two large nails had embedded themselves into our off-front tyre. No trouble changing this and onwards to Bled, picturesquely situated along the shores of a very clear bluey-green lake with an island in the middle, with a white church nestling amongst trees. Bled and its lake are surrounded by steep wooded hills. We spent four days here, staying in a small 'pension' where we had pre-booked our accommodation. We had a view of the lake from our room but were sad not to have a verandah on which we could have our breakfast. We had left behind the attractive Austrian chalets. Here in Yugoslavia, houses were all white plaster villas. Ours was simple and unpretentious but adequate for our needs. On two of the evenings when we were not tired out from tramping the hills, we danced to a good band at the main hotel.

During our stay in Bled, the weather was rather unsettled but both of us managed to swim (I found the water rather cold) and explore the surrounding mountains. Above Bled was another very scenic lake, Lake Bokinjako Jezero, with a bubbling river running out of it. My husband had been told there was fishing to be had here and as he was a keen fisherman we sought out the permit office. For a small sum you could buy a day's fishing and give up your catch or pay a larger sum and keep your catch. My husband bought the former and enjoyed the sport immensely, fishing the river whilst I read a book on the banks of the lake and then tried my luck as well—unsuccessfully.

On another day we took a strenuous three-hour walk to the top of a mountain which formed part of the frontier with Italy. The lower reaches were again through meadows full of wild flowers and here we came across wild strawberries and bilberries, so we dallied a while, picking and eating these. As well as a stupendous view from the top of our mountain, south towards the sea, and west into Italy, we found edelweiss in clumps which gave us special delight. On this walk we also came across little clumps of blue gentians. I was reminded of this glorious day years later when tramping the hills behind Tbilisi in Georgia.

On leaving Bled, it was now goodbye to the hills and dales and mountains for ten days of sea air and four days of swimming in a translucent sea. After an almighty and terrifying thunderstorm and deluges of rain on the way to Susack, the rather messy port at the head of the Adriatic, we embarked on the *Dedinje* to cruise all down the picturesque mountainous Dalmatian coast. Kotor was our destination at the head of an inland loch and situated at the foot of sheer bare rocky mountains which immediately rise 4,000-odd feet up, and on top of a rocky crag is perched a castle with a wall like the Great Wall of China climbing round it. Here we took a car up to Cetinje, the old capital of Montenegro. The road goes up 3,000 feet sheer from the water's edge in a series of impressive hairpin turns, which put even the Gross Glockner Strasse in the shade.

After a quick round of sightseeing in Cetinje (not much to see except the tombs of maiden aunts of the late king!) we returned to Kotor and had time to explore the cathedral which had some interesting works of art and reliquaries of saints. The *Dedinje* arrived back at Dubrovnik at 10 p.m., and here we disembarked at 8 the following morning for a delightful four-day stay in the Excelsior Hotel opposite the old harbour of Ragusa, the original name of Dubrovnik.

We had been joined on this trip to Kotor and Cetinje by a great friend from Tokyo days. He was a Frenchman full of ready Gallic wit and now serving at the French embassy in Belgrade. This rendezvous with Maurice Pérègne had been arranged weeks before. Here in Dubrovnik, he introduced us to the French Agent, a Yugoslav in Dubrovnik who owned a large sailing boat. He and his Yugoslav lady friend took us to a local fish restaurant for a delicious lobster meal and invited us to sail with him the following afternoon. I remember it was very hot with insufficient wind, but a pleasant way of lazing away an afternoon before a refreshing dip in the wonderfully clear sea. That evening we went to an open-air performance of *Carmen*. The background was the entrance to a large cave. The tavern scene in the last act was amazingly realistic in this setting.

Dubrovnik is built on two sides of a rocky peninsula. The old town of Ragusa, with its ancient harbour in a small bay, is on the southern side. The town is a mixture of medieval and renaissance stone architecture within encircling ramparts, with forts at the angles. Of an evening, all Ragusans strolled up and down the wide Corso which bisects the town. An excellent café-restaurant had been conjured out of the old ship-building yard and jetty with a vaulted ceiling. Only a few fishing boats and other small craft bobbed up and down in the little bay. Excellent food was served there and we enjoyed a couple of evenings there watching the leisurely evening activities in the harbour. On our last evening we walked all round the ramparts and watched the sun set. The view across the old town is very picturesque, and near at hand one caught a glimpse of Ragusan life as one peered down upon yards and balconies of the houses near to the walls. Red and white oleanders, purple bougainvillea, morning glories in all shades, occasional palm trees and ilexes all helped to add to the charm of this ancient and proud port. Memorable within the town was the old Benedictine monastery with a very peaceful cloister with finely carved and fluted colonettes.

The modern busy shipping port of Dubrovnik is on the northern side of the peninsula. Plenty of modern buildings here and this is where the cruise ships stop and pick up and spew out their passengers.

For me, the highlight of this holiday was our stay in Ragusa. The memory of swimming in the warm translucent and clear waters of our bay has remained with me to this day.

At the end of our third day we said goodbye to our French friend who now had to return to Belgrade, but we had another day of glorious swimming and enjoyment of Ragusa. A year later we were devastated to learn that Maurice had been killed in an air accident in his own region of Bordeaux.

We sailed from Dubrovnik at 8 the following morning on the *Alexander*, a lovely boat, the pride of the line. It was a hot, sunny day and we spent most of it on deckchairs enjoying the scenery of this lovely coast. We had brief stopovers at various small picturesque ports, but a half-hour stopover at Split enabled us to stretch our legs along the quayside. Our last port of call was Sibenik, which we had visited on our cruise south and had had time to explore on that occasion. The town clings to the lofty hills behind it and consists of very narrow, steep streets, some of them being nothing but steps. There is an attractive old church with a sweet little baptistery with carved columns. We had watched a funeral procession; the men were all in front of the coffin carrying long white candles, where the women walked behind and seemed to be enjoying themselves—that is, all but, presumably, the widow, who kept up a rather curious wail. We sat on the low wall of the churchyard as they all filed past and then heard them singing in the church. We were struck by the excellence of it. Our impression of Sibenik was that it was a rather messy little town, though picturesque of course. Now it looked lovely in the sunset. We stayed long enough to see the town gradually light up and some Italian destroyers equally light up. It added to the effectiveness of the scene.

The following morning we disembarked at 7 o'clock at Susak and immediately made for the Park Hotel where we had left our car. After breakfast here we drove off for a visit to Plitvice with its fifteen lakes. We had a lovely drive south along the coast, with views of the sparkling blue sea of the Adriatic and its pretty islands. At Senj we left the coast and began a two-hour climb up an excellent road with many serpentine bends. The day had become very hot and the drive was tiring. Eventually we reached the top lake of the series, all cascading, one into the other, with waterfalls but curiously not from over the brim but from fissures in the cliff walls.

We were dismayed to find all the hotels in Plitvice, which is situated close to the shores of the lowest lake, full up. However, we found a wonderful haven in the house of a widow who had known better times but now took in a few guests. We were the only guests of this very motherly lady who made us extremely comfortable and cooked us the most splendid meals, the mainstay of which were lampreys which abound in the lakes. As Croatia had been for centuries part of the Austro-Hungarian empire, her natural language was German. We were taken aback by her vehement anti-Serb sentiments. We spent three nights with her and lazed much of the time in her pretty garden. But in the earlier part of the morning and after 4 in the afternoon we explored the various lakes all with the clearest water imaginable. My husband swam each day, but I only the once—I was so horrified at seeing the swaying tentacles and legs of innumerable lampreys walking beneath me on the floor of the lake, that I thought my foot might be grasped by one of them. The lakes were lovely with their blue/green limpid waters and surrounded by beech trees with an occasional pine. They must look lovely in autumn.

Our time was now up. We had to turn for home.

Total amnesia has taken over my mind relating to our journey back to Berlin. Just two specks of light emerge from this void of memory. First is of a tightrope walker standing on a rope way up above a square, the rope attached to a church steeple and a castle. On his bowed head is fixed a twirling fire-wheel, and on his back is strapped a packet from which coloured rockets rise with a bang. It was terrifying and spellbinding. My husband's diary of our holiday tells me this was at St Wolfgang am See, where we stopped on our way through the Salzkammergut.

The other is of walking on top of the wall which surrounds

the little medieval town of Nordlingen, almost dead centre of Germany.

I recall nothing else of our journey across the Alps through Corinthia and the Salzkammergut and all the way up the centre of Germany. Very strange! I surmise that for me the holiday was now over and I was now hankering to be back home to see my toddler—perhaps too, such a plethora of events during the succeeding years have chased away recollections of those five days' drive back to Berlin. It appears it was a journey of sunshine and downpour, stalked by thunderstorms, and that we camped out three times.

Happy Weekends

Another very enjoyable memory of those two years in Berlin was the friendship we struck up with an aristocratic (junker) family who owned an estate some thirty miles east of Berlin. They lived in what in today's parlance would be termed a medium-sized stately home. They received a letter introducing us to them, but I have no recollection as to who might have sent it, though I do remember our astonishment at suddenly receiving an invitation to luncheon on a certain Sunday in late October, a month after our arrival in Berlin. We accepted with pleasure and a 90-minute drive brought us to the Hardenbergs' home. It was a cold but sunny day on that appointed Sunday. The magnificent trees on the drive up to the house were now shedding their leaves, but there was still plenty of lovely autumn colouring. We were very courteously received by our host and hostess and quickly warmed to each other. They had five children ranging from an 18-year-old daughter to a boy of five. The eldest daughter had married that summer and her parents told us they were expecting their first grandchild the following June. The young people lived in a cottage on the far corner of the estate and the news of the expected happy event obviously delighted the family. We met three of the children at lunch, two girls about 11 and eight and the little boy. We learned that a boy of 14 was at a boarding school, way down south by the shores of Lake Constance. We expressed some surprise at this. 'We live too far away to send him to a Berlin day school,' was the explanation. 'A teacher comes here to teach the girls, and Hansi goes to the local village kindergarten school for the moment.'

We received a second invitation in December, for lunch on the second feast day of Christmas (our Boxing Day). 'If you could get to us by 11 o'clock, and the weather is fine, we could take a walk to foster our appetite for lunch.' The letter continued to say they would suggest our leaving for home by 3 o'clock so that we might get back to town before dark. We accepted with pleasure, and all went according to plan. Once again we were lucky in having a sunny day. The grounds were now deep in snow but our walk took us along cleared farm tracks and we certainly developed a hearty appetite for the excellent venison and red cabbage, which was the main course of our luncheon menu.

On a side table in the dining room were laid out a number of wrapped parcels which the children distributed at the end of the meal. It was explained to us that although gifts were distributed within the family on Christmas Eve, a parcel for each child was retained for the second feast day, the traditional day for inviting guests, who would be offered a gift. The children would then join in with the guests in the opening of presents. We had also brought a gift for our host and family. It was a very happy day and we reached home as darkness fell.

We had a further invitation in April 1938 (after the Anschluss). This time it included an invitation to stay the Saturday night. It was a very enjoyable visit, and we had a lovely walk through burgeoning woods and drifts of wild flowers here and there. This time Countess Hardenberg showed us all over the house, and she took me into her bedroom to show me her special bed—very wide and I imagine extremely comfortable. It had an ingenious contraption which could transform it into two single beds.

We had no further meetings during that very fraught year, until early in December we received an invitation once again to come for lunch on the second festive Christmas day, and to stay for two nights. What a lovely invitation—we accepted with alacrity. We left our toddler son in the care of our very competent Swiss nanny. I arranged with my cousin to keep in touch with them. In fact she gathered them in for the whole day we were away, fetching them hither and thither.

My outstanding memory of this visit, which sadly was our last one, was of the hip bath brought to our room before dinner on each evening. 'The bathroom would be rather cold for you,' said the Countess, 'but it will be all right for your husband!'

There was a glorious fire in our bedroom. The hip bath was brought and placed on a special large mat—three cans of hot water plus a can of cold water were placed alongside it, plus bath soap in a dish and an enormous bath towel. It was a glorious experience!

On our visits to the Hardenbergs, the political scene remained a more or less taboo subject. Inevitably, however, on this second Christmas Day visit at the end of 1938, the threat, though averted, of imminent war could not be totally ignored. The Count and Countess were full of praise for Mr Chamberlain and his efforts for peace. They were obviously immensely pleased that this had been achieved in Munich. Indeed, apart from diehard Nazis, these sentiments were echoed throughout Germany, and all British folk working in Germany now found themselves very popular.

In 1939 we had no further contact with this family. I can well visualise their dismay, apprehension and anxiety as events slowly unfolded.

Their son's school on Lake Constance closed and the visionary headmaster, Kurt Hahn, moved to the East Coast of Scotland where, in 1933 when Hitler came to power, he opened a school which has acquired much fame—Gordonstoun, alma mater of the Duke of Edinburgh, Prince Charles and his brothers.

I have often wondered if the Hardenberg family survived the war—their estate would have been overrun by the Russian armies, and after the war it would have found itself in East Germany.

The End of the Second World War and the Three Conferences

By the end of 1941 the war, which had begun in September 1939 between Nazi Germany and the British and French, became global. In June 1940 Italy had joined Germany, in June 1941 Germany attacked Russia and in December 1941 Japan attacked Pearl Harbor, bringing the United States into the war and in less than no time the war spread worldwide.

During the war and before the end of the war in Europe in May 1945, the three main allies, Great Britain, the USSR and the USA, met together at three conferences to discuss the further conduct of the war in the first two and, at the third conference in Yalta, the terms of peace and the new shape for Europe and indeed of the world, based upon a United Nations, the brainchild of Roosevelt.

The conferences took place in Moscow, Teheran and Yalta in the Crimea. My husband was a member of the delegation both in Moscow and in Yalta.

Moscow

It was at the Moscow conference that he had his first professional encounter with Russians and his first sighting of the

British embassy which he would know intimately four years later. His workload was so concentrated, with very long hours, however, so he saw nothing of Moscow, other than the superb view of the Kremlin from the embassy house.

Yalta

My husband kept a diary of the fourteen days he was away from home as a member of the British delegation to the Yalta conference in February 1945.

Our delegation was 40-strong. They brought everything with them, including personal valet and cigars for the Prime Minister, cars with chauffeurs and one or two mechanics for all transport, typewriters and their expert operators, and a few cases of fine clarets and whisky to stimulate and relax the grey cells when required.

Accommodation and catering with excellent food, which included caviar for breakfast as well as for other meals, was provided by the Russians together with Georgian wine and Armenian brandy at the occasional dinner parties which punctuated the eleven days in the Crimea. The Big Boys (Stalin, Roosevelt and Churchill) took it in turn to host a lavish dinner party for each other during this period.

The delegates were housed in three of Crimea's palaces which had belonged to the top aristocratic families in Tsarist days. The largest and grandest palace was the 'Livadia'. This was where the American VIPs of their delegation with Roosevelt in his wheelchair were housed; but the Livadia palace was also the conference centre where the plenary sessions between the three Big Boys with their respective foreign secretaries and military bigwigs met, seated around a central table with their respective advisers seated at long trestle tables behind them. Further delegation officials would twiddle their thumbs in an adjoining chamber waiting to be

THE END OF THE SECOND WORLD WAR

called into the conference hall to provide in-depth data as required.

The diary commences with a description of the journey via Malta, where our delegation had a two-day stopover and the opportunity of discussing the forthcoming conference with members of the American delegation, ahead of the arrival of President Roosevelt on board a large American cruiser, which, as it entered the harbour, was saluted by the bands and the marine guards on all the British ships. It was extremely impressive.

Following is a description of his drive from the aerodrome where his plane touched down in the Steppes of the Ukraine to the Vorontsov Palace at Yalta:

Watched the sun rise over the Black Sea. Landfall at about 7.30 and touched down uneventfully a quarter of an hour later. The aerodrome was vast, 6 or 7 giant 4-engine planes had already arrived and there were another 14 or 15 behind us, spaced out at 10-minute intervals. Molotov and Vyshinski met us on arrival and we were shepherded into two tents and plied with vodka, sandwiches, tangerines etc. After a long wait we eventually got away on our 100-mile drive to our destination. The first part of the journey was over limitless Steppe, covered with a bright powdering of snow. Every 300 or 400 yards were Russian soldiers on guard and so on the whole extent of the journey. There were no houses, so I suppose they slept where they stood in the open.

After Simpheropol, we started to climb over a pass. It must have been 2000 or 3000 feet high with a good many hairpin bends. When we got over the other side, the whole scenery changed. It became warmer and more Riviera-like with cypress and vineyards. After 3 hours' motoring we struck the shore of the Black Sea. The rest of the drive, some 2½ hours, was lovely, a real corniche road, twisting up and down along the coast. But it had been an exhausting day and we were getting too tired to enjoy it. By the time we reached the Vorontsov Villa, lunchless at 4.30, we were nearly deadbeat. (Actually, some members of the party did much worse, only getting in just before midnight, after various comic adventures on the way.)

The British delegation is split up into 3 parties: 1/ The PM, VIPs and officers in a curious Turko-gothic villa, with a superb position overlooking the sea. 2/ The Military in Sanatorium A, 10 minutes away by car and 3/ Ourselves, another 10 minutes on in Sanatorium B. Accommodation is pretty limited. We are five in a room on hardish beds with only a blanket. There are two WCs amongst 40-odd people. 3 showers at the end of the garden; and another walk to the restaurant. The pride of the establishment is the lady-barber, who haircuts and shaves admirably. I went in at 9.30 after supper and had a most refreshing shave with hot towels, eau de cologne spray etc, which made me feel much better.

Sunday 4th—A superb, sunny day. The sea sparklingly blue and everything looking lovely. Went up to the 'castle' where the place is stiff with VIPs, strolled down to the sea through a garden laid out with cypresses, arbutus and many other attractive trees whose names I do not know. No work to do. At 3 o'clock 'Uncle' came to pay an official call. At 3.30 three of us concerned with Germany went to the Villa Livadia, where the American VIPs are lodged and where the plenary sessions will take place. We had a very constructive talk with Harry Hopkins.

There was much to be discussed at the Yalta Conference, including, foremost, the forthcoming occupation of Germany from East and West to avoid disputes or even conflict between the allies; the rehabilitation of Poland as an independent sovereign state with a democratic government; reparations; the future configuration of Europe with new frontiers; the speedy end of the war with Japan; and, very important to Roosevelt, the future of the world based on a United Nations organisation more comprehensive than the League of Nations set up after the First World War, for now it should include Soviet Russian and American involvement.

The conference proved very wearying for all the delegates. The three secretaries of state had daily meetings at noon. Briefs for these with special points to be discussed had to be drawn up by the officials of the respective foreign offices and delivered to whichever of the three castles the meeting was to take place. Every afternoon a plenary meeting at the Livadia Palace took place. Much driving was involved. On the sixth morning, my husband woke up with a heavy cold and feeling distinctly unwell. Luckily for him the plenary meeting that afternoon did not concern him so he had a quiet day. The following day he once again had a free afternoon as Polish affairs were being discussed.

Following is another extract from his diary:

We have had a pretty hectic 5 or 6 days, keeping very late hours, driving many miles over twisty, hilly roads waiting around for long periods in stale, overheated rooms. It is beginning to tell on us all.

Went for a walk in the park behind Vorontsov—very attractive, laid out with paths, ponds, grotto etc and lots of jolly coniferous trees, whose names I do not know. Up behind tower 4000ft mountains, the last 2000ft being sheer rock face with a sprinkling of snow on the top. The 'Crimea Riviera' lies along the lower slopes of the mountains, running down to the sea. It is a kind of austere Riviera, with rugged coastline. There are many relics of a bygone age in the form of luxurious villas and palaces of attractive and formal design. But alas, they were very thoroughly 'scorched' by the Germans as they withdrew, and 90% are just empty shells.

BERLIN 1937–1939

> *Saturday 10th—woke up with a roaring cold and fiendishly busy all day till late in the evening.*

Halfway through the conference the diary states:

> *At 4pm had a superb view of the Great Men in the conference hall. There was great photographing and during it we all crowded round. Uncle Joe was quite imperturbable, Winston smoked a cigar, at least 9" long, Roosevelt was wheeled in his chair, an impressive and 'sympatique' figure, but looking tired and old.*

The final plenary meeting at the Livadia Palace took place the following day at noon to discuss the communiqué drafted until late the previous evening by members of the delegation. The entry in my husband's diary reads as follows:

> *Whole delegation is in the last lap—the conference hall was the dining room of the palace, a very attractive rectangular room with a beautiful ceiling. A round table stood in the middle at which sat the great men and their 3 or 4 chief advisers. The rest of the delegation sat in a second row immediately behind their great man and moved forward to advise when their subjects came up. Roosevelt was far and away the least impressive of the big three. Winston was the most talkative. Uncle Joe didn't talk much, but what he said was always very much to the point. He has mellowed a lot since the earlier meetings. He never gives anything away (like the PM does), but he can on occasion yield gracefully. The communiqué and conclusions were agreed in principle in the morning and it was left to the Foreign Secretaries to complete the details in the afternoon after a gargantuan luncheon.*

> *Returned to Vorontzov about 7pm and after tidying up and a good dinner, retired to bed at a fairly reasonable hour.*

The Aftermath of the Yalta Conference

So the conference ended and the delegates departed from the Crimea in a state of general euphoria. But not so Winston Churchill. He left Yalta in a gloomy mood. He had failed to make any headway on the question of Poland. The rehabilitation of this country as a free democratic sovereign state had been a priority for him. But this had not been so for Roosevelt, who had little interest in Poland or generally in Eastern Europe, and Stalin had already made up his mind regarding Poland's future. For centuries Russians had wanted to dominate that country and now was their opportunity. Poland should now embrace communism under the aegis of Soviet Russia.

Stalin extended lavish hospitality and amicable cordiality to his two wartime allies and he did concede little points here and there as the conference progressed. He even conceded the point that the Polish Prime Minister, Mikolajeski, who had run a Polish government in exile in London, should be allowed to return to Warsaw and fight his corner in a general election for a new post-war government, though he knew perfectly well that nothing other than a communist regime would in fact be installed.

Churchill distrusted Stalin. He had not forgotten Stalin's double-crossing manoeuvres in August 1939 when, behind the backs of the French and British delegates in Moscow, at the time negotiating a treaty of friendship with the Soviet Union, he agreed to sign a pact of non-aggression with Hitler which gave Hitler a free hand, having vanquished the Poles, to switch the bulk of his armed forces westwards for the attack on France and the British army in May 1940.

Four months after the Yalta Conference, Germany surrendered and peace was declared on 5 May 1945. A conference in Potsdam to implement the principles agreed at Yalta was immediately arranged for July. Roosevelt had died two months after Yalta in April and Churchill lost the general election in Great Britain so only attended the first half of the conference. Stalin now had two new and unknown leaders as his opposite numbers. The amiability he had shown in Yalta and at the previous two conferences was now replaced by strict formality. A spirit of non-cooperation with his wartime allies now prevailed. Ever-increasing friction developed between Russia and these erstwhile allies, in spite of the fact that the principles agreed in Yalta were endorsed in Potsdam. Berlin, now utterly devastated, was divided into four zones of occupation and France was allotted one of them. They were under military administration.

Such was the friction that developed that Russia within the year withdrew all cooperation with the other three partners and before long the Cold War was in place and effectively divided Europe into two camps. It was to last for many decades.

II

Moscow 1947–1949

Prologue: My First Russian Experience 1930	44
Mid-Twentieth Century Moscow	49
From Tilbury to Moscow, October 1947	51
Our Arrival in Moscow, October 1947	52
Settling into Skatertnay Pereulok	54
Autumn 1947	55
December 1947	57
Turn of the Year 1947–1948	60
Leningrad (St Petersburg), January 1948	63
Terror 1947–1949: The Volga Germans	67
Emma and Amalia	68
Moscow 1948	71
Journey back to Moscow, July 1948	75
Autumn/Winter 1948	77
To Tbilisi, October 1948	78

MOSCOW 1947–1949

Return to Moscow from Tbilisi	85
Our Social Life in Moscow 1947–1949	91
Cultural Activities, Moscow 1947–1949	94
The November 7th Celebrations and Parade, 1947	101
Memories from Skatertnay Pereulok	105
— The Afghan Ambassador	
— The Milking Cow	
— The Cresta Run	
Uncle Frost—Dadya Maroz	109
General Arrested	111
Last Months in Moscow, 1949	113

Prologue: My First Russian Experience, 1930

I first became interested in Russia as a teenager in Teheran, where my father was British Minister, though after the Second World War he would have been called ambassador. Teheran was full of refugees from the Russian revolution. There was a posse of gifted musicians amongst them, all trying to earn enough money to take them on to America or at least to a western European capital city, and it was a pianist from amongst them who came to give me piano lessons. As I was recovering from an operation, he would play Schubert impromptus and sonatas and Beethoven. He loved talking to my mother about his country and his harrowing experiences and I loved listening in. So I became aware of this great country just the other side of the mountains north of us, and was duly thrilled three years later at the prospect of travelling overland from London to Teheran via Moscow and Baku, where a ship would transport my brother and

PROLOGUE: MY FIRST RUSSIAN EXPERIENCE, 1930

myself down the Caspian Sea to the Persian port of Enseli, as it was then named. In late July 1930 my aunt bade us farewell at Victoria Station and pressed a box of Karlsbad plums into my hands. 'You may enjoy these on your journey,' she said. A further gift was pressed into my hands at the top of the great staircase in the British Embassy, Moscow, by our then ambassador, Sir Esmond Ovey, with the words, 'One never knows what may happen in Russia. You youngsters may find this German salami a good standby!' No truer words were ever spoken.

It had been a very hot day in Moscow (at the end of July, 1930) and Sir Esmond had laid on a busy programme for us. We saw the outdoor exhibition of French impressionist paintings, looted from rich industrialists who lived in grand houses in Moscow. We also watched the demolition of the great nineteenth-century cathedral on the banks of the Moscwa River, just downstream from the Kremlin. The Kremlin itself was now the seat of government and closed to the public. However, there is no better view of the Kremlin with its golden domes and pepper-pot cupolas of its great churches together with the great nineteenth-century palace of the Tsars, which dominates the scene above the great Kremlin wall, than from the British embassy. We had also tramped around a great deal, so by the time we were settled in our compartment on the Baku train we were ready to snuggle down on our respective bunks, much wider and more comfortable than their counterpart in western Europe. I had the upper berth lengthwise over the window, whilst Robbie's berth was crosswise from door to window. Our luggage was stowed in a cupboard in the ceiling of the corridor. A closed washstand, with the legend in French '*un vase se trouve sous le lavabo*', was in the corner by the door.

We fell into grateful sleep, conscious in our dreams of the haunting sonorous sound emitted by Russian trains every so often to announce their presence to the neighbourhood, or their arrival at a station. The train moved at a leisurely pace and every now and again would stop at a village. In the morning our carriage attendant brought us glasses of tea (tchai) and presently we dressed and emerged from our compartment to search for the dining car and breakfast. It was only after struggling through several carriages, all groaning with humanity, that the penny dropped and we realised there was no dining car attached to our train. The awful truth now dawned on us. These frequent stops, the slow pace of our train, had just one explanation—we were on a *Bummelzug*, German for a slow train, as opposed to the express train to Baku we should have been on. It was to take over eighty hours to reach Baku, instead of the scheduled sixty hours of the express train—and no food other than our salami sausage and Karlsbad plums, washed down by endless glasses of tchai. Some comestibles were being touted by peasant women walking up and down the platforms at some of the stops, but they looked utterly unappetising. Moreover, neither of us knew a word of Russian. Robbie had an unsure idea of the relative value of the roubles he had been handed by Sir Esmond in Moscow for 'emergencies' and was afraid of being hooked by these women. So, it seemed best to reserve our energies and hopefully manage to eke out our salami. We retreated to our bunks and immersed ourselves in our respective books: Robbie with some Swedish saga and Tolstoy's *War & Peace*; I with the entire *Forsyte Saga*, a parting present from my headmistress. We had reached steppe country—it was vast, flat and featureless—it had up to the revolution been the bread basket of Russia, exporting grain to Europe. Since the revolution, the old farming habits of the countryside had been utterly ruined and now, in 1930, it was on the verge of its second devastating famine. Our train stopped at innumerable hamlets, for what purpose I really do not know.

We were greatly relieved to find on our eventual arrival in

PROLOGUE: MY FIRST RUSSIAN EXPERIENCE, 1930

Baku a young man on the lookout for us. Misha had come to meet us as a result of our non-appearance off the Baku–Enseli boat three days earlier in Enseli. My father contacted Moscow and the story of our having been mistakenly put on the slow, rather than the express, train was revealed. He escorted us to a hotel, where we were dismayed to find there was no food available until 7 o'clock that evening, when the restaurant on the roof terrace would be open. Misha was a kind young man, a student of English. He disappeared and returned with a packet of very dry and hard biscuits. The day was hot and airless. He said he would return to us at 4 o'clock and take us to see the Caspian. We duly ambled along the promenade and past a jetty with rowing boats moored alongside. We noticed the sea was bespattered with oil and smelled of it too.

We returned to the hotel hot and sticky from our walk. There was no en suite bathroom to our rooms. Nevertheless, we each enjoyed a complete wash down from our basin and a change of clothes. On the dot of seven we were the first arrivals at the roof restaurant.

On a fine evening it is always fascinating to fly over a city after dark and see all the twinkling lights below, but the fascination is all over too quickly and one has landed. So dining on a rooftop terrace on a warm July evening, overlooking the illumination of a city spread out at one's feet, is extremely pleasurable—and Robbie and I thoroughly enjoyed our first Baku evening. We were ravenous, but though I have no recollection of our menu, whatever it comprised it certainly satisfied us and halfway through our meal a chap appeared and strummed on a balalaika. We were happy—then the bill came and anxiety replaced pleasure. Half the wad of roubles now went in one fell swoop—we had two whole days ahead of us to cater for and what would our hotel rooms cost?

Robbie was now extremely troubled, but luckily he was

able to find out the following morning that the cost of our hotel nights had been paid by Intourist in Moscow, so if we ate very frugally and kept a little money back for incidental expenses, we should get by—and we did. Our next square meal was dinner with the captain on board our Caspian steamer. I have forever thought that the roast chicken we ate that evening was the best and tastiest I have ever enjoyed.

Baku in July is intolerably hot, with the disagreeable odour of oil assailing one's olfactory senses at every little waft of air. Two experiences remain in my mind of our enforced time spent in this city.

We longed for a swim. 'Why not try and hire one of those rowing boats we noticed tied to that jetty, and row out to sea into clear water and swim from the boat?' suggested Robbie. 'Yes, yes,' I agreed enthusiastically. How naïve we were! We managed to hire a boat and out to sea we rowed, but the globules of oil followed us unremittingly. It was very hot, Robbie tired, I tried to take over, the oars were heavy, I was inept. We stopped, dispirited, then we heard the purr purr sound of a motor boat approaching us—sure enough, it was Misha. He was quite steamed up at our having given him the slip. In fact, we had congratulated ourselves on this feat! Now we felt rather like naughty children caught out in a glorious escapade. A rope was attached to our rowing boat and we were ignominiously towed back to the jetty. 'If you wish to swim, I will take you to a beach tomorrow,' promised Misha.

There was no enjoyment in the following day's jaunt to a Baku beach. The beach itself was an ant heap of teeming, sweaty humanity. Any desire to swim evaporated instantly. You could hardly see the water for bobbing heads. It had taken us forty minutes to reach this 'paradise'. We had been squeezed into one of three carriages in a little puff-puff train, which every so often emitted a cloud of evil-smelling dirty smoke. Latecomers for the departure of the train hoisted

PROLOGUE: MY FIRST RUSSIAN EXPERIENCE, 1930

themselves onto the roof of the carriages and their legs dangled down over the windows.

It was a ghastly experience and our thirst was overwhelming. Misha bought a watermelon—with his pocket knife he carved off chunks, brushed off the black pips onto the sand to mix with the other debris there and handed them to us. We sank our jaws into the pink flesh—it was wonderfully cooling and refreshing. Curiously, since that day, I have not relished watermelons.

It was bliss crossing the gang plank onto our steamer at 7 p.m., to wash down from a small amount of water in our tiny basin and then to tuck into a wonderful dinner with our jovial captain, who obviously considered us a great joke. How glad we were to leave Baku. It was seventeen years before my next experience of Russia.

Mid-Twentieth-Century Moscow

We now move into the Russian room of my gallery of memories which is partitioned into two separate sections, the first relating to the years 1947 to 1949 and the second to 1965 to 1968.

There are two links between these two periods: first, the climate—six months of cold, snowy weather, bitterly cold at times, with the temperature sometimes as low as $-24°$ centigrade; in between, there were days of rain and thaw with resulting slush which would subsequently ice over, making it very slippery underfoot, four months of hot summer are interspersed with mighty thunderstorms, and finally there are two months of lovely autumn. Spring as we understand it is non-existent. No daffodils and other spring flowers to gladden the heart, just one week separating winter from summer.

The second link was the invisible barrier between Russians and foreigners (unless of a satellite country), except on a purely professional basis. During Stalin's lifetime, contact with foreigners was stringently forbidden and enforced. In 1947–1949 the only contact we ever had with Russians was when meeting them at national day receptions, and then only very few officials turned up at these unless hosted by a satellite country, such as Poland, Bulgaria, Romania, or East Germany, when crowds of Russians would turn up.

This barrier between Russians and foreigners within the Soviet Union was matched by the barrier between the two blocs into which Europe now found herself divided—the communist eastern bloc dominated by Russia, and the western block comprising separate sovereign states, all with strong anti-communist convictions, bar a small minority of their citizens.

The countries of eastern Europe were nominally independent but in fact they were all under the Russian yoke. They were known as the satellite countries and by the end of 1948, Czechoslovakia, which for three years had withstood communism, was brutally invaded by Russian troops and found itself absorbed into the Russian orbit. With the signing of the military treaty known as the Warsaw Pact, between Russia and her satellites, the Cold War was now born. There was a veto on citizens of the eastern bloc travelling to any foreign country. This presented great hardship and anguish to Germans who often had relatives on both sides of the divide. The Berlin Wall was erected towards the end of the fifties as a measure of containment for eastern zone Berliners who repeatedly attempted clandestinely crossing the frontier.

During our first period, with echoes into our second period sixteen years later, there came up the question of Russian wives of British personnel, largely servicemen who had been caught up in Russia during the war. The men had had to return to England, leaving their Russian wives behind, and endless parleys took place between the ambassador, his senior staff and Russian officials trying to extract permits for the wives to rejoin their husbands, but from Gromyko downwards, *'niet, niet'* was the uncompromising Russian riposte.

Keeping in touch with family and friends throughout both periods was through the medium of the weekly King's messenger (or, since 1952, Queen's messenger). This gentleman belonged to a corps of mostly retired military, air and naval men who travelled the world carrying official documents between the Foreign Office and other government ministries to missions overseas. These couriers plied to and fro on a regular basis, carrying not only official documents but also the personal mail of individuals on foreign stations. By international agreement, government couriers and the bags in their charge had diplomatic immunity and were not subject to foreign interference and customs.

From Tilbury to Moscow, October 1947

The most rewarding way of visiting a beautiful city is to approach it by sea where possible. I had the luck thus to see Venice and Rio de Janeiro for the first time and this is how we first saw Leningrad (only recently reverted to its real name of St Petersburg).

It was a bright sunny morning on 14 October 1947. Slowly we glided up the estuary of the river Neva on our Russian boat. The passengers were all on deck, eyes trained on the goal ahead. Soon we saw the two golden spires of the Admiralty and the St Peter and Paul fortress glinting in the sunshine. We tied up at the docks, a short way downriver from the Aurora, a Russian navy frigate, on board which the Russian revolution of 1917 began.

By lunchtime, our two boys aged 7 and 5, their governess and us, plus a pile of luggage, were installed in the Astoria Hotel opposite St Isaac's Cathedral. This was our base for the day. That evening we were to take the night train to Moscow. Our afternoon was free, so we hired a car and an Intourist guide and did a quick tour around the main sights of Peter the Great's city. Like everyone else, we fell under its spell and vowed to come and visit it properly at the earliest opportunity.

When we sailed from the Tilbury docks early in October, England was enjoying an Indian summer. Leaves on the trees were beginning to turn, but when we reached Stockholm most leaves had already fallen and in Leningrad the trees were bare. As we steamed away from England, the temperature fell steadily and now our day in Leningrad was distinctly chilly, particularly by the river.

Our train pulled into its Moscow terminus at 7.15 a.m. on 15 October 1947. Snow was falling; we were in a white world. For the next two and a half months, we scarcely ever saw the sun. The sky remained an opaque grey until December when the great frosts came; a daily pattern of snow, sleet, rain, thaw, slush, frost and back to snow, seemed to be the order of the day. Our spirits drooped. Then in December the serious frosts took over, the thermometer plummeting to $-24°$ centigrade on Christmas Day.

Our Arrival in Moscow, October 1947

On arrival at Moscow Station we tumbled out onto the platform and shivered. We were met and driven to the Imperial Hotel of nineteenth-century splendour, rather akin to the Savoy Hotel in London, with suites of rooms upstairs and a huge cafeteria bar and restaurant on the ground floor. A grand suite allotted to us comprised a lobby and a fairly large sitting room with gilt chairs and sofa all upholstered in damask silk. A glass chandelier dangled from the ceiling and china ornaments were dotted around. It was all redolent of a

OUR ARRIVAL IN MOSCOW, OCTOBER 1947

past age. Beyond this room was a dining room, a small study and a bedroom with a large double bed, and there was a bathroom with a single basin.

'Are we all going to sleep in this big bed?' asked my five-year-old. Well, there were five of us: my husband, myself, the two boys and their governess. We were assured that further beds would be provided and placed wherever we wished. But the immediate priority now was breakfast and the boys were impatient to unpack the hamper provided by the Astoria Hotel in Leningrad, ordered by Mr Kostaki and placed in our train compartment. Mr Kostaki explained to us that he had ordered this hamper as he knew it would take us a full two hours to obtain any breakfast at the Imperial Hotel. However, tchai would be immediately forthcoming as there was always a bubbling samovar on each landing of the hotel.

So we ordered tchai and unpacked the following out of the hamper: two whole roast chickens, 1lb of ham, 1½ lbs of butter, 1lb of sugar, 1lb of cheese, 2 enormous loaves of bread and an excellent currant cake. The only snag was, all this was in bulk form and we only had two small pocket knives between us to deal with this bounty. But we dealt and enjoyed our meal. There was enough left over for the governess and the boys for high tea for the next two evenings.

Mr Kostaki, of Greek origin, was a highly efficient employee of the British embassy. Administrative questions arising between the embassy and the Russian authorities were always satisfactorily negotiated and eased through by him. (Eighteen years later, when we returned to Moscow, Mr Kostaki was still there). He had been sent up to Leningrad, not just to meet us and ease our onward journey, but also to meet our ambassador and Lady Peterson, who were returning from home leave and who had travelled with us from Tilbury. They had a great mound of luggage, of which only about a third was personal, the rest being stores, mostly food and medicines, destined for the British Mission in Moscow as a whole. It was up to Mr Kostaki to field all this and accompany it to Moscow. This he successfully accomplished and by our second Moscow day, all was safely deposited within the confines of the British embassy.

Settling into Skatertnay Pereulok

After a week spent in the splendiferous lustre of the Imperial Hotel, we moved into the ground-floor flat of Skatertnay Pereulok (Table Cloth Street). This we inherited from our predecessor, Frank Roberts and his wife, who had assured us that the flat was much too small to accommodate a family (they were childless). We had, however, seen a plan of the flat whilst still in England and had concluded that we could squeeze in the boys and a governess. It certainly was a tight fit, like sardines in a tin, but at the end of our second week I wrote to my parents, 'We are now more or less installed and unpacked—getting in was rather like stuffing a fat pillow into a clean pillowcase.' Furniture was moved around and a small lumber room, used as a repository for trunks by our predecessors, was given a thorough wash down, followed by a coat of paint, and a window was prised open. A comfortable divan bed for the governess and two suitable smallish beds for the boys were moved in to the flat.

At the end of a chaotic week I wrote to my parents, 'Here we are, settled in and shaken down and in fact we think we are really pretty snug. I am sitting on our comfortable divan/sofa with my back against the delicious warm tiles of our wonderful Russian stove.' The flat was bisected by a long corridor with excellent cupboards all down one side. Four Russian stoves were built into the wall at each end of the corridor. At 9 a.m., two stoves diagonally opposite each other were lit, the flues wide open. Emma, our wonderful inherited Volga German maid, fed them for the next half hour with logs bundled together in two great heaps. When the floor of the stoves was covered in ashes Emma closed the flues tight, spread the ashes quickly and evenly around, closed the door of the stoves tightly, and the two tiled walls facing into two separate rooms slowly and gradually got ever warmer as the day progressed, and even retained warmth the following day. The flat was wonderfully heated in this way and so economical on fuel.

Autumn 1947

It was now two and a half years since the end of the war, and although Russia had finally triumphed and defeated Hitler and had reached Berlin ahead of the American and British armies, the cost in human life had been colossal. Moscow was now largely a city of widows and grandmothers. The dearth of men, particularly young men, was quite striking. It was the women who seemed to do all the hard labouring jobs, such as demolishing half-ruined buildings, which you would normally expect men to be doing. It was the women who kept the streets relatively clear of the winter snow and ice by shovelling it all to the side as fast as it fell, so that traffic moved freely, and with picks and shovels they did their best to keep the pavements clear enough for the pedestrians. These women, armed with their tools, would work away, night and day, hacking and shovelling all the mess into separate mounds along the streets, presently to be scooped up and thrown into lorries which turned up every so often, and when full, would then drive down to the river, there to tip it all into the water. The flow would carry it away, but when the river froze over the now dirty snow would coalesce into blocks, not to unfreeze until the great spring thaw did at last arrive. It was a back-breaking job but these women were tough. Black bread, the only unrationed food, was their staple nourishment—all other food was purchased in 'gastronomes', the Russian word for a food shop, where there were always long queues.

The shelves of these emporiums were largely empty. Food, other than meat, was hidden out of sight under the counters. Different categories of food entailed separate queuing, three queues for each category, Queue 1: Enquiring as to an item's availability. If yes, you collected a cost ticket. Queue 2: Paying for the item at an enclosed pay desk with your ration card. Queue 3: Return to back of Queue 1 to collect your package in exchange for your receipted cost ticket. Up to December 1947, all food was rationed.

Foreigners living in their own accommodation rather than in hotels (largely journalists) had the facility of shopping in their own special shop, and this is where during the autumn of 1947 we bought our bread, butter, meat and poultry and a very restricted selection of groceries, such as flour and sugar. Every so often you could purchase a tin of top-quality caviar.

About once a week a market operated in Moscow with stalls of a few vegetables stocked from community farms—potatoes, carrots, white cabbage and dried mushrooms threaded on strings. No other vegetables or fruit were ever seen. The scarcity of everyday commodities and of basic groceries led to the British government setting up a small commissariat to operate from an outbuilding within the precincts of the embassy compound. This was stocked with a number of consumer necessities for its personnel in Moscow, and comprised milk for babies and concentrated orange juice for children, toilet paper and soap (both toilet and laundry), a small amount of basic groceries such as flour, sugar, porridge oats, tea and coffee, and a very restricted number of frills such as tinned milk, marmalade and jam, dried fruit, whisky and chocolate.

All these items for consumer consumption were imported under a quota system fixed by the Soviets of goods that a foreign country was allowed to export per annum into the Soviet Union, but for the use of their own nationals resident there. The quota had to include furniture, crockery and glass for households as well as office furniture and stationery and all the other equipment for running an office, plus necessary tools and electrical equipment for communication purposes. The quota was very tight, and was roughly the same for all countries, large or small—it was arbitrary and grossly unfair to countries like ourselves, the French and the Americans, the wartime allies of the Russians. We all had sizeable missions in Moscow, military as well as civil, as against much smaller countries, like Switzerland or Scandinavia.

December 1947

In December 1947 a sudden bombshell exploded in our midst—utter consternation struck our world, affecting Russians and foreigners alike. There had been no inkling of this at all. Rationing of food would cease forthwith, the special foreigners' shop would close and the rouble would be devalued to the tune of 1 new rouble for 10 old ones.

Once the fact had sunk in that ration cards were no longer necessary, the Russian women went quite mad. Food that for long years past had merely been dreamt of was now available, so they descended like locusts on the gastronomes and they bought and bought and bought and carried off all manner of foodstuffs to hoard in their exiguous apartments. They spent their last rouble on food without thought for the morrow.

But now the penny dropped. Suddenly they realised that for 1 new rouble they had to cough up 10. Their savings all disappeared in less than no time and a fresh bout of misery engulfed these long-suffering Russians, so it was a stressful end-of-year scenario, not only for them but also for those foreigners who relied entirely on their diplomatic bag to bring them produce from the outside world, and of course on the foreigners' food shops.

It so happened we had planned to give our first cocktail party on the evening of the bombshell, followed by a second party two days later. These parties were a return of hospitality received by us from our own mission colleagues and also from our foreign colleagues following our arrival in Moscow. So the day of the bombshell was a very busy day for me and my household. When my husband returned for a quick snack at two o'clock between shifting furniture to make space for our guests, he told me briefly what had happened but it was only from the voluble chatter of my guests later in the day that I fully learned of this new decree. It certainly gave everyone at this party and the subsequent one a wonderful topic of conversation.

The greatest wailing and gnashing of teeth was on the subject of the monetary loss which we, together with the Russian population, were now to incur—sheer robbery on the part of the Soviet government. Luckily my husband and I between us stood to lose only about £15 (at 1947 prices). Many members of staff, and in particular junior members, were seriously affected, so my husband drafted a letter to the Foreign Office suggesting that they should consider reimbursing the loss incurred by embassy personnel.

On the food front, I wrote to my parents on 16 December, saying, 'I don't know what Christmas cheer we shall be able to conjure up for Christmas Day, apart from plum pudding which Amalia has already made. Whether there will be any fresh meat or poultry available, only the Gods may know. Three days ago Amalia managed to purchase some beef, and to eke it out she has stuffed white cabbage and also made delicious "piroshkis" (little stuffed pastry rolls—a Russian speciality). We may have to make do with a couple of tins of ham and tinned vegetables from my store cupboard. On

Christmas night we are bidden to the Embassy with the rest of the staff for a buffet supper, but Lady P doesn't know yet whether she will be able to get the necessary food.' Unfortunately a letter recounting the outcome of this Christmas fare dilemma is missing and my memory is blank. But somehow we must have survived!

Our catering problems were compounded by the dreadful weather which prevented aeroplanes landing at Moscow airports. For three weeks no King's messenger arrived bringing us coveted stores for individuals and for the commissariat, no eagerly awaited letters from family and friends, no Christmas cards or presents. Our commissariat was seriously depleted. There was no coffee and we ourselves had also run out. Entertaining had come to an abrupt halt. Understandably many people became quite seriously depressed. We all felt like forgotten exiles in a distant land. People with children weathered this difficult month more easily than single people or childless couples.

Christmas 1947 may have been rather bleak but the year ended on a happy note. The King's messenger at last arrived on the 29th, after three weeks of non-appearance and, like Baa-Baa Black Sheep, he came with three bags full. To everyone's grateful satisfaction the Foreign Office agreed to reimburse the monetary loss we had all incurred and he brought our longed-for mail, plus Christmas cards and presents. A very happy tea-time and evening was enjoyed by the family in the ground floor flat of Skatertnay Pereulok.

Another effect of the devaluation of the rouble was that shops, known as commission shops, filled up with all sorts of goods—rugs and textiles, clocks, watches, porcelain (practical and ornamental), pictures, jewellery and household goods galore. All these things were brought in for sale by impoverished Russians. The shopkeepers accepted these goods for sale on a commission basis. They would value the items and agree with the owner the asking price, but were allowed to bargain with a potential buyer. If the owner had second thoughts he could always remove the objects.

Visits to these shops by us foreigners was a quite usual Sunday occupation. One could often pick up quite valuable items at relatively bargain prices. I bought an attractive nineteenth-century French clock-cum-barometer which was subsequently stolen from me by a thief in the night forty years on.

Turn of the Year, 1947–1948

Our first two and a half months in Moscow from mid-October 1947 to the new year of 1948 had been devoid of enjoyment, but it was a busy time and there was no time to mope. Getting settled into our cramped flat, getting the boys into a routine of lessons and leisure with their teacher-governess, getting to know the ropes of living in Moscow, starting up with Russian lessons, meeting a mass of new people; all this made for a very full timetable. The one glow of satisfaction was that we were snug and warm in Skatertnay Pereulok—the outside world was uninviting! Snow, rain, frost, slush, grey skies, mist and fog and never a gleam of sun until Christmas Day, when a sudden plummeting of the thermometer to $-24°$ centigrade was accompanied by three glorious hours of sunshine around midday. It had not been unduly cold till now, and after all we were inured to cold at the end of the 1940s. We had actually walked on the North Sea off the coast of Belgium the previous winter. But the burst of sun on Christmas Day boosted our morale no end and it marked a turning point. December, up till now, had been a particularly difficult month but the year ended on a happy note. At last the King's messenger arrived on the 29th and we felt we were once more in touch with family and

TURN OF THE YEAR, 1947–1948

friends back in England and there was the promise of much enjoyment during 1948.

What made Christmas especially gratifying for the boys was that they were now in possession of skis like their parents, who had brought some out with them. (They dated from pre-war days in Berlin.) Yes, I had been very lucky: on Christmas Eve I had been tipped off that skis for youngsters would be on sale after 5 p.m. at Dietski Mir (Children's World), the large three-storey building in Derjinski Square, right opposite the dreaded Lubianka, the headquarters for the NKVD (the secret police). Dietski Mir catered for all children's needs, from babyhood to school leavers, their clothes, toys, uniforms and sporting gear. All these items were only spasmodically and individually on sale and one acted very much on tip-offs, so at 6 p.m. on Christmas Eve, our driver drove me to Derjinski Square, parked the car on the curb (easy in those days!) and escorted me to the sports department where, wonder of wonders, with his help, I managed to purchase skis for each of the boys. Thus I had a super present for them for Christmas Day. Items I had brought out with us for this purpose now remained stowed away until February when they both celebrated their birthdays.

Four days later they were able to try them out. Fittings and straps had been fixed onto the skis by a handyman at the embassy garage workshop. We had been advised that Tzaritzina would be a good place for a first go at skiing. Tzaritzina was Catherine the Great's hunting lodge and nestled on a wooded hillside beside a lake about twelve miles out of town. Both in summer and in winter, it was a favourite spot for Russians and foreigners alike, for walking and picnicking in summer, and for walks on skis through the woods in winter. There were some gentle slopes there, suitable for gliding down, and our driver knew their whereabouts and so out we went on the morning of the 29th. After much tumbling over and initial frustration, the boys did manage to find their balance and even to slither down a gentle slope. Tired out but exhilarated, we returned for a very late lunch and heard the news: 'The King's messenger has arrived.' Hurrah—so ended a very happy day. On New Year's Day we met Dadya Maroz, Uncle Frost, a bewitching experience. He helped to start the coming year of 1948 on an encouraging note.

There had been no highlights of enjoyment during our first three months in Moscow, but 1948 was to prove different. There was much to enjoy that year, culminating in a trip to Tbilisi in Georgia, where we enjoyed five gorgeous autumn days in October.

On our arrival in Moscow in October 1947, we had been lucky to find amongst our embassy colleagues another family with three sons, each a year younger than our own, and with the eldest son left back at school in England. Father was the assistant military attaché. Unfortunately they lived out at Perlovka, some twelve miles outside the city's boundary, a 40-minute drive along an atrocious road. The transport situation was too difficult for these boys to join our schoolroom class, but weather permitting, we spent some happy Sundays out at Perlovka, and once our boys had skis we would join up with this family and drive a further five miles to some treeless slopes suitable for skiing down. Competition between the boys was very keen, and was a wonderful stimulus to their respective performances. Though a little younger than our boys, they were much the same size, and when not skiing they had much fun together in the grounds of Perlovka.

The boys were now settled into a routine of lessons and play. Australian twins and the daughter of an embassy colleague had joined our schoolroom class.

The sun was now making a very welcome occasional presence, though *snow* now prevailed for the next couple of months. No more thaws and slush, just new falls of snow keeping our world pristine white. So off we went for a freezingly cold weekend to Leningrad at the end of the first week of January 1948.

Leningrad (St Petersburg), January 1948

After the Russian Orthodox Christmas there was a welcome lull in activities and my husband was able to take a Friday off and on the Thursday night, we scrambled into the night train for Leningrad. We had three days to enjoy the city before returning to Moscow on the Sunday night train.

Leningrad was now in the grip of ice and snow, and intermittently small snowflakes would flutter down from the leaden sky. The Neva was frozen over, resembling the lower reaches of a glacier with great lumps of ice strewn around. Walking along its banks was such a cold experience; one snuggled into one's warm coat, one's fur hat and muffler and hardly noticed the beautiful buildings one was passing. No question of lingering.

Once again, we hired a car and, accompanied by an attractive Intourist guide, we toured around the city and went further afield than on our arrival day in October. What struck us so pertinently was the emptiness of the streets—hardly any traffic at all, just a few pedestrians well wrapped up in padded clothing, the men in fur hats with ear flaps down, the women well encased in their padded coats with great shawls over their heads and half covering their faces. Thick felt boots, '*varlinkis*', on their feet as they hurried along. The silence of this city was all-pervading, away from the Whitehall–Westminster arena with its palaces and grandiose buildings. The streets seemed long and grey and empty and the cold was intense.

In the afternoon, our guide took us to the Hermitage. We

had expressed our desire to see the French Impressionist paintings, looted by the government from their owners, mostly rich industrialists living in splendid buildings in Moscow. The British Embassy is housed in one of them. A sugar king had built the house bang opposite the Kremlin—the best location in town!

These Impressionist paintings were hung in three low-ceilinged galleries right at the back of the Hermitage on the top floor. Looking out of the window, we had a splendid view of the great circular parade ground behind the Hermitage. On the far side of the great circle was the lofty gate through which the peaceful demonstrators streamed to petition the Tsar for a democratic parliament in 1905. They were mown down by the military, an act which shocked the world and contributed greatly to the outbreak of the revolution some years later in 1917.

We had three French Impressionist galleries to ourselves, a quite fabulous collection, re-housed in the 1960s in a Moscow picture gallery.

On the following day a rickety old car and an elderly male guide were provided for us to drive out and visit the great country palaces belonging to the Tsars and Tsarinas and members of their family. They had been bombarded and overrun by the Germans in 1942 and now stood in various stages of ruin. These palaces are situated some fifteen miles to the west of the city.

The main road was passably good on beaten-down snow, but the turn-off road to the palaces was atrocious: ruts, bumps and pot holes for some three or four miles. The first palace we visited was Tsarkoie Selo, the family home of the late Tsar Nicolas II with nearby Ekaterinburg, built by Peter the Great's sister and then greatly added to and embellished by Catherine the Great.

Half the walls were down, rooms open to the sky, pillars, balustrades, statuary flung around amongst rafters, bricks

LENINGRAD (ST PETERSBURG), JANUARY 1948

and rubble—a sorry mess. It was heart-rending. We tramped over the ruins and discounted any idea of the feasibility of restoration. Ekaterinburg though badly battered was mostly still standing but Peterhof, Peter the Great's summer palace, was almost utterly destroyed. Our guide told us that in due course, yes, they would all be restored. We did not believe him.

Cold and depressed, we rejoined our car and ate our packed lunch provided by the Astoria Hotel and were glad of a swill of vodka to warm up our innards. We then set off on our return journey. Bumpity-bump, we rejoined the main road and some two miles along it, our rickety car hiccuped and then conked out. We were now in the middle of nowhere, flat snowbound desolate country all around. No sign of life anywhere and bitterly cold. We got out of the car, stamped our feet, and leaving the chauffeur and our old guide with their heads buried in the engine, began to walk down the long straight road towards Leningrad, thinking the car would soon catch up with us.

But quite soon we saw a strange car approaching us. We waved frantically and the car stopped beside us. A lone man probably in his late 30s was driving it. He was obviously an intelligent and educated man and we quickly discovered that in spite of our two and a half months of Russian studies, we had little expertise in the language, but we also soon discovered that we could communicate with him in German. He said he had passed our car and had told the two chaps that he would report the breakdown as soon as he reached a telephone. 'But you people, if you would like a lift into town, hop in.'

My husband sat beside him and I scrambled into the back and almost immediately this friendly unknown individual and my husband were engaged in a lively conversation.

It appeared that our new friend was a senior hydraulic engineer working on the construction of the Volga Don Canal way down south and he was home now for a few days' leave. He was thrilled to find that we were Brits.

As we neared the City it was by now dusk, and he asked us whereabouts were we lodged. When he heard the answer, his whole manner changed. He shut up like a clam and then said, 'It will be extremely dangerous for me if it is discovered that it was I who gave you a lift. When I stop the car, please get out as quickly as possible; I will stop at a corner, please walk straight ahead without further word to me, then cross the road and take the next turn to the left. You will have about a 15-minute zigzag walk to your hotel. Everyone knows where the Astoria Hotel is.'

Silence now reigned, as we realised at once the implication of what he had said. 'I am stopping at the next corner.'

We hopped out quickly. He turned the corner and accelerated. We walked straight ahead as instructed. Our spirits sagged. We understood only too well what lay in store for him if the authorities discovered his name—had the two chaps of the rickety car taken his number?

It was a sad and depressing day and I have often thought about our charming rescuer and wondered whether his identity was ever discovered and then what? Uncomfortable musings with a thread of guilt through them still haunt me from time to time.

Our last day was a little more benign and we spent some time exploring around and about us and then a further morning and afternoon at the Hermitage. The night train landed us back in Moscow at 7.15 a.m. and we were back in our flat for breakfast on the Monday morning.

Our three days in this beautiful northern city had depressed us. It had also given us a far deeper understanding of the impact of three years of siege with hunger, cold and mourning. Although by and large the core of Peter the Great's city had been spared, there was ample evidence away from this core of the ruin and devastation of war.

The Russians are a tough, resilient people and they were coping; but we were also deeply aware of the ever-present

KGB and of Stalin's malignant power. This awareness stayed with us for the entire two years we spent in Russia at that time.

Terror, 1947–1949: The Volga Germans

After the agonies of the war years and up to the time of Stalin's death in 1953, Russia was again in the grip of terror as it had been in the late thirties. Spy mania and denunciations not only gripped Stalin himself, but were widespread amongst the general population. No one was secure from being reported for a carelessly expressed thought or for some imagined misdeed. These could land a close relative, even a parent, in trouble. Those in authority, with distorted minds, would accuse their own citizens of a potentially treasonable purpose if seen conversing with a foreigner unless they had official sanction to do so. The unfortunate individual would be taken to the Lubianka, the notorious headquarters of the KGB, as the secret service was then named. He or she might be tortured and then packed off for years of hard labour in a Gulag in Siberia or else shot.

Diplomatic households in Moscow had one or two Russian servants assigned to them who did the cleaning, laundering and possibly cooking and, if so, most of the household shopping. The Volga Germans among them were intelligent and literate women and would develop friendly relations with their foreign employers. However, on a given evening of each week they had to go and report to their Soviet masters overheard conversation or unusual behaviour, squabbles, bad temper, and so on, on the part of their employers.

Before the revolution in 1917, the unmarried daughters of Volga-German origin who were good needlewomen would find employment with aristocratic families in St Petersburg, where they would become the personal maid of their mistresses. They were also much in demand with diplomatic families. When the capital was transferred to Moscow, these maids were allowed to accompany their foreign employers to the new location. Gradually over the years they were able to introduce younger relatives from the Volga villages to follow in their footsteps. But with the war this all came to an end.

The Volga Germans were so called because the communities they came from emanated from German settlements along the middle reaches of the river Volga. These German settlements dated from the days of Peter the Great, who, in recognition of the splendid work German engineers and craftsmen had done in the building of his dream capital, had donated tracts of land along the banks of the great river for them to send for their families and settle them in these fertile lands. The settlers came and built churches and schools and gradually constructed villages that mirrored the ones back in their homelands. They were hard-working and industrious people who generally inter-married amongst themselves, rather than linking up with Russians (although of course some of them did). These villages became pockets of German culture within the vast confines of Russia.

During the war, as the German armies came ever closer to Stalingrad, the German settlements along the Volga came under suspicion of colluding with the enemy. Stalin gave the order to eliminate them. The villages were torched and families disbanded and transported in cattle trucks to Siberia, where they were dumped to struggle as best they could.

Emma and Amalia

In 1947 there were just six or seven of the Volga-German women in service with senior diplomats in Moscow. We were lucky to inherit two of these: Amalia and Emma. Amalia was our cook and Emma the all-purpose maid.

EMMA AND AMALIA

Amalia was a very large woman in her forties. She was rather dour and suffered from indigestion. This necessitated dessert spoonfuls of bicarbonate of soda every so often. My predecessor had asked me to bring half a dozen large drums of this product with our luggage and during our two years I obtained replenishments from London via the King's messenger. Amalia was very frugal in her eating, though. Maybe she was a finger dipper, as all good cooks and chefs are. Certainly the food she cooked for us was always excellent; real chef cooking. She was renowned amongst our colleagues as the best cook in the circuit and they always relished coming for a meal in the ground floor flat in Skatertnay Pereulok.

Emma was gaunt and tall and a bundle of nerves, very superstitious and a staunch believer in telepathy (since Moscow days, I too have become a believer in this ethereal form of communication). A superstition of Emma's has haunted me all these past years. I asked her one morning whether there was any caviar left over in the fridge from a recent dinner party, as I had dreamed about it. All colour drained from Emma's face and she stammered, 'No, no, you didn't really dream *that*, did you?' 'Yes,' I answered, 'why?' 'Oh, *lieber gott*, there will be a death in the family.' The following day I received the sad news that my father had died.

Every Thursday evening Emma and Amalia had to report on us to their Soviet masters. Emma would be jittery all day. She was always terrified she might not return to us. During our two years in Moscow, two other Volga-German maids did not indeed return home from their interrogation. One of them worked at the embassy and was a close friend of Emma's. Endless polishing, cleaning, touching up the paintwork—these activities all seemed to bring her solace. She was extremely efficient in all she undertook, from being a parlour maid to a laundress.

These two servitors were real paragons and such nice women too. Their one drawback, especially for me, was that as they were bilingual and always conversed in German with each other, and both my husband and myself were fluent German speakers, I was never able to pick up any Russian from them. My trouble with learning this very rich and difficult language was compounded by three successive teachers being apprehended. It was not until eighteen years later that I began to make progress.

Five years on after our departure in autumn 1949, there were no more Volga-German maids in Moscow. What happened to Emma and Amalia?

One incident that springs to mind, that occurred while there were still Volga-German staff at the British embassy house, was relayed to me by GWH. It concerns the tale of the hens in the attic.

As chatelaine of the British embassy house, Lady Kelly, who succeeded Lady Peterson in this role, naturally wished to be shown the attic floor as well as the rest of the house. On the north side of the long corridor were utility rooms, but on the south side were the bedrooms of the Russian Volga-German staff (by the sixties these had all been replaced by British staff). All but one door was opened for Lady Kelly's inspection, so she sent for the key of the locked door. When the door was opened, she was not greeted by four-and-twenty blackbirds, singing away as in the nursery rhyme, but by the cluck-clucking of roosting hens in cages. It appears that a former butler had installed these birds and was selling the eggs at black market prices to diplomatic families. There was a chronic shortage of eggs in Moscow at the time. Apparently the yolks of the eggs were as white as the shells, for complete lack of light! Lady Kelly had the hens and coops immediately evicted.

I had already left Moscow, but my husband wrote and told me of this incident which became the talk of the town at cocktail parties!

Moscow 1948

The food situation was now largely stabilised, although there were a couple of hiccups in the course of the year, but these were more amusing than stressful. Basic food requirements were, by the end of January 1948, available from the gastronomes, though it was a time-consuming business getting them. Our embassy commissariat concentrated on stocking comestibles not locally obtainable, though they did try to keep a small stock of basics such as flour and sugar against contingencies.

In April 1948, flour completely disappeared from the local shops with no indication as to when it might become available again. Our commissariat quickly ran out of their small stock so they immediately put an order for flour to be added to the next consignment of goods expected a month hence. We were advised to order some on our own account to come by bag with the King's messenger, which we all did, but inevitably there would be a delay of at least two weeks before we could expect it to arrive. So, cakes and pastry were now excluded from our menu, and Amalia husbanded very carefully the remaining stocks we had. A month later she heard via the grapevine that on a certain day the following week a ration of flour would be available to each individual to be collected from certain distribution centres in town. So, on the appointed day, Amalia, our chauffeur and myself duly stood in a queue in a draughty, puddly (from thawing ice) open space close to a building site. After a half-hour stand, we reached the head of the queue: we proffered our wrists and a number was scribbled on it with an indelible purple pencil. My number was 187. We were told that flour would be on sale from 2 p.m. onwards, according to our numbers. Amalia judged pretty accurately the probable time when our numbers would be called between 2 p.m. and 2.30 p.m. And so it was that at the end of some fifteen minutes of queuing, it was our turn and we each came away with 250 grams of flour already packaged up.

The following week our commissariat was stocked up with flour. The gastronomes had to wait until the next harvest had been gathered in before they once more had flour for sale.

In the autumn, a ration system was imposed on the sale of poultry. We never fathomed the reason. To purchase a whole chicken, four people had to present themselves as each chicken was chopped into 4 portions. So once again, Amalia, the chauffeur, myself plus one of my boys queued in a shop to buy a whole rather skimpy chicken. I decided it wasn't worth the trouble, so there was no more chicken on our menu.

Perlovka was an adjunct to the British embassy for accommodation purposes. This came about when the transfer of the capital from Petrograd (as St Petersburg was re-named immediately after the revolution of 1917) to Moscow led to an immense demand for accommodation for the government workforce, for both office and living space. Foreign missions thus had enormous difficulty in obtaining necessary dwelling quarters for their personnel; and after the war it was even more difficult.

In the 1930s a small group of British electrical engineers working under contract for the Russians were living here. They had leased this compound with its two Swiss-type chalets and outhouses, once stabling, now garages, as their work was in a factory complex in the nearby village of Perlovka. They had a tennis court built within the quite spacious wooded grounds. In the mid-thirties, however, to the world's bewilderment, Stalin unleashed a reign of terror. Most of the top generals in the army were arrested and shot. A vast number of civilians belonging to the educated classes—academics, scientists, authors, musicians—were arrested on trumped-up charges, tried, and after impossible confessions of wrongdoing under torture, were either shot or sent off to the notorious Gulag camps in Siberia. Few of them survived to tell the tale—Solzhenitsyn did.

Amongst those arrested were the British engineers, accused of spying. After several months of incarceration they were finally expelled back to Britain. The British government took over the lease of the Perlovka compound and held it until it ran out in the late fifties.

The upper floor of the larger chalet made an excellent family flat, with two deep verandahs on two sides. The kitchen was on the ground floor and shared between the family and three bachelor members of the embassy staff, lodged on the ground floor. Two further bachelor members shared the smaller chalet.

Senior staff, either diplomatic or defence, had a two-year posting in Moscow but all junior staff had a mere year, so there was an ongoing turnover of staff. The assistant military attaché and his family were due to return to the UK in early May, their two-year assignment being completed. As their Perlovka flat would now be empty we asked our admin section if we might move out there for the summer months, if the flat was not immediately otherwise required.

Happily it was not, and by the end of May we were installed in this nice country 'dacha', as the Russians call out-of-town escape chalets. For the next three months we led a very enjoyable outdoor life. Meals and lessons for the boys were on the verandahs (except of course on rainy days!) Amalia and Emma remained in town and I shared the cooking with the local Russian maid who attended the flat for a couple of hours each morning. My husband set off for the office at 7.45 each morning and would return around 6.30 in the evening, the car laden with provender supplied by Amalia, including dishes and cakes prepared by her, thereby giving me the minimum of trouble. Ice and snow, cold fog, mist and slush were forgotten and my memory recalls only warmth and sunshine.

MOSCOW 1947–1949

Very sadly I lost my father in March 1948. I had not been able to return to England at the time. It so happened that Gromyko was visiting London that fatal week and my husband was detailed to accompany him and to attend the meetings with Mr Bevin, our foreign secretary and Foreign Office officials. We could not leave our boys in Moscow without a parent. The Cold War was now on and the general political situation was dangerously unstable. My father died during that week my husband was in London and he was able to attend the funeral. I promised my mother I would return in July and spend three weeks with her prior to collecting our eldest son at the end of his summer term and bringing him back to Russia with me for his summer holiday.

I kept my promise to my mother and very conveniently there was a Russian boat sailing from Leningrad to Tilbury in the first days of July. So, off I went greatly looking forward to a break from Moscow life. I might not have been so relaxed at leaving the boys out at Perlovka, alone all day just with the governess, but by a happy string of coincidences this problem was solved.

During April a new air attaché, with family, arrived in Moscow and moved into the flat above ours in Skatertnay Pereulok, as its predecessors had left. We were already friends with this family as we had been recently together in Brussels. There were two little girls, aged six and three. The elder one joined our school class in September. The two bachelors housed in the smaller Perlovka dacha returned to the UK early in June and the dacha was not required until September, so the Ogilvie-Forbes family were able to take possession and join us out at Perlovka. Mary Ogilvie-Forbes became a lifelong friend and I knew she would be keeping an eye on my boys, with whom she would be in daily contact, and she had a real knack with children, devising games and activities. It would also be companionship for Miss R, the governess, until such time as the fathers returned from their offices. Also, with the other bachelors from the ground-floor flat, tennis was now on the agenda.

My planned three weeks in England in July worked out admirably—helped by excellent weather. Parents' day at my son's school, a weekend with my in-laws, a flit up to London for dentistry and shopping and an overnight stay with my sister-in-law and husband, combined with helping my mother to sort out her life. Then back to Moscow with John.

Journey Back to Moscow, July 1948

We took a boat across North Sea, a train across Sweden, a boat to Helsinki and from there travelled on to Leningrad. It was a very enjoyable journey but at times almost too hot. The North Sea, which in my experience is usually grey and turbulent, thought it was the Mediterranean at its best. The sea was as calm as a millpond. Our overnight journey from Newcastle landed us early in the morning in Gothenburg. We had two hours' shopping time before catching our train for Stockholm. John was in great need of cool summer clothing. In the UK clothes rationing was still in force and males, whether adults or school-age boys, never wore cotton shorts. (Service personnel would have knee-length khaki or white shorts.) Shirts all had long sleeves. The ubiquitous T-shirt had not yet been invented. Scandinavians and continentals all had cool summer clothing though and our shopping spree was crowned with success. We just had time to purchase provender and drink from a platform vendor before clambering into our coach for a six-hour baking hot journey to Stockholm.

My memory of the difficulty we encountered in obtaining help with luggage in Stockholm is very vivid. This was my first experience of the utter lack of porters at stations and ports in Sweden. It was 'self-help' every inch of the way, even with a child in tow. We had no slack time before boarding our Swedish boat. We just made it and an excellent dinner was served immediately on leaving port. We gobbled it down as fast as possible and hastened up onto the deck so as not to miss a moment of our zigzag passage, threading past all the islands that throng the Baltic and Gulf of Finland between Stockholm and Helsinki. It was a magical journey on a warm evening, with a cloudless sky and a fantastic sunset and dawn with a bare 15 minutes between them, and no night at all. Though weary from a long hot day, it was difficult to tear oneself away and go down to one's cabin for a sleep. Since childhood I believed implicitly what I had been told: the sun rises in the East and sets in the West, yet here in front of me was the sun rising from the horizon, not more than 20 to 25° to the right of where it had dipped 15 minutes earlier.

Next morning there was a 3-hour stopover in Helsinki; time enough for a quick sight-seeing tour. Then we sailed on to Leningrad, caught the night train to Moscow, had a bumpy drive out to Perlovka and once again the family were united together for three happy weeks, which galloped by like lightning. My memory of that summer was of glorious sunny weather with daily excursions, together with the Ogilvie-Forbes family, into the lovely woods some 10 to 15 minutes' walk along a little stream in which the local children would be paddling. Stuffed into rucksacks were picnic fare, liquid refreshment and balls of various sizes. Mary devised wonderful games—a special favourite was cops and robbers. Sadly John had to leave us for England at the end of three weeks as he had the opportunity of joining a family returning to the UK on a boat sailing from Leningrad to Tilbury. There were no further embassy staff departures due until later in the autumn. Direct flights between London and Moscow were not established until several years later.

Autumn–Winter, 1948

By mid-September our two families were back in Skatertnay Pereulok. The weather was still superb and it was a wrench to leave airy Perlovka for stuffy Moscow. However, within two days the weather broke and rain and chill were in the air. Although we had double-glazed windows, Emma immediately got busy and spread 3-inch thick rivers of cotton wool in the 8 inch gap between the outer and inner windows (the traditional Russian larder) and also stuffed strips of cotton wool down the jambs of the inner windows. Now only one little pane at the top of one window could be opened to let in a modicum of fresh air. Modern double glazing was of course fitted in all new buildings.

School started up again with the addition of Cecilia, the daughter of the family above us. Sadly our Australian twins had returned to Australia but we still had our other girl pupil. Cecilia competed with Michael in arithmetic and with Bruce and Mandy in dictation. All other subjects were shared together. I had subscribed to the excellent PNEU programme for overseas British children and Miss R followed it meticulously. Lessons lasted from 9 until 11.45 with scarcely a break. But now it was time for the mums to take over, and the time for fresh air and exercise. In the course of the winter of 1948–1949 we explored all the various parks of 'Rest and Culture', as they are called in Russia, reaching them by the superb underground network installed by the Soviets. The 'Culture' was centred on a variety of theatres and open-air stages in the summer months. Plays and concerts and variety shows were staged and there were occasional mini exhibitions of pictures. All the parks would have some cultural activity, but most were centred on Gorki Park, the largest park in Moscow at the foot of the Lenin Hills, along one bank of the river Moskva. Here too was a fascinating alcove, surrounded by a high hedge. You squeezed in and, lo and behold, worthy citizens of mature age would be sitting on benches crouching earnestly and silently over chessboards, with other worthies of all ages standing and watching the game in progress. There were usually three separate games being played. Whereas the open-air stages and theatres closed and were boarded up in winter, the aficionados of chess would play on, apparently oblivious of winter cold. There they sat, huddled in their padded coats, fur hats clamped on their heads. I was always fascinated watching this scene. The players mostly had straggly white hair and beards. Although I had discovered this corner of Gorki Park in 1948, I had more time to dally and observe during my second Moscow incarnation when I was free of young children intent on running and snowballing.

Our favourite park for them was the Sokolniki Park on the very boundary of the city. A wide path followed the boundary within the fence of the park, with paths quartering the park and meeting in the centre around a fountain with a boarded-up central statue in winter. All these paths were frozen over and kept swept to form a superb skating course. It was a jolly scene at weekends, like a Dutch picture of people skating on canals, and obviously enjoying themselves. Our kids lacked skates but enjoyed running freely and snowballing. There were footpaths for non-skaters alongside the frozen tracks.

Before the arrival of winter, my husband and I had had a wonderful ten days' break away from Moscow. We went to Tbilisi, the capital of Georgia.

To Tbilisi, October 1948

I found living in our ground-floor flat in Skatertnay Pereulok quite claustrophobic. Sunshine never penetrated into any of our rooms and we had no greenery to look out onto. So our move out to Perlovka for three summer months was a great boost to morale, and these months had been happy and enjoyable. Nevertheless the prospect of a week right away from Moscow was a thrilling idea.

The opportunity of a week in Tbilisi (previously known as Tiflis), the capital of Georgia, came in October. It proved to be one of the happiest of memorable 'get aways' of my life. The last one had been the drive south from Berlin to the Dalmatian coast in June 1938. The sea, the mountains and general scenery of that picturesque coast and the drive through the Alps to reach it had a therapeutic quality to offset the stress of life in pre-war Berlin up to the outbreak of war. Equally in Moscow, with the years still so close to the end of that extremely destructive and horrific war, and now with the start of the Cold War, life did entail a certain background of stress.

When the Petersons went off on their annual leave, my husband was left in charge of the embassy and whilst I relaxed out at Perlovka, he had an extremely busy two months cooped up in the office in the heat of a Moscow summer. The whole of this first year had been very gruelling and he badly needed a break. On his return from his holiday the ambassador recognized this and granted him a week's leave to sample the air of Georgia.

American colleagues had recently been given permission by the department of the Russian Foreign Office that dealt with us foreigners to visit Tbilisi, so we applied in our turn for a similar permit. It was granted and on 23 October at 11 a.m. we boarded the 'Russian Riviera Express' train for Tbilisi, a distance of roughly 1,500 miles. It took sixty-eight hours, almost the same amount of time as that other journey eighteen years earlier with my brother from Moscow to Baku. I was strongly reminded of that journey, and mindful that we had had to exist on one salami sausage and a box of Karlsbad plums, we brought ample provisions along with us. This time, however, there was a restaurant car right next to our carriage. As before, a samovar bubbled unceasingly at the end of the passage. The train emitted every so often the same low-pitched haunting sound as of yore and did not appear to travel any faster, around 25 mph, but this time it only stopped briefly in towns set at considerable distances from each other, with vast tracts of empty space between them. On that previous journey our train had stopped at every little hamlet.

Looking out of our train window, we saw the scenery change from the forested country of North Russia with cultivated clearings and rather miserable-looking little villages to the vast steppe lands stretching into the Ukraine, flat as a pancake, not a tree in sight. The grasslands were now brown and shrivelled, and the cultivated land was all ploughed up. This vast endless land was very depressing in the rain. In summertime though, this one-time bread bowl of Russia, with standing corn swaying in the breeze, might have a certain allure.

On the third day we reached the western hills of the Caucasus and for the greater part of the day we skirted the eastern shores of the Black Sea, the sea on one side and the hills on the other. The sea was rough and uninviting, and the clouds were low on the hills so we got no glimpse of the higher mountains, but even with the rain teeming down it was an agreeable change from the forests and plains of the north.

Our train stopped at various resorts along this Russian riviera. Amongst them was Sochi, where, during a lull in the storm, we managed to stretch our legs. This is where Stalin had a villa (inherited by his various successors) and where, very sensibly, he spent much of the autumn and winter. On our return trip by air we touched down at two airports along this coast. It was now a sunny day and the country around and about looked most attractive: wooded hills, pretty villages, lots of flowers and the higher mountains just peeping out behind.

TO TBILISI, OCTOBER 1948

At 7 the next morning we emerged from our train in Tbilisi, a bit dizzy and our legs a bit wobbly after all those hours of rattling and bumping. Half a gale was blowing but the sky was blue, the sun was shining and there to meet us was Cecilia from Intourist; with her olive skin, dark hair and finely moulded features and beautiful eyes she conformed to the famed good looks of Georgians, akin to those of their neighbours, the Armenians. We were very taken by Cecilia, who was lively, spontaneous and charming. She spoke excellent English. The Georgian men we met during our week we thought were all tamed brigands, with their handsome, flashy good looks. The contrast between Russians and Georgians could not be greater.

We were driven to the Orient Hotel situated in a tree-lined avenue. We had a suite with bedroom, sitting room and bathroom. The first two well-furnished and comfortable, but the bathroom was true to the Russian stereotype—bunged-up drains, loud gurgling pipes, dripping taps (no plug in the basin, perhaps just as well) and the bath with an emery-like surface, so that one was quite sore when one got out. 'Nichevo,' as the Russians would say, meaning, 'No matter, you'll survive.' We enjoyed our ablutions and after breakfast Cecilia took us on a tour of the town—actually, three separate towns. The old town nestled against the flanks of the Caucasus to the north. The new town lay across the turbulent Kura river to the south. Here were good administrative and office buildings including our hotel in tree-lined boulevards. Here also was the university and old and new apartment blocks. Cecilia told us all new buildings had to follow the traditional Georgian style. Our impression was that new Tbilisi was an attractive city. Finally, the third town was the industrial and factory quarter of Tbilisi, situated downstream to the east along the banks of the fast-flowing Kura as it wended its way through a gorge, eventually reaching the Caspian Sea, just south of Baku.

The Old Town

The old town was picturesque; rather tumbledown houses, with outside staircases and many of them with wooden balconies. The streets were narrow and often steep, with washing swaying in the breeze stretched across them. There were little piazzas and courtyards and plenty of dark-haired, bright-eyed children playing around and about. It had a distinctly Mediterranean feel.

There are many churches in Tbilisi and in more or less good repair and seemingly in use. We visited a couple of very ancient ones as well as two castles, one in ruins, the other an erstwhile grim prison, now a museum.

Upstream in a rather dominating position by the river was a handsome circular building. 'That's the circus,' explained Cecilia, then quite casually she added, 'Georgians don't like circuses, Russians love them and thought Georgians might change their minds and enjoy this type of culture if they had a purpose-built circular building, hence this building, but Georgians still don't like circuses, but the children enjoy them.' 'What *do* Georgians enjoy?' enquired my husband. 'Drama,' replied Cecilia. 'There is a historical play being performed in our theatre this week. I am sure it is good, would you like to go? I would tell you the story beforehand and explain as it goes along.'

We both agreed: 'Yes, we would like to do that very much.' So, on one of our evenings Cecilia escorted us to the theatre, an attractive miniature of Covent Garden, where we saw a play with the splendid name of 'Hells Berry Gotcha', an old historical tale with the sort of heroic theme favoured by Racine and Corneille. It was well acted and staged, and with Cecilia there to translate it was quite understandable and interesting. A 'hells berry' is a Georgian high priest and chieftain of a mountain village tribe. 'Gotcha' was the name of the priest around whom the play centred. The actors were all dressed in very becoming old Georgian costumes. Mount Kasbek, the highest mountain of the Caucasus, was the backdrop to all the scenes. We enjoyed our evening very much.

Tbilisi Park of Rest and Culture

By our second day in Tiflis, the wind had completely abated and the sun shone. Cecilia suggested we might like to visit the local Park of Rest and Culture situated on the summit of the bluff overlooking the Kura River as it entered the gorge to the east of Tbilisi. This bluff marked the end of a spur of hills stretching away to the south towards Armenia. A funicular takes one up to the top of this bluff. We settled into a roomy empty compartment of the funicular and were presently invaded by a large class of chattering and excited seven-year-olds with two teachers on an outing to the park.

It so happened on that particular morning some hitch occurred in the running of the funicular. We were immovably clamped with all these kids in our compartment for some forty minutes before the train finally moved us up. The children were very good and well behaved. The mistresses made them sing songs to keep over-excitement and boredom at bay. Some of the songs included rhythmic clapping alternating with humming. We enjoyed this free show and we thought the kids very cute and attractive, all alert and lively and neatly turned out. They all had such amusing and roguish little faces. One touch which amused us greatly were some of their names. There was a Genghis, also a Tamerlane, which both gave one a curious whiff of past history and also a realisation of one's geographic position. The Persian Teymour seemed very common.

At last our funicular started up again. The hillside had been planted with a variety of shrubs and a number of maple trees, all ablaze in their autumn colouring. At the summit a splendid panorama unfolded itself. Opposite, with the city below, were the foothills of the great Caucasus mountain range, whilst to the west the country opened out towards the horizon. The Park of Rest and Culture was also ablaze with the vermillion and gold colours of autumn. It was beautifully laid out and most attractive. Whilst we wandered around, the children raced each other to the refreshment building.

Our hilltop was the spur of a long ridge, gradually rising as it merged with the hilly country beyond—all very barren and dry. No lush vegetation here as on the coastal area adjacent to the Black Sea. Here in the hilly and mountainous country the climate is quite different, with no humidity. The scenery of bare hills and distant views of mountains was very reminiscent of Persia and it brought back nostalgic memories of afternoon rides beyond the confines of the city walls of Teheran in the 1920s and those lovely summer camps in the Lar Valley at the foot of Mount Demevend.

We had a great desire to stretch our legs and a path up the ridge beckoned us, but it was already past midday, so back down the funicular we went and that afternoon was spent wandering around the shopping area of the town, now unescorted by Cecilia. We noted that shops had no more to offer than back in Moscow, but the streets were full of people walking here and there, seemingly quite relaxed and minus that strained look of the inhabitants of Moscow.

On each of the succeeding days bar one, we went up on the funicular and had an hour or two's tramp on the hillside beyond the Park of Rest and Culture. Finally, on our last day we took sandwiches, half a bottle of Georgian wine (excellent) and a bottle of water and set off up on the funicular and enjoyed a superb day walking all the way up the ridge. We encountered flocks of fat-tailed sheep tended by grizzly old men with large floppy sheepskin hats on their heads. What the sheep found to eat I really don't know. Blue-headed thistles and here and there patches of autumn croci seemed to

TO TBILISI, OCTOBER 1948

be the only vegetation. It was a glorious clear day and so warm we walked in shirt sleeves and cotton blouse and ate our lunch and dozed on top of a hill with a glorious view below, beyond and around us. We could see the whole range of the Caucasus, with Mount Kasbek and all the other snow-capped mountains. It was a far cry from Moscow.

Our fourth day in Tbilisi entailed a foray into the Caucasus mountains up the Georgian Military Highway. The ancient capital of Georgia is Mtskheta. It is picturesquely situated at the confluence of two rivers, the Kura and the Arakui. As they emerge from the mountains, one turns east and empties into the Caspian Sea, the other west into the Black Sea. A most interesting eleventh-century cathedral and a few buildings of a monastery all forming a close surrounded by an old wall were the focus point of our visit. Cecilia told us that two octogenarian monks still lived there and tended the cathedral. The old kings of Georgia are buried here. There is an old fortress atop a craggy hill, overlooking the rivers. We revisited Georgia nineteen years later, so I will leave further description of Mtskheta and the Georgian military highway to a later chapter. Suffice it to say that we had a most interesting and enjoyable day.

Bronzed from our tramping the hills above the funicular, we spent our final evening in Tbilisi at the opera, a Georgian version of *Carmen*. At daybreak next morning, we boarded a plane for our return to Moscow.

Return to Moscow from Tbilisi

The plane took off at dawn the following morning. As it climbed up and up we had a fabulous view of the high mountains, the sun just catching the snowy peaks. The sky was blue and there was the promise of another beautiful day. We flew towards the Black Sea and touched down at two airports, where we picked up several passengers, all Moscow-bound. We then headed north, skirting the Caucasus mountains to Rostov-on-Don. The blue sky gradually gave way to an increasingly opaque grey one and on landing at Rostov we were informed that Moscow was engulfed in a snow blizzard and fog, the two airports were closed and it had not yet been decided whether we should stay overnight in Rostov or continue to Voronesh, a town about two hours' flight short of Moscow. After a couple of hours' wait the decision was taken. We re-embarked on our plane and three hours later dived down alarmingly through a snow-laden cloud but made a perfect landing in Voronesh. We had no safety belts and fellow passengers continued smoking despite a notice forbidding it, and there was a considerable amount of unsecured freight at the back of the plane. This was my first experience in a Soviet plane but apparently was quite normal form on Soviet airlines. I experienced exactly the same forty-five years later on a flight in a small plane in Uzbekistan.

Voronesh was quite an experience. We humped our own luggage to the new shell of an airport building. My husband and I transformed ourselves successfully into mute and humble sheep and stuck firmly to the 'herd'—our fellow passengers were quite a large herd, for our plane carried a full complement of passengers, quite well dressed and well-to-do-looking people. We were some five miles from the centre of town—we were told that the hotel there was full and anyhow there was no transport to get us there. We stood around or sat on a few hard benches. Our limited Russian was just sufficient to get a drift of proceedings. We all just waited for something to turn up and in due course after about one hour an antediluvian bus with seats for sixteen people drew up outside the airport building. About thirty of us crowded into it and we set off for the centre of the town, asking to be put down outside the hotel. When we got into the hotel we found a seething mass of humanity round the reception desk together with that pungent odour which is encountered whenever a small number of Russians are gathered together within their own country. In due course one of our number reached the desk and asked what could be done for us all. Firstly, he explained that there were 'two foreigners' in our party. My husband was at once called forward and after he had shown our identity cards we were led off by one of the reception clerks, a woman of around fifty, and climbed up the stone staircase to the third floor, where we were asked to wait a moment. The good lady then walked down the passage and went into one of the rooms, from which we shortly heard sounds proceeding of a violent altercation. She emerged some five minutes later, looking rather hot and dishevelled, and asked us to wait another moment. She then returned with the manageress of the hotel, and after a further interval they emerged from the room with an irate colonel between them, he was clearly being ejected to make room for us. After the manageress had been introduced to us there was a further interval while the sheets were changed and we then took possession of the room. It reeked so pungently of sweaty feet I felt quite ill. However, past experience came to the rescue—my husband remembered the same smell had pervaded Chancery in Tokyo during the hot and very damp Nubai season. It came from plaster which was sweating from the prevailing humidity. So I felt I could cope with that. This is a good illustration of the psychology of suggestion! The window was of course hermetically sealed up against the winter. We tried 'airing' the room by leaving the door open onto the passage, but this was of no avail, for it was always shut again whenever one of the large females who seem to be constantly roaming around Russian hotels happened to pass by. Apart from that, both the room and the twin beds were clean. Twin beds, two hard chairs and two small tables were all the furniture provided. A small alcove by the door with two hooks sufficed as hanging space and there was no washbasin. I would find one two floors down, I was told. Furthermore, there were no toilets within the building. Outside, at the rear of the building, there was a hut divided into gents and ladies. Within, for the ladies, nothing but a hole in the ground and lit with just a hurricane lamp. It was a pretty desperate experience, especially after dark, with just one's own pocket torch to light the way and supplement the hurricane lamp. I desperately wished I was a boy.

Our hotel was located within a very large building with an imposing façade and we reckoned there were probably some 200 bedrooms. Apart from the reception hall and a restaurant, there were no other reception rooms. As I have indicated, plumbing was as yet non-existent. (To the Russians this is always a quite unimportant detail!) Of course this hotel was not yet completed and not earmarked as an Intourist hotel for foreigners, but more as a transit stopover for Russians, such was the shortage of housing whether for dwelling, business or factory purposes. In Russian cities that lay within the recent war zones, the buildings were all impressed into use long before they were ready.

The German armies had smashed their way through Voronesh on their way to Stalingrad and what had not been destroyed then was left in ruins on their retreat. It was only four years since this had all happened. On our five-mile journey from the airport to the town centre we passed remains of tanks, guns and other detritus of war and lots of ruined buildings. On the outskirts we noticed blocs of new workmen's flats in the process of reconstruction and in the centre of the town, where our hotel was located, a number of imposing buildings, including a theatre, were nearing completion. Our hotel formed part of the largest building, with an imposing façade, but as one stepped inside one was brought to earth with a bump.

Having taken possession of a room, and as there was still

daylight outside, we decided to go out for fresh air and a bit of a walk. The huge building which incorporated our hotel was situated at the start of a boulevard leading out of the square where we had noted obvious municipal buildings and a theatre not yet completed. We wandered down this boulevard and came upon a 'gastronome' and a general store. We walked into this and noted the same paucity of merchandise, and what there was was identical to the items for sale in Moscow and Tbilisi. Amazing, that this should be so in three cities so very distant from each other. On the other side of the boulevard were the gates of a Park of Rest and Culture.

It was now dark and very cold. We returned to our hotel and then tried to get a meal, but the restaurant was not yet open. From a buffet, however, we managed to get some dry bread, and surprisingly cream, and not very appetising sausage and, of course, tchai. Just to add a touch of romance to the scene, the lights gave out and we were plunged into stygian darkness for about half an hour—so we just sat tight. Luckily the chap at the buffet had a stump of a candle. Back in our nifty room, we managed to round off our meal with apples and chocolate. The remaining bully beef sandwiches, left over from our lunch (origin: our Tbilisi hotel), we were keeping for our early breakfast, for we were told to be ready to leave the hotel by 6 the following morning. However, after our night in this stuffy, smelly room, the taste of sweaty feet or damp plaster in our mouths was too strong for us to stomach a bully beef sandwich. When we reached the airport, the cold crisp air of an early November morning in the middle of Russia soon gave us an appetite and we gobbled up our sandwiches with relish.

We now had an irksome wait, a repeat of the previous day, involving much standing around. The hard benches could only accommodate a few of us. The clouds were low and we were told the weather reports from Moscow were still bad. Finally, however, at 9 a.m. the outlook appeared slightly better and we took off. We rose above the grey misty cloud and flew very smoothly in a clear wintry sky for about 1½ hours and then dived down again, alarmingly through the cloud into a snow storm, but made a perfect landing—our pilot was excellent. The ceiling was not more than a couple of hundred feet, and I was all of a tremble as our plane taxied a short distance before stopping for us to disembark. Here we had a further wait before our car came to collect us. It seemed particularly strange to be driving over ice-bound roads through such a wintry landscape after the glorious warm sunshine of two days before in the hills above Tbilisi. Skatertnay Pereulok gave us a gloriously warm welcome, though. It was great to be home.

After a year of living under the restrictions and curious isolation of life in Moscow from October 1947, our Georgian holiday had provided a wonderful break, a real tonic for both of us. Bronzed and relaxed, we were ready to face our second winter. As the King's messenger with bags for London was due to leave Moscow within a few hours of our return, I hastily scribbled the following note to my mother:

> *We are back! Our trip to Tiflis was an unmitigated success—we thought Georgia a jolly country, picturesque scenery, lots of interest and peopled by lively and amusing types. One felt far from Moscow and Russia, in spite of it having been under Russian domination for almost a century and a half and of course Stalin is a Georgian. We had glorious weather and on our last day we walked for miles and miles along a ridge with wonderful views all around and quite especially of the Caucasus. Today, 30 hours later, here we are in Moscow all under snow and freezing pretty hard—what a comedown. Next bag for a detailed account of our trip.*

Our Social Life in Moscow, 1947–1949

In those early post-war years in Moscow, right up to his death, the paranoiac personality of Stalin dominated the scene and the terror of 1937 once again stalked the land.

There was an intangible feeling of fraternity between us foreigners of the western bloc, all staunchly anti-communist. A similar feeling of fraternity existed between the members of the communist bloc. During the years when Stalin held sway, our lot were a relatively small group who all became good friends and who enjoyed each other's company. Nationality, rank and social background made little impact—we all coalesced. The chief form of entertainment was the cocktail party, but small dinners for those of us who had domestic help were also quite frequent, especially between those of us who were bridge players.

There was a flourishing Catholic church in Moscow, and a greater number of foreigners in the western bloc were Catholics. Ministering to them were an elderly French 'Père' with a magnificent beard and his acolyte, a small English Canadian chaplain. They made an incongruous pair; they stuck together like limpets and were present at almost every cocktail party. We were told that, interestingly, Sunday services in the Catholic church were always packed out with extremely devout Russians!

In those years there was no religious provision for Anglicans, so Lady P did her best to redeem this lacuna by inviting us to a substitute little service on feast days in the ballroom of the embassy where, on Christmas Day and at Easter, we would gather and sing 'Hark the Herald Angels Sing' or 'Christ is Risen, Alleluia', whilst one of the typists would thump out at breakneck speed the relevant tune on the piano. There was talk of an English padre about to be appointed to Helsinki, where there was an English church, though not yet reopened since the war. The idea was that he should come to

Moscow every now and again and take a service. This did in fact occur between our first and second incarnations.

Lady P thought Christmas wasn't Christmas without carols. So each year some of us were bidden to a meeting to discuss the carols we should choose to sing, and we then did our best to give tongue to these. Just one note was played on the piano for the pitch, which we then hummed, and we were off. A notice was sent around the office and also displayed on our commissariat noticeboard, saying that there would be carols at 6.30 in the ballroom of the embassy on such and such a date. Rather sadly for Lady P, very few people turned up on the given evening. The lady typist thumped the tunes out and such of us present would self-consciously warble 'Noël, Noël' and 'In the Bleak Midwinter'. We had all voted for the latter carol. It seemed so very appropriate to Moscow. One little trait of Lady P which both amused and startled us ladies of the embassy was her schoolgirl habit of keeping her hankie in the leg of her bloomers. I remember our suppressed giggles during our carol practice. I found it rather endearing.

A year in Moscow was punctuated by national day celebrations. The venue would be either the relevant embassy house, if the premises were large enough and there was a sufficiency of domestic backup, or else in the suite of rooms in a certain restaurant. Here the evening might end with a sit-down supper to which heads of mission and other guests, seemingly chosen at random, would be invited. It was a toss-up as to whether one was chosen or not.

My husband and I were once roped in by our Hungarian hosts (it is not just the ambassador who is the host—on national days all the staff are co-hosts). We found ourselves seated side by side and marooned amid a galaxy of guests who could only speak Hungarian or a Slav language. Further down the table we spied our Mongolian colleagues who were equally marooned. We noted with interest that they relished the ice cream offered at the end of the meal—Mrs Mongolia asked for four separate helpings.

At this party my neighbour was a Pole. It was astonishing that Russian was his only foreign language. His predecessors, both the ambassador and his number two and their wives, were fluent English and French speakers and probably German ones as well. But they had been members of the pre-war foreign ministry. It was not until the end of 1948 that Russia dominated all aspects of Polish life. It had been a gradual takeover. So, in fact, during our first fourteen months in Moscow, the members of the Polish mission easily integrated into our western bloc. The Ambassador and wife, and his number two and wife (the Zaleskis) were extremely nice people with whom we became great friends. Sadly for us, at the turn of the year they were replaced by hard-line communists. Subsequently we heard that the Zaleskis had emigrated to Chile. They came to visit us nine years later in Rio.

Sadly after that visit, no further opportunity of meeting each other presented itself and gradually we lost contact. It would take a further forty years before the birth of emails and for the ability to fly hither and thither across the world to be no more difficult than clambering into a car for an out-of-town weekend trip. And so it was that we lost contact with many other friends of those Moscow years—something I have greatly regretted. Among these friends were the ambassadors and wives of Burma and China—the missions they headed consisted only of themselves, plus a secretary. Both couples were middle-aged, small in stature and very gentle and soft-spoken people. My father would have called them 'dear old pets'. In my mind I bracket them together, though they represented two very different countries.

When Mao Tse Tung set up the 'People's Republic' in 1949, the Chinese couple abruptly left, but I have no idea what the future held for them.

The atmosphere in the living room of the Burmese couple

was warm, friendly and oriental. It had embroidered hangings and many Burmese artefacts with a very beautiful and serene Buddha in a little alcove of the room. In both households we were never more than six couples and we would be served delicious dishes from their own country. These evenings were always cosy and enjoyable.

Cultural Activities, Moscow 1947–1949

An individual can be both actively and subjectively affected by culture. Being actively affected entails study and absorption, while the unconscious absorption of influences around one is more subjective. A deeper understanding of the rich Russian culture had to wait until our second tour. For study requires leisure, a commodity I did not have much of in those years of 1947–1949. Like dogs and horses, my boys required regular outdoor activity and during the winter months this required a good deal of effort. They were too young to take to museums or to visit the two great monasteries, the Novadevichi on the banks of the Moskva River at the very door of the city, and the other great monastery-cum-fortress of Zagorsk some forty-five miles north east of Moscow, which we as foreigners were allowed to visit having first obtained a special permit to do so.

In the early spring of 1948, together with another embassy couple, we spent a wonderful Sunday visiting Zagorsk. The road was only cleared by snowplough for the first twenty or so miles. For the rest of the way we were in and out of deep snow ruts, so it was a very bumpy ride. But the country around is attractive, partly wooded with deciduous trees, reminiscent of parts of the New Forest. The sun was shining and as we emerged from the woods, there ahead of us was this glorious monastery. The eye is first caught by the blue-painted pepper pots surrounding the golden dome of one of

CULTURAL ACTIVITIES, MOSCOW 1947–1949

its many churches. The brightness of the blue and the gold contrasted most vividly with the soft rosy hue of the lovely impressive old walls with funny lookout towers projecting above them every so often. With the sun shining and snow lying around, I felt this was really Russia as I had visualised it.

Zagorsk and Novadevichi were the only two 'working' monasteries, in 1947–49 Zagorsk being also the only seminary in Soviet Russia. I visited Zagorsk on a number of occasions during our second tour as it was one of the highlights of a Moscow visit of family and friends visiting us during our three years there from 1965 to 1968.

There are many old cities in Russia with interesting churches and monasteries but during the two years 1947–1949 they were all out of bounds to foreigners and we had to wait until we returned to Moscow in 1965 before we managed to visit a number of them.

Monasteries were not just centres of devotion and learning, they were also asylums for the elderly and refuges for the citizens around and about when threatened by enemy aggression. Wood was the usual building material in mediaeval Russia. Houses were all timber-built and strong barricades were erected around monasteries. But these were no protection against the Mongol hordes that suddenly erupted from across the eastern steppes in the thirteenth century, so towards the end of that century and during the next two, Italian architects and constructors were sent for. They built the fortified walls enclosing the many monasteries around Moscow, including the walls of Zagorsk, and towards the end of the fifteenth century they built the magnificent walls which encircle the Moscow Kremlin. However western Renaissance culture made little further impact on Moscow for the ensuing three centuries. It was Peter the Great who brought westernisation to Russia from the end of the seventeenth century by building his magnificent city of St Petersburg.

MOSCOW 1947–1949

Gradually throughout the eighteenth century mediaevalism was broken down. A further century on and the inherent native genius of the Slav people erupted in all fields of intellectual and artistic endeavour. Poets, playwrights, authors in all intellectual fields, musicians, both composers and exponents, artists, painters, decorators, craftsmen, all gradually revealed themselves as the century progressed, and by the beginning of the twentieth century western culture in its turn became ever more strongly influenced by the Russian output. In recent years this must include the fields of science and technology. This influence has increased rather than diminished since the revolution of 1917 with the great exodus of academics and artists in all genres to the Americas, where they have found the freedom and encouragement to develop their talents.

Culture for us was primarily concentrated on the performing arts. Russians are a gifted people full of zest and energy and talent. No doubt the Tartar influence brought to the Great Steppes by the Mongol invasions has implanted itself into the Russian psyche, so when we came to Moscow in the autumn of 1947, we may have felt depressed by the grey, cold landscape, the rain, slush and mess and the drab colourless street scene, but a visit to a theatre or concert hall, and we were transported into another world. If we were lucky enough to obtain tickets for an evening at the Bolshoi Theatre, cold, squalor and drabness were forgotten. The moment the curtain was raised, whether for ballet or opera, we were transfixed by the magnificence of the staging, and presently this would be matched by the performance of the dancers in ballet or the quality of the singing in opera. In ballet, the grace and precision and seemingly effortless execution of complex steps by the ballerinas and the corps de ballet, and the prowess and elegance of the male dancers were enthralling.

Up until then I had never seen a three-act ballet; they were not performed in the UK at that time, only excerpts from *Swan Lake* and *Sleeping Beauty* had come my way. I had enjoyed them tremendously. These three-act Russian ballets recounting an entire fairytale with their superlative performances were a bewitching experience. During these two years in Moscow we attended only one single performance of these two ballets, *Swan Lake* and *Sleeping Beauty*, and we also had the luck of seeing Prokofiev's *Romeo and Juliet* just the once before it was withdrawn from the repertory together with a number of his other works for not conforming to 'socialist realism' as decreed by the Stalinist government. It was not until after Stalin's death in 1953 that performances of his works were once again allowed.

Before our wonderful evening at the Bolshoi to see *Romeo and Juliet*, I was told that I should re-read Shakespeare's play in order to fully appreciate how closely the music with its inflexions together with the acting, interpretation in terpsichorean form adhered to Shakespeare's text. I did re-read the play and was duly amazed at the ingenuity of the libretto devised by Prokofiev together with two collaborators and the choreographer. It was a truly thrilling and very romantic performance; the part of Juliet was danced by the great ballerina Marina Semyonova in 1948 and by Galina Ulanova in the '60s. In the later '60s I saw Margot Fonteyn and Rudolf Nureyev dance the same parts at Covent Garden. It was just as romantic and thrilling as the Moscow performance some years earlier. Ulanova and Fonteyn shared the same ethereal qualities.

The one great historical opera seen by us during this Moscow period was Mussorsky's *Boris Godunov*. This too was a wonderful experience. I had heard the great bass Chaliapin sing Boris's final aria at a concert in London before the war and had marvelled at the wonderful tones of his voice. The Boris we heard that night at the Bolshoi also had a wonderful rich sonorous bass voice and was also an excellent actor, and unbelievably there on the stage was the forecourt of the great coronation cathedral on the great Kremlin square with its golden domes. It was so realistic. It was quite incredible that such scenery and opulent costumes should be staged at that very dour time. Like the rest of the audience, we revelled in it.

Tickets for first-class shows, particularly for the Bolshoi, were always hard to come by. The big boys of the Praesidium (the Politburo) and senior government officials had first pick for tickets, followed by the influential individuals of the professional and business world. Foreign ambassadors would be allocated two tickets for an evening at the ballet. They might on request get four. If an ambassador did not require his tickets they would be passed down the line in order of seniority.

There were other theatres besides the Bolshoi where opera and ballet were staged and where it was far easier to obtain tickets. We saw some excellent one-, two- and three-act ballets. The performers were mostly graduates of the Bolshoi Ballet School. The Bolshoi company could only take in a limited number of new young dancers each year, so many excellent dancers joined this rival company.

There were also theatres which staged variety shows with colourful folk dancing from different regions of the Soviet Union and which would include incredibly agile acrobats, these largely from the Asiatic republics. There were also excellent choir groups, amongst which was the Red Army choir, with excellent bass voices and energetic dancing: shooting out legs when in a squatting position is a great speciality, this coupled with corkscrew leaps in the air. The balalaika would usually accompany the singing.

Another 'cultural' attraction in Moscow was the puppet theatre. A university student had thought up the idea of manipulating almost life-size puppets from a pit below so there were no dangling strings. The ingenuity and cleverness of the performances he devised became recognised by higher authorities, until one day Stalin himself saw the show and became the special patron of this individual. He was given a theatre of his own. The show we saw was called 'The Concert' and represented an entire music hall concert with a lady soprano whose voice rose ever higher, just slightly flat, a tenor singing the toreador's song from *Carmen*, a child prodigy playing the piano, performing dogs, a group of gypsy singers and dancers, a negro jazz band and crooner; each item introduced by a compère whose references to current events brought the house down. Unfortunately, with only our limited knowledge of Russian we could not follow these. The whole show was incredibly well done, very clever and very funny, a superb skit of any music hall show.

There were also some excellent concerts but the pushing and shoving entailed to reach one's seat I found so unnerving that during these two years in Moscow, I only went to one. During our second period, the experience was similar. Even if you had a ticket, your life was almost extinguished merely trying to enter the concert hall through the street door. Elbows, hips and knees had full play. Once again I only went to one celebrity virtuoso performance. It was a recital by the renowned pianist Richter. I could not face another 'push and shove' experience. The maxim seemed to be 'never give way to anyone else'. I had one quite funny experience of this at a variety show. We were three seats away from the gangway when a female appeared flourishing her ticket with the number of a seat in our row. She shouted out this number—but another female was already seated in it. She got up and began to make her way across all our legs towards the gangway. However, the gangway lady could not wait a few more seconds and started her way into our row. The two ladies met right in front of me and I was afraid they would both land on top of me. An attendant had to come and order the gangway lady to back out.

MOSCOW 1947–1949

This episode illustrates the 'push and shove' attitude and bad manners the Russians evince so often in public. It was in sharp contrast to the very evident appreciation they have for beauty and excellence as expressed in all forms of artistic and literary endeavours.

Sometime prior to our arrival in Moscow, an enterprising member of our foreign community, finding exercise difficult to come by during the long winter months, had the idea of organizing a dancing class for ladies. Once installed in our flat, the other embassy mother of three boys mentioned that once a week she went to a class of Russian dancing, which started off with the warming-up exercises of classical dancing, led by a retired ballerina and revered teacher from the Bolshoi. 'It is great fun and wonderful exercise,' said my friend Rosemary Hulton, and added, 'Come and watch us and see if you would like to join. I will fetch you next Thursday at 9.30.' I went and Madame Lupova (not her real name) was very gracious. She said, 'You can join in now.' I joined and from then on Thursday mornings were always looked forward to.

Madame Lupova had turned seventy when she took charge of the foreign ladies' dancing class. Of medium height with white hair she held herself superbly and had a lovely figure. She wore heeled shoes and it was astonishing how, with a few hand gestures and a few little steps, she conveyed the framework of a dance. Our dances were very akin to Scottish reels, danced to the score taken from opera and ballet and played on the piano by a lady accompanist. We also danced traditional Russian folk dances. It was wonderful exercise.

Madame Lupova had great charm and personality and must have been very pretty in her youth. She knew the French ballet terms, but otherwise only spoke Russian. When she died in the late fifties she was given a state funeral. She had been awarded a Lenin prize.

The November 7th Celebrations and Parade, 1947

During my two Moscow incarnations I attended five 7 November parades, all of them impressive. Two of them remain vivid in my memory. The first one, in 1947, was three weeks after our arrival in Moscow, and was the thirtieth anniversary of the revolution in 1917. The fiftieth anniversary of the revolution fell in the year 1967—that was a very momentous occasion. Following is a description of the 1947 parade in a letter I wrote to my parents at the time:

November 7th is the most important day in the Soviet calendar and this year a very special 'do' has been made of it, for it is the 30th anniversary of the 'October revolution of 1917'. I haven't yet fathomed why the October revolution is celebrated on November 7th. These Moscow celebrations lasted for 3 days and 4 nights starting on the eve of the 7th with an important speech being delivered by Molotov at the Bolshoi. For the first time the Heads of Mission were invited to attend. The invitation only reached them on the 5th but the time was not indicated. Sir M Peterson rang up on the morning of the 6th about this, and the answer was: he would be told later! At 4pm a message was sent to the Embassy to say Molotov would be speaking at 6; just 2 hours' notice.

Afterwards an amusing bit of gossip was bandied around the dips corps, that the American ambassador clapped enthusiastically after the passage in Molotov's speech dunning the Americans. It is one of the curious customs in Russia that speakers are always clapped all through their speech and curiously here in Moscow, not just clapped by the Russkis present but also by the dips. It seems to me this custom should be discontinued, because really it is too absurd clapping away at something you don't understand, especially as the fellow may be saying the rudest things about you! I gather that 'faux pas' of this nature are continually occurring. However, as the American ambassador has such a dour personality, I feel rather disinclined to believe this otherwise rather good story.

The same evening as the speech, the fun and jollity really began with the whole of Moscow brilliantly illuminated, and the whole population in jubilant mood out on the streets. The illuminations were spectacular—the whole outline of the Kremlin's zigzag wall with the outline of the towers at the various angles of the wall all picked out with a continuous line of electric lights. Outstanding outlines of actual buildings within the Kremlin were equally picked out. It made the whole complex look like some wonderful fairy palace. We are told over a million bulbs were used just for the Kremlin alone. Then all the bridges across the river had garlands of red and yellow lights strung across as well as their actual arches picked out with the same continuous ribbon of light. Important buildings all over Moscow had various types of illumination fixed up against them, usually with large scale pictures of Stalin and Lenin and slightly smaller ones of Molotov and all the other blokes of the Politburo somehow fixed against the building. There were gorgeous effects of neon lights simulating cascading waterfalls and corkscrew pinnacles of light moving ever upwards all in coloured lights. In the big squares some centrepiece or other was rigged up with slogans and red flags and flood lighting. Driving through Moscow was a wonderful sight and at night, of course, all the dirt and the sadness of the tumbledown houses becomes invisible.

One of the features of Russian architectural design is to colour wash individual buildings, mostly in a warm creamy yellow with the woodwork of doors and windows and any ornamentation picked out in white. Sometimes they use a grass green wash together with the white paintwork. When

THE NOVEMBER 7TH CELEBRATIONS AND PARADE, 1947

it has all been newly done it is very attractive, but of course in this sort of climate it is really quite impractical, because in less than no time, the paint just runs and looks messy. When we sailed up the estuary and through the port of Leningrad, these colour-washed buildings were very striking and ditto the great palaces on the banks of the Neva and glinting in the sunlight one was struck by the beauty of the city.

The illuminations of Moscow lasted for 4 nights—on the Sunday night everything looked even prettier, for snow began falling in the late afternoon, and there was an extra glitter and sparkle to everything. The Kremlin looked even more ethereal than before.

November 7th 1947 was jolly cold with a mixture of sleet and snow. As I was well wrapped up this didn't bother me too much. It was a very impressive show—very theatrical. Red Square was packed with line upon line of soldiers all drawn up in separate squares and all very smartly turned out. They drilled, marched, saluted, cheered, all absolutely on the tick of the moment. As they marched out of the square, they were followed by a contingent of cavalry, equally smartly turned out and then came lorry loads of khaki-dressed soldiers followed by heavy tractors pulling larger and ever larger guns and then tanks came rumbling by—all this making lots of noise. Finally the purely military part of the parade was over, and the sporting youth took over. Young men and women dressed up in skiing trousers with either red, white, orange or yellow sweaters, but in massed colours and carrying millions of fluttering red and gold banners. It was a pity the sun was not shining for scenically it made a beautiful picture. We dips, heads of mission, their number twos and military, navy and air attachés, all penned within an enclosure bang next to Lenin's mausoleum with Stalin, generals plastered in medals and all the big boys of the

Presidium on top, all busily saluting away. Here in our pen, we met a number of our colleagues. As the sporting youth marched off the square, Moscow citizenry took over carrying flags and banners with anti-American and British slogans—this was the moment for us dips to leave. We had been in our pen for a good 1½ hours and the chill became ever more biting.

On the evening of the 7th we went to Molotov's annual party—the entire Presidium, influential people in industry, armed forces etc were present and foreign heads of mission and their number twos and attachés as in the morning were invited. I was told this was the only occasion we foreigners had of meeting Russians, but one really needed to speak the lingo. It took place in a large house which I gathered had belonged to a 'sugar' millionaire. There was no really large room—Mr and Mrs Molotov and the temporary head of the foreign office (Vishinski being absent) and his wife shook hands with us all—this taking some 45 minutes. There must have been a good 1000 guests who, after shaking hands, dispersed into various rooms on ground floor and first floor. Each room had a buffet in it.

One was able to wander around ad lib. In the largest room a concert took place but there were very few chairs. Arias from operas were being sung, but very few people could hear the concert and chattering never ceased— anyway food on the buffet tables was obviously the primary interest. The top nobs and wives and ambassadors were shepherded to one particular room and Molotov made a greeting speech to them all and then drank toasts to each Ambassador whilst Madame Molotova in a blue brocade evening gown was very gracious to the ladies. The Russian ladies had all donned their best dress, some in evening gowns but many in day clothes. When the first phase of eating was over the Molotovs circulated from room to room but separately and he would stop and toast selected individuals. He had a waiter with a bottle of vodka in attendance as well as a bevy of foreign office officials. Madame Molotova gathered a circle of Russian ladies in each room who all basked and smirked in her august presence whilst she prattled away at 19 to the dozen.

There was little intercourse between Russians and foreigners—such conversations as did arise were nearly always with the artistic and intellectual elements and of course fluency in Russian was a help—the foreign press were also at the party and they were all fluent in Russian. We could not participate very much, nevertheless it was a good party, everybody seemed to be in great form and it was amusing seeing all the Big Chaps.

Memories from Skatertnay Pereulok

In the first period during which we lived in Skatertnay Pereulok, three pictures immediately spring to mind—the Afghan Ambassador, the Milking Cow and the Cresta Run of Skatertnay Pereulok.

The Afghan Ambassador

Skatertnay Pereulok was a cul-de-sac out of one of the old tree-lined streets of Moscow, flanked with attractive patrician houses of the nineteenth century. At the end of our cul-de-sac was a high garden wall; one could see the top of a yew tree growing in this garden—our neighbour was the Afghan ambassador. Our front door opened onto Skatertnay Pereulok, whereas his opened on to the street running on the far side of our houses. Our back doors faced each other obliquely within a porch below an archway. The rooms above the arch formed part of his house. Access to the porch was from the street behind our houses. We met the Afghan ambassador for the first time three weeks after our arrival in Moscow. It was 7 November, the Soviet National Day, when every year the armed forces of the Soviet Union, plus a large portion of Moscow citizenry, paraded through Red Square beneath the gaze of the President of the Union (Stalin from 1947 to 1953) and the entire Politburo. These gentlemen had chairs on top of Lenin's mausoleum. An enclosure for diplomats and foreign press was alongside.

Having met our neighbour at the parade, my husband thought it polite to pay him a courtesy visit. He was ushered into the ambassador's study and was offered green tea and sweetmeats. My husband enquired politely if the ambassador had any family here in Moscow. 'My daughter is here—she cooks for me,' was the gruff reply. 'Your wife is back in Kabul?' enquired my husband. Pause, then in a sombre voice, pointing his finger at the yew tree in his garden, he replied: 'She is there, under the tree.' He paused. 'She was unfaithful.' History does not relate my husband's reply. At a later date when the ambassador, together with his very shy daughter (aged 18 or 19) came to lunch with us, I enquired of the ambassador, sitting next to me, if he had other sons or daughters. 'I have ten sons, thank God Modom, and one daughter.' I found conversation rather difficult.

The Milking Cow

One of the great surprises we encountered in Moscow in 1947 was our milking cow. She was owned by a peasant friend of Amalia, our cook, and once a week was led, whatever the weather, into our porch. A knock on our back door would bring Amalia out, pail in hand. The peasant woman produced a low stool and proceeded to milk the cow. This was our weekly provision of milk. Amalia would then place it on the stove, bring it to the boil and then simmer it very gently for twenty minutes, stirring it gently every so often until it was cool enough to strain into bottles and place in the fridge. As a family we all hated the taste of boiled milk, so coffee, cocoa, Ovaltine or whatever always had to be added to it for our consumption.

On that first National Day in 1947, we were bidden to a celebratory reception that evening given by 'The Big Boys'. We had just donned our coats when Emma, our Volga Russian maid, came bustling into our hall with a glass of milk in each hand. 'Please drink this milk,' she pleaded. 'It is necessary to line your stomach with milk to offset the effects of vodka with which you will be plied throughout the evening. The Russian hosts will meanwhile stick to water!'

We refused the milk—easy enough for me, as I would be sticking to fruit juice anyway, but my husband took the warning to heart.

The Cresta Run

Almost opposite our front door in Skatertnay Pereulok was a great slag heap, dusty and unsightly for half the year as debris from a half-demolished building was constantly being thrown onto it. There was a paling behind it which prevented planks and other large items being chucked over. Stones and swept-up rubbish were its main constituents. However, from the moment the snows fell in the second half of October, for the next five months until the great thaws of the following April, it became the St Moritz of the district with its famous Cresta Run. On one side was a gentle slope which younger children would slither down on their homemade toboggans, watched by their babushkas (grandmothers), but on the far side was what we called the Cresta Run—no formidable bends, but a long slope of packed snow, soon turning into ice as the local urchins with great dexterity repeatedly slid down it with whoops of joy, no doubt wearing out the soles of their varlinkis (felt boots)—the ubiquitous footwear of the Russian plebs.

There were shorter and longer slides on pavements, usually on the inner sides of Moscow streets, and no doubt in other cities as well, but the joy of the Cresta Run was that it was a downhill slope and required special skills of balance.

My young boys, aged 7 and 5, longed to join in the fun as they watched with fascination from our bedroom windows the antics of the urchins, but as soon as our front door opened, the militia on patrol at the corner of Skatertnay Pereulok would blow a whistle and bark out an order and, hey presto, the urchins would skedaddle away in less than no time.

We forbade our boys to attempt the Cresta Run, for fear of an accident due to their ineptitude.

A slide on the roadside of the avenue off which our cul-de-sac opened proved my downfall. The slide was invisible under a thin coating of snow. I stepped on it and the next moment found myself on my back with a very painful broken coccyx. No helping hand to my rescue, but a passer-by alerted the militia not far away and strong arms soon hoicked me up and I think must have more or less carried me to our front door, as I could not walk.

After lying prone for a few days, followed by painful struggles to walk, I was referred by our embassy doctor to the therapy department of the Russian poly-clinic established for foreigners in Moscow. Here I was introduced to the wax treatment for the rehabilitation of injured limbs—in my case, my injured lower back. I lay flat on a couch and several layers of hot liquid wax were painted on my lower back. This was then covered by a damp cloth over which were now deposited several thick wool blankets, topped by a heavy padded covering. I was left to stew for approximately forty minutes, after which time all was removed, the wax coming clear away on the dampened cloth. My back was now given a wonderful massage for a good twenty minutes. I rose like the phoenix, a new being. I had three such treatments, after which my back was as good as new. The lady who gave me this treatment was in her mid-fifties and could speak German. She was an extremely sympathetic individual. It was wonderful to thus have the opportunity of meeting a Russian!

Uncle Frost—Dadya Maroz

In Russia, New Year's Day is the great winter festival with feasting and jollity. Up to 1917, the religious festival of Christmas followed New Year's Day, for according to the Orthodox calendar, the birth of Christ falls on 6 January, but with the advent of communism, all manifestations of religion (of whatever denomination) were forbidden and abolished. Father Christmas, St Nicholas and Santa Claus were now personified by a new worthy gentleman named Uncle Frost (Dadya Maroz). An illuminated conifer, called by us (and all other Europeans) a Christmas tree (of Germanic culture origin), is called by Russians 'the New Year tree'. In Moscow, Dadya Maroz could be visited at one or two strategic spots in the city with a New Year tree close by.

On New Year's Day in 1948, a cold grey snowy day (just gentle flakes floating down), we bundled into our warm clothing, donned our boots and set off in search of Uncle Frost. We found him in an angle of one of the great bastions of the Kremlin wall. A New Year tree was behind him and towering above, atop the bastion, was a glowing red star—these were atop all the bastions or towers around the Kremlin. In a semi-circle at the foot of the tree were great painted cardboard figures of Dadya Maroz's retinue—a deer, a fox and a hare—the fox and hare in their white winter coats. Uncle Frost was also all in white, in his great coat with a white porkpie hat on his head. He held a great staff in his white gloved hand. Beside him was a brazier with glowing coals to warm him. Also on the ground beside him was a white box or sack and he would dip his hand in and pull out some little gift which he then handed to each child as he or she came up to him. It was a fairy-tale scene, but the crowd was too dense for us to approach at all near, so we were unable to see what Dadya Maroz gave each child—probably a little cut-out figure of an animal, to be cherished until next year.

Eighteen years later, in 1966, Uncle Frost and his retinue were now within the Kremlin walls. His stand was at the base of the great grassy bank which slopes down from the terrace on which stands the great nineteenth-century palace of the Tsars. Part of the Kremlin was now open to the public and a very agreeable walk was from the western gate, by the Armoury Museum, past the palace and on into the great square, on which stand the three great churches with golden domes and pepper-pot cupolas. The walk would take one out into Red Square across a drawbridge, the gateway being halfway between Lenin's tomb and the amusing and incredible St Basil's church.

Paths led down the sloping grassy bank in front of the great palace to the level area before reaching the Kremlin wall. A path with a few flowering trees and shrubs ran along the length of this area and at one end was Uncle Frost's special patch—but now he was fenced in. To approach him you first had to buy a ticket, which allowed you into the enclosure. You then handed your ticket to Uncle Frost, and he plunged his hand into his large sack and brought up a wrapped-up present for you.

The children were all now marshalled in school or pioneer groups—the latter were the equivalent of our Guides, Cubs and Brownies, membership of which was obligatory for every child of school age. Parents watched the proceedings from the top of the bank.

UNCLE FROST—DADYA MAROZ

New Year's Day in 1966 was a fine, sunny day and it was a colourful and interesting scene, but for me it had lost its magical fairy-tale quality it had had on that grey, gloomy and snowy afternoon in 1948.

General Arrested

The Novadevichi monastery nestles within the great elbow bend of the river Moskva about a mile downstream from the Kremlin. It was a strategic spot for the defence of Moscow in mediaeval times and the walls encircling the monastery were amongst the first stout brick walls constructed by Italian architects at the beginning of the fourteenth century. It doubled as a fortress in defence of the capital. Attached to the monastery is an enormous cemetery where all Russians who aspire to fame are buried. Joining the two banks of the river is a railway bridge with a footpath alongside it. Here the wooded Lenin Hills dip down and merge with the plain.

On a non-snowy or rainy Sunday morning just after we were installed in our flat, we took the boys to reconnoitre the area. In front of the entrance to the monastery is an open space down to the river. It was now covered with snow and the boys scampered joyously around like puppies let off their lead. A little distance away we saw a figure by the railway bridge. He stepped onto the footpath, pulled some field glasses out of a pouch and trained them on the Lenin Hills opposite. Presently we saw a number of men hastening towards him from across the river. They had emerged from some rather scruffy-looking buildings partly on the banks of the river and partly in the woods behind. There seemed to be a lot of barbed wire around and about. The man was escorted back to the buildings. 'Well,' we wondered, 'what was that all about?'

This elbow bend of the river, away from the city a short

distance behind it, is a picturesque and peaceful place. There were a few old-time timber Russian houses in the neighbourhood (eighteen years later they had all gone!). Although the sky was overcast we enjoyed our forty minutes in this open area away from Skatertnay Pereulok. It was now time to return to our Sunday lunch and a quiet afternoon reading our books. Towards the end of it the telephone rang—it was a call from the embassy to my husband. A matter of some urgency had suddenly arisen: a car was coming to collect him. The matter required immediate attention.

When he returned some hours later I was naturally curious to know the reason he had been called so suddenly. His answer was as follows: 'Do you remember this morning we saw a lone man standing on the footpath of the railway bridge by the Novadevichi monastery?' 'Yes, of course,' I replied. 'Well, believe it or not, it was our general, our military attaché.' 'Good heavens!' I exclaimed. 'What on earth was he doing?' 'Trying to discover possible slopes or tracks for skiing down the Lenin Hills; hence the field glasses. Unbeknown to him, and rather inconspicuous in the grey gloom, the scruffy buildings were in fact a factory, but of what, we haven't a clue. The Russkis arrested him for spying. They say he had trained his powerful field glasses on the factory. He was questioned for four hours before the embassy was contacted. To them his skiing story was incomprehensible and unbelievable. After much palaver with various officials, he has now been released.'

The story was splashed all over the Russian newspapers on the following day: 'British MA Caught Spying!' It also made headlines in the British press.

The general was now declared a *persona non grata* and the Russians asked for the general's recall. He had only been in Moscow since June. It had been a last posting for him before retirement. He left us soon afterwards. Seeing that this was Russia, we did all think his action had been rather naïve, but it made a splendid story for the cocktail circuit at this very gloomy period of the year. It generated a good deal of laughter at his expense.

Last months in Moscow, 1949

The winter of 1948–1949 passed without any stressful incidents. We had made good friends with various members of the Moscow international community and had enjoyed the various cultural activities very much. The boys were making good progress with their lessons and they had started to learn to play the piano. A very nice young teacher from one of the music schools had started both of them off with piano playing and with reading music. She only spoke Russian so I sat in during the weekly hour and somehow or other we all learned to understand each other. Irina taught them to read music with the help of an apple and a knife. By halving and quartering the apple she taught them the value of the notes from minims to crotchets and semiquavers and showed them how to write them down on the music staves, and she demonstrated the treble and bass modes. She was an admirable teacher and by the time they went to school in England, they could play simple tunes and had acquired a useful musical grounding.

In March 1949 I brought the boys back to the UK. They were both to start boarding prep school towards the end of April, the younger one just for one term as our next assignment after Moscow was to be London and I considered he was too young at seven to be packed off to a boarding school. He should rather attend a day school in London. It all worked out according to plan. Having installed the boys in their school where they joined their elder brother, I returned to Moscow for two months. Early in July I was back in England to spend time with my mother and be there for the summer holidays and to prepare for the birth of a new baby expected in August. In order to familiarise the 'Ruski boys' with school routine and rules, the three brothers initially shared a dormitory for three. However, we were told that such mayhem ensued that at the end of two weeks all three were separated and placed into other dormitories.

On my return to Moscow I was sad to find that Sir Maurice and Lady Peterson had bade their farewell to Moscow. Their three-year stint was up. The new ambassador, Sir David Kelly, arrived in June, but Lady K only joined him in July when I had already left. As we had got to know the departing couple on our initial journey to Moscow, being on the same boat from Tilbury to Leningrad, Lady P had thereafter taken a special interest in our boys. Each winter she invited them to a splendid tea in her private sitting room and she introduced them to the game of 'Happy Families', which they much enjoyed.

In September my husband completed his two-year assignment in Moscow and returned to London, where he was able to meet his baby daughter for the first time. Six weeks later and exactly two years after squeezing into our flat in Skatertnay Pereulok we installed ourselves in the top half of a house within walking distance of Regents Park and there we remained for the next seven years before packing up once more for another home, this time in the warm climes of Brazil—a great contrast to Russia. It was sixteen years before we were back in Moscow.

The author with her eldest son, John, on the balcony of their house at Kurfürsten Strasse, Berlin, 1938.

The church of Kolomenskoe, a popular site for a day trip from Moscow.

The Kremlin, as seen from the British Embassy across the Moskva River.

Suzdal, at the gateway to the Rizpoloz-Henski convent.

The Trinity-St Sergius Monastery at Zagorsk, which contains the tomb of Boris Godunov.

Picnicking in Georgia, 1967. Left to Right: Sir Geoffrey Harrison, the author, Simon Hemans.

The author visiting a school in Moscow, 1967.

A favourite painting of the monastery at Rostov, on the frontier of Moscow state.

Fireworks over the Kremlin on the 50th anniversary of the Russian Revolution.

The author on her 94th birthday, with sons (Left to Right) Bruce, Michael and John

III

Back to Moscow, 1965–1968

Back to Moscow 1965	117
— Setting the Scene	
— Arrival: 1947 compared with 1965	
New Features of Moscow	123
Our First Month in Moscow 1965	127
Diplomatic Calls	128
Weekend at Zavidova, end of September 1965	130
Zavidova, Winter Visit 1967	132
The Stewart Visit, November 1965	133
George Brown's Moscow Visits	135
The Wilson Visit, February 1966	138
— Recollections of a Non-event	
Moscow in the Sixties	145
— Khruschev	
— Brezhnev	
Leisure and Exercise	151
Encounters with Russians	153

BACK TO MOSCOW, 1965–1968

— Contacts
— Musical Encounters
— Living Conditions
— Madame Achmanova

The Royal Shakespeare Company and the National Theatre	163
New Horizons	166

— Return to Leningrad, February, 1966
— Yaroslav
— Early Summer 1966
— Queen's Birthday Party June 1966
— Vladimir and Suzdal

Visit of the BBC Orchestra, January 1967	184

— The Leningrad Concerts

Tour of the Hermitage, January 1967	191
Visitors and Travels, Winter to Summer 1967	195

— The Palace of Weddings
— More Travels

Siberia, February 1967	202

— Lake Baikal
— Irkutsk
— Bratsk

The Black Sea Autumn 1967	212

— Varna
— Odessa
— Yalta
— Sochi
— Batumi
— Sukhumi to Tbilisi

Armenia, Autumn 1967	225

— Echmiadzin

Georgia, Autumn 1967	233
The Central Asiatic Republic of Uzbekistan, 1966 to 1994	238

— The Russians in Central Asia
— Samarkhand
— Shahkrisabz
— Bukhara
— Khiva
— The Fergana Valley
— Kokand

November 1967: 50th Anniversary of Russian Revolution of 1917	256
1968	259
My Last Visit to Zagorsk, Spring 1968	260
Novgorod, June 1968	265
Leningrad: The Astoria Restaurant and the Arrival of Fluency	267
The Baltic States, June 1968	270
Karelia, July 1968	271
Day Trips from Moscow	272

Back to Moscow 1965

Setting the Scene

The time has now come to cross over to the further side of the partition which divides my Russian room. Much water has flowed in the intervening sixteen years that separate the two periods of my life in Moscow. In that flow there are many varied experiences including giving birth to a baby daughter, living in London with its notorious smogs of the early fifties, on to the lush warmth of Brazil and then to the mountains, deserts and outcrops of the moonscape scenery of Persia (called Iran since 1936), a country overflowing with centuries of history and culture, that had fascinated me since my teens.

It is now 1965 and we are about to live in the splendid British Embassy mansion, a far cry from our flat in Skatertnay Pereulok, our home in 1947–49.

The Embassy has the superb location of being right opposite the Kremlin with the Moskva River flowing between them. The Kremlin rises high above its superb great wall, built along the embankment with the beautiful nineteenth-century palace of the Tsars dominating the scene, and the golden domes and cupolas of its many churches was a view one never tired looking at.

I was extremely reluctant to return to Moscow. It was not only that I would not have small boys living with me—indeed, the boys were now all adult and into their own careers—but the fact that I would have no privacy. I would feel just like the Archbishop of York, David Hope, living in his grand bishop's palace in York. I would have to be sure I was clothed in my dressing gown—not, like him, to visit the bathroom, for there would be an en suite out of my bedroom—but to get items of clothing in fitted cupboards along the corridor opposite our private sitting room and bedroom; and my hair could not be in curlers—who might I not meet in that corridor? Since my birth I had lived in many different houses or flats, but once through the front door, each and every one of them was 'my home'. In Moscow I would be but a bird of passage living in that splendid house. It was not just the residence of the ambassador—it was the very nerve centre of the British mission in Soviet Russia. The ground floor and half the basement and the two wings on either side of the house were offices. As you entered the front door and stepped into the spacious but sombre hall, there on your right was a long counter with two British security guards vetting everyone who entered or left the house. To reach the front entrance, you drove or walked through a Soviet-guarded gateway of wrought-iron railings and on and round to the portico which sheltered the entrance door of the house set back a short distance from the embankment road. As you stepped into the hall, with its dark linenfold panelling, there at the back of the hall rose a magnificent wide staircase with impressive dark-wooded sculpted banisters. You mounted up and into a spacious lobby. Two magnificent tapestries hung on the walls on either side of the staircase. The lobby had doors on either side and a door and impressive fireplace on its back wall. The door on the left led into a corridor with a door at the end through which you found a staircase leading down to the ground floor and basement rooms of the offices. Two doors on the left of the corridor led to the two private rooms of the ambassador and his wife—nice large rooms facing the sunny south and overlooking the garden. On the right of the corridor were two doors, one leading to a guest room with what was known as the gothic bathroom adjoining it, and the other to one of the drawing rooms forming part of the handsome suite of reception rooms, the end one being the beautiful white and gold ballroom. At the ballroom's further end was a door leading to the second guest room. All these rooms had the glorious view of the Kremlin from their windows.

The door to the right of the lobby at the top of the grand staircase led into the very large dining room presided over by large and official portraits of past British monarchs: Queen Victoria, King George V and Queen Mary. George V looked so like his first cousin, the late Tsar Nicholas II, that Soviet guests were often startled and wondered why the British should have a portrait of their murdered Tsar. It was a fine room overlooking the garden; there was a connecting door between the dining room and the ballroom. Another door out of the dining room led into the pantry, with a dumb waiter lift to bring food up from the kitchen, two floors down in the basement. A door out of the pantry brought you to a steep and cold stone staircase connecting each floor from basement to attic. At ground level there was a back door into the drive from which there was access into the garden.

As there was no other dining room, this room was where the ambassador and his wife had to have all their meals (bar breakfast in the private sitting room), under the watchful eye of Victoria, George and Mary. The British embassy was not exactly a 'cosy' house to be living in! I remember a delicious breakfast here with my brother Robert on our journey from London to Teheran in 1930. In the evening, Sir Esmond Ovey gave us dinner and then bade us farewell at the top of the grand staircase before our departure for our onward journey to Baku, then by boat down the Caspian sea to Enseli, and by car over the mountains to Teheran. This dinner had been our last square meal for four days!

There was one innovation to the embassy house which had not been there in 1949—an innovation which we would greatly appreciate in summer time. This was the enclosure with canvas walls of the lateral sides of the balcony above the porch with an awning on top. It had access from the small drawing room through a French window. It was a lovely place to sit on fine summer days and evenings and watch barges and pleasure boats chugging up and down the river with the wonderful panorama of the Kremlin as backdrop. For me, relaxed moments here compensated a great deal for the inconvenience of the house.

Our Arrival in Moscow: 1947 compared with 1965

In 1947, in mid-October, we arrived in Moscow at 7.15 a.m. As we spilled out of our overheated train, we were struck numb by the sudden cold. It was snowing and it was a dark early morning. My first overwhelming reaction was gloom.

In 1965, it was mid-September when we flew into Moscow for our second incarnation—it was a lovely day, sunshine and blue sky. Our special aircraft brought not only ourselves and our luggage, but also several hundredweight of frozen meat which would be stored by arrangement in the city's deep-freeze depot. This supply was to last for a year and was renewed each year. We had been told we would be expected to give innumerable receptions, lunches, dinners for VIPs, delegations, academics, sportsmen, medics, technological experts and culture groups who would be periodically descending upon Moscow—what a new development since 1947–1949!

Also on board our aircraft were embassy staff members returning to Moscow from their leave. Amongst these we were pleased to become acquainted with our minister counsellor for economic and commercial affairs who had been to London on business. Alan Rothnie and his wife Anne became good friends, and remained so after retirement.

At Moscow airport we were met by senior members of staff and also by the Third Secretary, Andrew Wood, who was about to complete his stint as private secretary to the ambassador—within a fortnight he would be succeeded by Brian Fall, who would be arriving from London with his wife Delmar and their toddler daughter. They too would remain friends long after our Moscow days. Many years later and in very turbulent and changing times, Brian in his turn would become the British ambassador in Moscow. Private secretaries to the ambassador were all fluent Russian speakers.

Also greeting us at Moscow airport was, incredibly, Mr Kostaki himself, who had played the same role eighteen years earlier. His younger brother had the same job at the Canadian embassy, as head of Russian admin, though he also had a second string to his bow. He was friends with avant-garde Russian painters and collected their pictures which were stowed under his bed, until several years later he managed to smuggle them out to Paris, and he ended his life as a very affluent gentleman.

We shook hands very warmly with our Mr Kostaki and, together with Andrew Wood, we now proceeded to the embassy in the comfortable Rolls Royce, the ambassador's official car.

As the Kremlin complex with its imposing red brick wall, punctuated by impressive towers topped by their ruby-red five-pointed stars, hove into sight, there was the beautiful and white palace of the Tsars dominating the scene. To its right the golden domes and cupolas of the cathedrals, one cupola high aloft the campanile of Ivan the Great; all these gleamed in the sunlight, and my pulse quickened and I felt a surge of excitement and anticipation. I would be able to feast my eyes on this wonderful panorama whenever I looked out of any window of the embassy facing it.

We now drove through the iron gates and up and around to the portico—we had arrived.

Mr Moody, the English butler, was waiting for us. A footman opened the car door and Mr Moody ushered us into the hall. Andrew introduced us to the two security guards who emerged from behind their counter. We shook hands. Our domestic staff were lined up to greet us—Andrew introduced us to the four Russians: a cook, a chambermaid and two kitchen minions. Two English footmen who had carried a couple of bags and coats from the car were now introduced to us by Mr Moody, as well as the chef, Mr Wallace, and his wife. They were a nice couple, he an excellent chef and she ladies' maid and help to the ambassadress. We were sorry to see them leave at the end of the month, but the Batricks, who succeeded them, proved to be worthy successors. He too was a good chef, trained by Fortnum and Masons and experienced with the pressures of large-scale entertaining as he had frequently assisted at receptions and banquets at Buckingham Palace.

We proceeded up the grand staircase. The sun was streaming into our large square sitting room and there were a vase or two of lovely flowers. On the wall above a sofa was a painting by Lowry—I liked it immediately—it was all very welcoming.

A couple of hours later, having refreshed our memory of all the rooms on our floor, which had not changed at all in the intervening sixteen years, we hankered to stretch our legs, and Red Square beckoned. It was now late afternoon, but there was still plenty of time to cross the bridge and skirt around that exotic fantastic St Basils, one-time church, now a museum, and emerge into the historic square. Crossing the bridge we saw young people, some with linked arms, laughing, joking, enjoying themselves on this warm September late afternoon, and, surprise of surprises, what was this? People crossing the drawbridge and strolling in and out of the Sparsky Gate into the Kremlin? Ordinary people like ourselves—had we had time, we could obviously have done the same. To us it seemed there was an unexpected liberty abroad, which we had not visualised as existing. Definitely no traces of the terror which hovered in the last years of Stalin's reign. We felt cheered and returned home (willy-nilly, it was 'home' now) in a happy mood.

New Features of Moscow

Part 1

When we returned to England for our first leave in the summer of 1966, people asked me whether I had found any significant changes in the Moscow of 1965 compared with that of 1949 when I had left it? The answer was an emphatic 'yes'—many changes, in the city itself, in the general atmosphere and in the basic circumstances of my life, not just in the living conditions, which were very different, but also in the general social scene as it affected me.

I quote now from a letter I wrote in October 1965 to a great friend of mine with whom I had always corresponded regularly. She kept many of my letters, which were returned to me when she died.

In the city so much is new. Splendid great wide avenues with enormous characterless blocks of housing, all similar, radiate out in all directions. At ground floor level a few shops and gastronomes (food shops) every so often. Gaps between the blocs will usually lead into 3 or 4 sided courtyards, with doors and staircases leading up to flats. The buildings facing the avenues are quite tidy—but the courtyards behind generally pretty messy. As the avenues extend out to the city limits, even more buildings are being erected and being put to use (for housing mostly) before ever being completed just as had been the case 16 years earlier in the war zones, with construction rubble and mess lying untidily around. Of course when the snows come this mess will all be covered up by snow and forgotten but goodness knows when it will ever get cleared.

One quite new feature and within walking distance from the embassy, a feature which fascinated me, was the vast circular swimming pool attached to an indoor one; these were just downstream from the Kremlin on what had been waste ground during most of the thirties and forties and I don't know for how long after that before this amenity for Moscow citizens was constructed and established. The extensive waste ground was where the great nineteenth-century cathedral of Moscow had stood and which my brother Robbie and I had watched being demolished way back in the summer of 1930. The water for the outdoor pool was heated during the winter and in sub-zero temperatures with snow and ice everywhere around, it was incredible to see what appeared to be a whole lot of coloured balloons—yellow, green, red, blue, white—bobbing around on clear water; but they were not balloons, but the coloured bathing caps clinging tightly to the heads of swimmers. To reach the outdoor pool they had had to swim from the indoor pool down a channel under water and under a barrier. (Now in 2005, the pools have all gone and have been replaced by a new splendid cathedral, re-opened with great pomp and ceremony by the hierarchy of the Russian Orthodox Church).

Other features which punctuated the skyline of Moscow were what we called the 'wedding cakes', because they had tiers of masonry piled one on top of t'other. They rose to a height of around 22 storeys with a spire and a red star on top and were adorned with fussy little towers and much statuary. I reckon the building of them must have started during 1948, for Stalin is reputed to have so admired the first one, that he ordered a further five or six. Who occupied them, I never discovered. Moscow University, which extends along the first half of the Lenin Hills from which Napoleon is reputed to have watched Moscow burn, has certain similarities and was also a new feature for us.

Part 2

In my first Moscow incarnation I only once managed to penetrate the security of the Kremlin. A guided tour had been laid on for members of the embassy, for us all to tour the great nineteenth-century palace. It was an end-of-the-year treat in 1947. Now in 1965, the most scenic part of the Kremlin was open to the public, while the cathedrals with their golden domes surrounded by four golden pepper-pot little domes were now open as museum pieces. A great new white building had been erected along one side of the great palace and wedged between the palace and the cathedral square. Luckily it did not intrude on everyone's tableau of the Moscow Kremlin. It was called the Congress Hall and it doubled as the annual meeting venue for the delegates from every region of the Soviet Union, here to be harangued by the Big Boys (and a few ladies) of the Presidium, and also as the second theatre of the Bolshoi. The platform on which the Nobs sat was the front of an immense stage, excellent for the great lavish productions of the historical operas, but we always thought it much too large for ballets, some of which were also performed here. We much preferred seeing these danced at the Bolshoi itself.

To us it was obvious that, little by little, old Moscow, which had much charm, was being replaced. The immediate neighbourhood of the Kremlin remained more or less inviolate, and this included a small quarter behind our embassy. A small branch of the Moskva River flows past the back of the house beyond a miniature park before rejoining the main river, before it reached the Lenin Hills. In fact, our building was on an island. The little park was a peaceful haven where the babushkas (grandmothers) of the district could come, often with a great, red or blue padded bundle in their arms, and sit on a bench however cold the weather. They were sometimes accompanied by two or three small children with their toboggans. These might be neighbours' children whose parents were at work and who had not got an old babushka of their own. If you peered closely enough at the bundle, you would see two little eyes looking up at you.—a Russian babe out for its airing—there are few prams in Russia. If you ever see one, it has probably come from abroad. There are crèches and kindergartens in Moscow, but there are not enough and many parents prefer the services of their old relatives. The small children are equally well wrapped up like so many humpty-dumpties. The babushkas would foregather in this little park for a good gossip. In another clime an analogous scene could be observed until the mid-fifties in the London parks. Uniformed nannies foregathering with their friends or rivals and pushing beautifully sprung and turned out high prams with enormous wheels, equally accompanied by one or two young children. I refer to Regents Park and Kensington Gardens.

The further bank of the little river at the rear of the embassy house was fringed by a row of picturesque cottages—the bulldozers and town planners had not yet reached this little quarter of Moscow. It had a particular charm. One of the very few working churches of Moscow was in a street behind. It was well known for its excellent singing. I visited it on a number of occasions if I had a friend to escort me. In wintertime, after the trees had all shed their leaves, its four green pepper-pot domes were just visible from both our sitting room and our bedroom.

Our First Month in Moscow, 1965

On returning to Moscow in 1965, I found not only were the material circumstances of my life utterly different from those of eighteen years previously when living in Skatertnay Pereulok, but the social setting was now completely different. The personnel of our own embassy had now tripled in size; with wives, we were now around 180 souls. I am not sure of the total number of foreigners who now worked in Moscow—but foreign colleagues alone made up a throng. In the old days with Stalin at the helm, we all coalesced; nationality, rank and social background made little impact. But now in 1965 we were very much divided into specialised work concerns, diplomats, defence, commercial, information and cultural. The members of each group would meet and socialise with their foreign colleagues of similar work interest. Amongst the diplomats, protocol with a capital P ruled the roost. It was as rigid as at the court of Louis XIV at

Versailles. The more senior your rank, the more restricted was your social life. At dinner parties we seldom met anyone other than a fellow ambassador, perhaps his number two and possibly the most senior of one or other of the three defence sections, army, navy and air. I found this very irksome and boring. Time and time again I would find myself seated next to the same ambassador. However agreeable and nice an individual he might be, topics such as family, countries one had served in or current shows one had recently seen were soon exhausted.

Once a newly arrived head of mission had presented his letters of credence to the head of state, he would then proceed to call on all other heads of mission, and his wife would do the same and call on the wives. Time and date of calls were first arranged.

It took us the best part of a month to complete all these calls, but at last they were almost completed and the weather was fine, so we decided to go off for a country weekend. The Soviets had now set up a country installation for members of foreign missions. It was some eighty miles up the road to Leningrad. Following is the newsletter I wrote about it to my family after our first visit. It is preceded by a description of my calls on two African colleagues.

Diplomatic Calls

This week I have been continuing my calls. This has included Uganda and Tanzania. The first was hard going—poor Mrs Uganda; very tall, very ungainly, with short fuzzy hair, speaking and understanding rather little English and no other language, is miserable here. They live on the top floor of one of the immense blocks. The entrance (always through a messy back yard) stairs and lift are identical in all Russian blocks. It's all very sordid

DIPLOMATIC CALLS

and very depressing and the lift is very rickety and consequently to me alarming. However if one has to visit someone on the 12th floor one has no choice. I was ushered into a rather bare room with a few black leather swivelling chairs and one or two black tables. Mrs Uganda and I then sat down on opposite sides of one of these tables and drank passion fruit juice (disgusting!) followed by black coffee. Conversation was very difficult. Mrs Uganda's efforts were limited to whether I knew Uganda and to 'You like lions?' I tried hard to embroider on these themes and then switched to children. Six was the answer, four in Uganda all quite little and two here, a boy with a hole in his heart in hospital here, and a 16-month-old baby. I asked if I might see her—Mrs Uganda beamed. This was a great success. She was rather a sweetie brought in by the Russian maid.

When I got up to escape, Mrs Uganda cried out 'you no finish juice', but I'm afraid I just couldn't oblige. Mrs Tanzania was much more fun. Her outlook on life was less tragic. She's a cheerful soul in herself, but my goodness life is difficult for these poor Africans here. Mrs Tanzania admitted as much in a rather disarming way: 'Not easy for you white people here in Moscow, but we are only poor Bantus, very much difficult.' Mrs T received me in her African clothes, whereas Mrs Uganda wore a quite smartly cut earthy brown European suit. Something which struck me was how fluently Africans of erstwhile French colonies speak French—whereas those of erstwhile British colonies can hardly speak any English at all. Mrs Tanzania however wished to speak English to me although she was fluent in well-pronounced French. She had studied it during the three years she had spent in Delhi before coming to Moscow, and she managed remarkably well. She told me she was now attempting to learn Russian so that she could go shopping on her own.

BACK TO MOSCOW, 1965–1968

Weekend at Zavidova, end of September, 1965 (Extract from my Newsletter)

Still very glorious weather. We went and sampled the Diplomatic Dacha last weekend. When it clouded over last Friday and began to drizzle we were very afraid that the weather was going to be beastly for the weekend—but not a bit. It was beautifully clear and sunny. However a biting north-west wind which on the Sunday morning was more north than west fairly pierced one through and through, and of course coming from this over-heated house we hadn't at all visualised how nippy it was going to be and did not in consequence really have quite the right clothing with us. Luckily I did at the last minute slip in a coat into the car and a wool head scarf, so I just got by without completely freezing up! It so happened that the Saturday night was the coldest as yet with some 3 degrees below zero (centigrade). I had been told by a chèr collègue that staying at this place was rather like being a guest in a concentration camp. Indeed there is something in this. One drives through great gates set in a 10ft high iron fence, and they are closed behind one. The property about 1¼ acres (the size of Gulahek) is on a promontory at the mouth of a tributary of the Volga. The situation is really rather beautiful and very peaceful. One has the impression of being on a lake with great woods on the far side, fir and deciduous, very lovely now in their autumn colouring. There is a small hotel with some 9 double rooms, a dining room (restaurant), billiard room and a central hall sitting room. A highish square tower with a glassed-in platform all round rises from the centre of this building, and we noticed that there were search lights up there. Apart from this hotel club house there are about 8 little wooden dachas dotted around. We had reserved one of these. It was beautifully clean and comfortably arranged. Everything

WEEKEND AT ZAVIDOVA, END OF SEPTEMBER, 1965

there for one; crockery, cutlery, pots and pans, a gas cooker and a fridge. One could bring one's own food and fend for oneself entirely if one wished. We did, except for dinner which we ate over in the restaurant and had quite a respectable meal there, but it was nice being on our own otherwise.

It was fairly cold in our little house when we arrived. They had only just lit the stove in the kitchen which supplied both central heating and hot water, but there was a glassed-in veranda facing south and in there it was like being in a greenhouse. Seeing our great fence all round, we asked the good lady who seemed to be in charge of the place where we might walk. 'You must take a boat and cross over to the far side of either the Shoja (the tributary) or the Volga and then you can walk where you please.' 'Is there nowhere this side?' I asked her. 'Just inside the boundaries', was the answer. So after lunch we went down to the jetty where there was quite an assortment of boats with a number of boatmen in attendance. The wind was keen so we chose to sit in the motor boat with a closed in cabin and over the Volga we went. We had a glorious walk and GWH was like a child out of school, so jubilant to be right out in the country and 80 miles away from our Embassy house.

As I knew it would be, it is pretty ghastly living on top of the offices. One has no sense of privacy in the Embassy house at all and one just cannot feel at home. Nowhere ever have I had such a sense of being but a bird of passage as here. It is only one degree better than living in a hotel, and this feeling of being constantly under supervision, and everyone knowing exactly where one is and what one is doing is pretty inhibiting. GWH misses the freedom of his weekends frightfully, and this was the first time since leaving England that we felt free and on our own, even though the Russkis knew exactly where we were of course.

BACK TO MOSCOW, 1965–1968

Zavidova, Winter Visit 1967

During our three Russian years, 1965–1968, we escaped three or four times to the diplomatic ghetto, as a colleague called it. It was always a refreshing breath of fresh air, giving one a sense of freedom and relaxation away from the eyes of the many humans who peopled the embassy precincts. One of the weekends was in the depth of the cold winter of 1967. We drove the eighty odd miles in order to see the Volga covered in ice and snow. A letter to my mother written immediately on our return to Moscow from the weekend reads as follows:

> *We had clear sunny weather (end of January) and it was very beautiful and a great experience. We especially chose to go there when we did because we wished to see the Volga covered in ice and snow. Not only did we see it thus but we actually walked straight down the middle of it! Admittedly it was devilishly cold—it made my eyes water and then icicles formed on my eyelashes! Very uncomfortable. We did this walk on the afternoon of our arrival. On the following day we crossed to the further side of the Shoja River (the tributary) and had a walk through woods where it was much warmer than in the wide open spaces of the great river. It was a very enjoyable weekend and our little wooden dacha all to ourselves was very snug and warm.*

A month later we were off to Siberia, and there we would see a much greater river than the Volga: the awe-inspiring mighty Yenisey, seen from the great dam at Bratsk.

The Moscow–Leningrad highway (probably the most important in Russia) was a good road of evenly packed snow. It was regularly patrolled by efficient snowploughs which shoved the snow to one side or t'other, there to form great banks of freezing snow. One saw wooded areas here and there but no great forests, and the little dachas under their mantle of snow imparted a feeling of snugness and were picturesque, many with painted fretwork and wood carving around window frames; the eaves of the roofs equally painted to match. Squalor and dirt were no longer visible. Isolated, ungainly and out of keeping with the countryside—a three-to-five-storey-high building would suddenly protrude out of the landscape. One wondered: why on earth was it there? Then we remembered having passed perhaps half a kilometre back a collection of low sheds and buildings, or they might be half a kilometre beyond it. Together they formed a collective farm—the little enclave of low sheds and buildings were for farm animals and all the necessary implements and machinery like tractors for running a farm and snowploughs would also be housed here—for cleaning both the highway and the immediate surroundings of the farm. The ugly isolated building was for housing the farm labourers. Presumably there was a communal dining room—a pretty grim existence, I would imagine.

The Stewart Visit, November 1965

Our weekend at Zavidova gave us the breathing space we needed before being plunged into our official role in Moscow. Immediately following the 7 November celebrations, with the parade in the morning and the Kremlin reception in the afternoon, our foreign secretary Michael Stewart and his wife came on an official visit to Moscow, accompanied by Sir Paul Gore-Booth, head of the Foreign and Commonwealth Office and a delegation of 29 individuals. We had been just seven weeks in situ, with an unrehearsed domestic staff.

The Stewarts and Sir Paul were house guests and we were to give our first official dinner for some thirty-six guests plus a lunch party. So for me it meant organising and supervising our staff for these events. It would also be my first opportunity of meeting the wives of the Soviet hierarchy. These ladies took charge of Mrs Stewart and her programme, quite different from that of her husband's. They entertained her plus myself and took her on three special visits—tours of the Kremlin Palace, a kindergarten and one of the special English language schools where, from the age of seven, children would spend their entire school career. I accompanied Mrs Stewart to two of these visits, the kindergarten and the English language school. I knew I would have plenty of other opportunities of visiting the Kremlin Palace and I had plenty to do at home.

The visit to the kindergarten in the late afternoon was delightful and the visit to the English language school extremely interesting. In these seven-year-olds' first year, an hour a day was devoted to English, and all other lessons were in Russian. In the fifth year, however, when the children were 11 years old, all lessons were now in English, including maths and science. There were a number of these special English language schools in Moscow as well as an array of special language schools devoted to the teaching of European, Asiatic and African languages. Other Soviet cities also had these schools. Thus, once the children were grown up and had continued their studies in their special language at university, a cadre of men and women proficient in most world languages was available to be sent to countries all around the world where they could promote Russian interests and spread the gospel of communism. Children for these special schools were selected at kindergarten stage.

We sat at the back of the class for seven-year-olds taken by an attractive young teacher. The hour was divided into a number of different sections. In one of these both Mrs Stewart and I were asked to read through an ABC book (*a* for apple, *b* for baby, etc.). She read the first half of the alphabet, I the second. Our readings were recorded for our accent. Mrs Stewart, a teacher by profession, found the method of teaching young pupils a foreign language extremely interesting. We then met 13- and 14-year-olds during break time and were impressed by their fluency and the way they expressed themselves in English. Presently they acted a scene from *As You Like It*—excellently.

The visit of the Stewarts was an excellent exercise for our whole embassy. It was the precursor of the expected visit of our Prime Minister, Harold Wilson, in February 1966.

We were pleased with the way our young chef had coped. He had been given a practice run the previous week when we entertained twenty-two senior members of the embassy for luncheon. Two days later we gave our first diplomatic dinner for our Canadian colleague and his Brazilian wife who had welcomed us very warmly within days of our arrival in Moscow.

George Brown's Moscow Visits

During 1966, George Brown succeeded Michael Stewart as Foreign Secretary. He visited Moscow on two occasions, the first time accompanied by Mrs Brown, but the second time on his own. On both occasions he stayed at the embassy.

The Soviet ladies, the wives of the great and mighty, Mrs Brezhnev, Mrs Kosygin and Mrs Gromyko, rallied round Mrs Brown as they had around Mrs Stewart and would around Mrs Wilson. This time I did not accompany them on the trips to various places of interest that they took her on, all exclusive of any sightseeing. However, of paramount interest to me was the banquet laid on for the Browns in the Granitovaya Palace in the very heart of the Kremlin complex. Although called a palace, it consists of just one square chamber to serve as audience hall for the Tsars. It was the first building other than the cathedrals to be built of stone, rather than wood, and dates from 1491. Responsible for its structure were Italians who had the engineering know-how of building with stone and bricks, and in fact Italians built the Kremlin walls and those of monasteries such as Zagorsk to withstand onslaughts by the Tartars. The great Moscow cathedrals all owe their existence to the Italian architects and building experts; they gave them a Russian flavour with the cupolas and their interior design, having visited Vladimir and absorbed the style which suited their Russian employers.

The outer walls of the Granitovaya Palace are built of faceted stones (hence its name) and it is entirely mediaeval in concept. The vaulted ceiling centres onto a massive rather squat circular pillar rising out of a 2½-foot-high brick, rectangular base. On entering it I felt I was entering a kind of Aladdin's cave, not sparkling with jewels but richly coloured all over with historical scenes and decoration and the different coloured marble floor was equally striking. This interesting audience chamber was not open to the public in our day, nor usually shown to visitors, so I felt it was a great privilege to be entertained in this palace. The menu for our meal was, by Russian standards, relatively simple and straightforward, and the meal did not span a four-hour period with innumerable toasts.

There was a great deal of difference between George Brown's Moscow visits and those of Harold Wilson and Michael Stewart. Wilson had already visited Moscow as Minister of Trade in the Attlee government of 1948 during our first tour there. People of small stature tend to be blustery towards others, perhaps to give themselves an aura of self-assurance. This was certainly the case with both Harold Wilson and George Brown. Harold Wilson, however, was immensely interested in Soviet Russia and maintained this interest throughout his career, and he visited Moscow on several occasions. Michael Stewart had a schoolmaster's interest in the country. But George Brown's mind was almost

GEORGE BROWN'S MOSCOW VISITS

entirely focused on America and the Vietnam war. His other interest was the ever-present troubles which rule the Middle East. Russia and her relations with Europe and the Cold War were all secondary problems to him and he had no time for other aspects of Russia. He thought he had all the answers to the world's problems and he knew everything much better than anyone else.

The cartoonists of the British press had a field day with his Moscow visits.

During the forthcoming week your prayers are particularly asked for HM Ambassador in Moscow.

BACK TO MOSCOW, 1965–1968

The Wilson Visit to Moscow, February 1966

The visit in November 1965 of British Foreign Secretary Michael Stewart and his wife was the precursor of a visit in February 1966 of our Prime Minister, Harold Wilson, accompanied by Mrs Wilson and a great posse of Foreign Office officials led by George Brown who had succeeded Michael Stewart as Foreign Secretary and Sir Paul Gore-Booth, head of the Foreign & Commonwealth Office. It was Sir Paul's second visit.

Following is the newsletter I wrote to my family after the event.

Thank God, the visit is over and we are left with two immense photos of Harold and his Mrs in green tooled leather frames. She all blurry and he looking just like Chi-Chi the Panda. The party came laden with gifts for great and small and to our considerable amusement, we found these portraits (18" × 14") had been left for us. Luckily the problem of where to put them is solved by the presence of what we now call the Prime Ministerial Desk. I think in my last letter I mentioned that we discovered this enormous and very handsome writing table mouldering in the attic. It scrubbed and polished up beautifully and spent its first three days peregrinating around the room allotted to it. Everywhere it looked so overwhelmingly huge. However, suddenly it found its niche across one of the corners of the small sitting room and it really looks so good there that we shall keep it there. It will do splendidly for all our subsequent guests, and now it is the obvious resting place for these two vast photos!

We'd been warned that the PM likes to feel everyone is bustling around—so we all bustled. Couldn't help it in fact, we were just carried along with the prevailing tidal wave. It started from the word 'go'. There we all were, at the VIP

THE WILSON VISIT TO MOSCOW, FEBRUARY 1966

airport; Embassy staff, foreign ambassadors, all the Soviet Big Nobs, guard of honour, all waiting apprehensively. It was a thoroughly English day; not cold but damp and drizzly with an ever-thickening mist and plenty of snow around. On the dot of the scheduled time we were told the plane was overhead. We all trooped out, the guard of honour marched into position—we all gazed into the opaque whiteness. Suddenly the plane was heard, louder and louder, quite close—invisible. Mme Gromyko, beside me, squeezed my hand. Then the sound of the plane grew fainter; it was gone. Almost at once some Russian called out, 'The plane has gone to Sheremetev' (the civil airport). 'Come on, off to Sheremetev,' called out Mr Kosygin, and we all dashed and scurried to find our cars. Led at a spanking pace by the half dozen leading Soviet cars, we hurtled for some 35 miles along or rather around the double tracked outer ring road, to arrive quite breathless at Sheremetev. There we found the party surrounded by photographers and minor officials sipping tea. The DT had a good description of all this.

With our arrival, tea, photographers, minor officials were all swept aside—in so far as you can ever sweep aside a press photographer! Mr Kosygin embraced Mr Wilson. Mrs Kosygin ditto to Mrs W, and they were immediately swept away to the cars. In the meantime, the American and one or two of the South American Ambassadors had by now arrived from the other airport, but I'm afraid, poor things, they were just swept past by the leaders. GWH and I hastily and apologetically shook them warmly by the hand and off we went again too. We ourselves followed the leaders to the villa allocated to the distinguished visitors; a villa perched on top of the Lenin Hills with a most glorious view across Moscow. When we got there, we all discarded our coats and then sat round a table and sipped champagne. The Russian party then withdrew and Mr W at once said, 'Where are all the boys?' 'Oh, they have all gone straight to their various lodgings.' 'Better get hold of them quick, tell them to come here at once, we'll have a meeting'. Then ensued a very funny sort of dumb crambo act. Geoffrey explained it would be better for everyone to turn up after dinner at the Embassy. It would perhaps be a better place for discussions. Everyone then put their fingers to their lips and pointed around the room at the walls etc. The PM growled his assent and we then parted to foregather about 45 minutes later for dinner here at the Embassy. With some of our senior staff and with the senior members of the delegation, we sat down 24. The rest of the party then came in after dinner, and the men presently withdrew for their meeting, leaving us ladies to make polite 'converzatione' to Mrs W for about two hours!! A bit of a strain, for all concerned. She was obviously very tired, she naturally had been terrified at the landing, but somehow she couldn't bring herself to firmly say 'I'll go to the villa and so to bed', which I am sure Mrs Stewart would have done. But she was extremely friendly and pleasant and quite easy to talk to. One just really ran out of topics. However the evening at last came to an end and with a sigh of relief we went to bed. 'I'll be round at 9 to read telegrams' was the PM's parting shot. But Mrs W would not be round till 10 to pick me up en route for the Bolshoi Ballet school.

Mrs Wilson's program was in fact very similar to that of Mrs Stewart, but with slight variations. As I had missed the Kremlin tour at the time of the Stewart visit, because of it having been on the same morning as our dinner party, and because on that day we also had to arrange to be a party of 6 for lunch, I took the necessary measures to tack onto the Kremlin tour this time. I cunningly arranged for two of the Embassy ladies to come in that morning to 'do' the flowers. These, tulips, freesias, daffs, hyacinths and

THE WILSON VISIT TO MOSCOW, FEBRUARY 1966

narcissi had come on the plane with the party. I got Mrs. Batrick to bed them all snugly down in the larder in buckets of deep water and I'm glad to say they survived. In fact freesias and tulips are still going strong.

But I am jumping ahead. On the Tuesday morning it was the Bolshoi ballet school, and this as you can imagine was enthralling. We saw boys and girls at various stages and it all ended with a very gay Russian dance. We just had time for a quick brush up here at the Embassy before going off to the official lunch at the Kremlin given by the Soviet Government. I'd never had a meal there before and I don't suppose I shall again. The mise en scène is superb. The lunch itself was held in the old throne room of the old Kremlin Palace all painted with biblical scenes! It dates from the 16th century, a great big square room with windows on three sides and a vaulted ceiling, also painted. In Tsarist days, when the tables were no doubt adorned with magnificent plate and the company bejeweled and sumptuously dressed, it must have been very splendid. Nowadays all grand silver ornamentation is banished and sits behind glass doors in the museum, and one now eats with very plain silver cutlery with the Soviet crest and off dull white china plates with a narrow gold rim and again with the Soviet Emblem. Tidy but dull. Down the table were low bowls of flowers. But if the table furnishings were simple, the meal certainly wasn't. Course followed course. Through chunks of crab dished up, with the carcass of the crab somehow propped up on the dish, smoked fish of several varieties, through blinis with the best quality caviar, such as I haven't seen since Persia, through delicate deer's tongues, excellent fillet of beef, through grilled chicken, wait a minute I left out the Siberian grouse before the beef—all these dishes 'garniert' as the Germans would say, to finally the ice cream. All this of course liberally washed down with vodka and wines. We ate from 1 till 4 *(this did include the speeches) and then adjourned to a neighbouring splendid room where we all sat around various tables on heavy gold and brocaded chairs for fruit, chocolates and coffee.*

I sat around the table with Mrs Wilson, Mrs Kosygin, Mrs Brezhnev and other high-ranking Soviet ladies. As before, I found them all very cosy and easy to talk to and very forthcoming and friendly. Mrs Kosygin talks quite passable French and she really made great efforts. Our Mrs W also made efforts too, but one could see she was obviously very tired and her role doesn't come easily to her.

After the lunch, most of us feeling pretty gaga I would think, the ladies took Mrs Wilson to a kindergarten. A picture gallery had been on the agenda but luckily we got this changed. The kindergarten was effortless. It was obviously a fairly showy piece. The children seemed quite accustomed to visitors, and put on a singing and dancing show. It was already late in the afternoon and many children had already been fetched home, but these Russian kindergartens remain open till 7, and the music teacher was still there, hence there seemed to be no difficulty in conjuring up about 20 children to perform.

Hardly home from this, we hastily changed and went off to the ballet. Unfortunately not at the Bolshoi, there was nothing suitable on there that evening, but to the immense new theatre-congress hall in the Kremlin. There are only two boxes there, at either side and so far back from the stage and at such an acute angle that one could only see half the stage and the dancers were so remote that one really would have done just as well watching the ballet on TV. Moreover, apparently 'The Fountain of Bakchisarai' is the one ballet which always appears to be on whenever Wilson has been to Moscow. He told me he had seen it about five times! I expect Kosygin has also no doubt seen it innumerable times. I think it is a lovely ballet, but I think

THE WILSON VISIT TO MOSCOW, FEBRUARY 1966

it loses by being staged there instead of at the Bolshoi. During each interval (three) we sat down to a variety of cold foods. I don't think anybody, Russians anymore than ourselves, had the slightest desire to eat any thing, in fact Wilson and K were so busy jawing away, at least Wilson was whilst K looked poker faced, that I don't think they did eat. And so NOT to bed, at least NOT for the British men folk, for W insisted on returning to the Embassy which he didn't leave till just after 2am. Two of our most senior members of the staff didn't in fact get to bed at all that night, nor indeed did these two gentlemen get more than about 3 hours sleep the following night! I can't help feeling that the final result of the visit, as published in the Communiqué, was hardly commensurate with all this prodigious effort in terms of all-night vigils!

For me actually, things were quite easy. Not having a lady guest actually in the house and very few meals to cater for (quite different story when the Stewarts were here), my only real concern was to see that the PM's study was aired, tidy and ready for him when he turned up in the mornings and then of course we had our dinner on the Wednesday night. As the form was exactly the same as at the Stewart dinner, the servants did know more or less how to lay it all up. I was able to tack on to the Kremlin tour on the morning of the dinner, but I did cry off Mrs Kosygin's tea party. I had in this way the whole afternoon to see to things. It all went off most easily, the dinner was quite good and the atmosphere was relaxed and the after dinner period did not last too long. We put Wilson and Kosygin sitting next to each other with their respective ladies on either side, just as though they were monarchs, and they with 12 others sat at the top table, whilst the rest of the party were at four round tables. Geoffrey arranged for 3 'non-eating' interpreters (great joke this in the Embassy against the poor non-eaters) to sit on stools at strategic points around the top table group. These non-eaters are our most fluent Russian speakers. The official interpreters were at the round tables and were able to dine in peace. They were only called upon at the end for the set speeches.

I found the Kremlin visit most interesting. We were shown Lenin's private apartments which are seldom shown to foreigners, and then we toured the whole of the big palace where we had lunched, followed by a lightning visit to the museum and finally, by special request of Mrs Wilson, we visited the mausoleum which is Lenin's tomb in Red Square.

And that ended the visit as far as I was concerned. I didn't tack on to the programme arranged for the Thursday morning. It was identical with what had been done with Mrs Stewart and the Soviet ladies fetched Mrs W straight from her villa. Mrs W did then come here and spent about half an hour chatting to me in our sitting room before going back to the villa for lunch, and immediately afterwards they were off.

I've written this with innumerable interruptions and I am hastily finishing off now at 4pm and the Tapsells leave in 20 minutes.

I hope the PM felt we'd all bustled around. Certainly our front hall gave the impression that Piccadilly Circus had forsaken London and taken up its location right there. For three and a half days it appeared to contain a solid core of dark suited gentlemen who successfully blocked entrance and exit to the front door, and weaving around and through this bloc were other gentlemen and lots of ladies all carrying papers and boxes and all looking harassed and busy. And to help this atmosphere of general clutter was the background of prodigious fur coats, hats and galoshes on the coat stands provided for this occasion.

THE WILSON VISIT TO MOSCOW, FEBRUARY 1966

Recollections of a Non-event

Before leaving Moscow, Harold Wilson invited Mr Kosygin to come to London for a return visit and for further discussions on outstanding problems. Mr Kosygin agreed that such a visit would be very useful. On his return to London, Wilson discussed the matter with the Queen who said she would give an evening banquet for the Russian visitors. An invitation was sent to Moscow inviting Mr and Mrs Kosygin and Mr and Mrs Gromyko to come for a three-day visit to London in early May. This was accepted and my husband was to accompany the Russians, and I was invited to come along too.

I was thrilled at the prospect of being a guest at a Buckingham Palace banquet and told our chef Mr Batrick, as he had on a number of occasions helped the palace chef to prepare such a meal. I had a suitable evening gown—it was ironed and ready for packing with appropriate shoes and bag, about a week before our travelling date. But just then, the Embassy was told that Mrs Kosygin had fallen ill with a chest infection. She hoped however to have recovered in time for the visit. Alas, no, she was not well enough to travel to London. We were only informed of this just two days before our departure.

The London response to this was that I should not come either! I was thus denied my Buckingham Palace banquet. It was a hard blow.

I have always thought this was extremely mean of the Foreign Office.

Moscow in the Sixties

That very first walk on the late afternoon of our arrival back in Moscow in early September 1965 alerted us to the fact that

BACK TO MOSCOW, 1965–1968

the atmosphere of Moscow was now, in 1965, very different to what it had been eighteen years earlier in 1947. There was now a new boss presiding over the Presidium, and a new lot of men running the Politburo of the Communist Party. Moreover the paranoiac evil and feared dictator Stalin and his sinister henchman Beria were dead. This was a new world with new challenges. So our natural reaction on our return to Moscow was that a great gush of fresh air had blown through the city. We also sensed a great easing of tension between Russians and foreigners.

We had been told before leaving London that we would find a number of British students of Russian studying at the Universities of Moscow and Leningrad, also music students studying with maestros at the Moscow conservatoire of music. We were also told that professional groups from the scientific and medical world had been invited to attend conferences and would be coming to Moscow in the course of the next year and into 1967. The BBC Orchestra with members of the Hallé orchestra under Sir John Barbirolli would be coming in January 1967 and the Shakespeare Company with Laurence Olivier and Joan Plowright were also booked to come in December 1966 for a few days each in Moscow and Leningrad.

This was all quite exciting for us and we looked forward to an interesting three years in Moscow. However, it did not take us long to discover the unfading truth of the maxim of the Marquis de Custine written over a century earlier in 1839: 'Plus ça change, plus c'est la même chose' (the more things change, the more they remain the same). The Berlin Wall had been built in the late fifties. At the same time, Russian troops had marched into Hungary, encountering much bloody resistance, deposed the existing government and replaced it with a Russian-controlled communist regime, as the communist regime in place in Budapest since the end of the war was too liberal minded and not sufficiently subservient to

Russian wishes. So now Hungary was firmly incorporated into the Eastern Bloc. The Cold War was now on and very much a reality, resulting in much activity in the sphere of intelligence. Europe was firmly divided as it had been eighteen years previously into two blocs—the Communist Bloc versus the Western Democratic Bloc. The Secret Services of both blocs were kept busy and this in Great Britain gave rise to the thrillers of Ian Fleming with his romantic, handsome and dare-devil hero James Bond, and of John Le Carré with his mild-mannered secret agent George Smiley. We found the following facts to be operative—facts which had evolved and changed in a number of ways but basically were the same as two decades earlier:

1.) Freedom of close social contact between Russians and foreigners was by and large impossible. As soon as Russians in a gastronome became aware that you were a foreigner, more often than not they would turn their backs and shun you. 2.) Russian nationals and those of the satellite countries were forbidden to travel to foreign countries. 3.) Consumer goods were still in hopelessly short supply and people relied largely on imports from the satellite countries, so when a consignment of some desired commodity arrived, say of boots and shoes from Czechoslovakia, news would be passed around by word of mouth, just as previously, and the boots and shoes would all be sold within 24 hours. 4.) Restriction of movement for foreigners beyond a fifty-kilometre limit from the boundaries of the city of Moscow was in force. The limit in 1947–1949 had been twenty-kilometres, so to us this was an appreciated concession. Moreover, now special permits were readily granted if asked for in order to visit a special monastery or even an interesting old town which might involve a night or two away—and there was no difficulty in obtaining a permit to travel to a distant region of the USSR, like Kiev in the Ukraine or Georgia or the central Asian areas of the union. The fact was the authorities just wanted to keep a tab on one. There were certain areas in the vicinity of Moscow which remained forbidden territory for foreigners. This included Nijni-Novgorod, now named Gorki, for Andrei Sakarov, the eminent and dissident Nobel prize-winning scientist, was exiled there and was forbidden to have any contact with foreigners. But we understood that he and his wife had a comfortable flat, and from time to time she was allowed to come to Moscow to see relatives and friends.

The fundamental fact was that the present generation of Russians now in government, together with the leaders of the armed forces, had been teenagers on the threshold of adulthood at the time of the 1917 revolution and during Lenin's life, and they had grown to maturity during Stalin's reign. The ideology of Marxist–Leninism was the only creed they understood, and they believed in it implicitly. Just as the youth of Germany venerated their Führer, so these men had revered first Lenin then Stalin, and for decades, successive generations of children continued to be indoctrinated with this creed, from nursery school through to adulthood, and all in the Soviet Union in the mid-twentieth century firmly believed that if only the whole world became communist, the sooner would world peace be assured and Russia would lead the world in this endeavour. The present-day leaders had been clever and ambitious young men, and luckily for them they had been favoured by fate, for many of their peers had been eliminated in Stalin's incomprehensible purges in the terror days of the mid-thirties and again during the post-war years up to his death in 1953. His demise must have come as an immense relief, for right up to the end, the sword of Damocles had been an ever-present threat as it dangled above their respective heads to fall at any moment at the whim of their paranoid dictator and master with the connivance of his greatly feared henchman, Beria. So, not surprisingly, when Stalin died, the clique of men closest to Stalin and all members of the Politburo immediately ganged up together, on news of his death, to kill Beria before he succeeded in realising his ambition and step into the shoes of his master.

In 1965, people like ourselves who had experienced Stalin at the helm rejoiced with the Russian people that Stalin was no more, but as foreigners we were still under supervision, with a number of restrictions. However, a chink of door had been partially opened into a friendlier world. For this we have to thank Khrushchev, who immediately preceded Brezhnev, the number-one boss during our three years in Moscow in the sixties.

Khrushchev

Khrushchev was an intelligent individual but he had a split personality. Imbued with ambition, he managed after two years of manoeuvring, following Stalin's death, to achieve the coveted goal of becoming supreme boss. In many ways, he was a visionary with liberal ideas. He recognised that his fellow countrymen required greater liberty in their lives and better living conditions. He also realised that cultural and technical exchanges with the western world would be beneficial to all concerned. He could, however, also act in savage ways reminiscent of Stalin, not shooting those who annoyed him but packing them off to the Gulag in Siberia. He was also an impetuous gambler, and this proved to be his undoing. He will be remembered on three counts: 1.) He instigated the building of the Berlin Wall and the invasion of Hungary, thereby intensifying the Cold War situation. 2.) He was the first Russian individual to denounce Stalin and to expatiate on his crimes during the two terror periods before and after the war. This denunciation was naturally to the great consternation of his colleagues and of those Russians who learned of this (both radio and the press remained silent) and of course to the consternation of the outside world. 3.) He will also be remembered for the Cuban crisis of 1962, which brought Russia to the brink of war with the USA. This was more than his fellow members of the Politburo could stomach. Some of his behaviour at conferences in western Europe had already alarmed them, but this crisis was unacceptable and in 1964, whilst he was abroad on holiday, they removed him from office and on his return, banished him to a dacha they gave him as a parting present, away from Moscow.

Brezhnev

After the disposal of Khrushchev, intrigue and manoeuvring took place again. Brezhnev, a one time protégé of Khrushchev, now in 1965 finally emerged as First Secretary of the Politburo with Kosygin as Prime Minister, Gromyko as Foreign Secretary and Podgorny as President, a figurehead position with no executive power. It was to him as Head of State that my husband presented his letters of credence. Mikoyan and Brezhnev had both filled this post for two years each in Khrushchev's reign. It had given Brezhnev the opportunity to travel abroad and to become acquainted with the leaders of foreign countries. It also gave him a taste for prestige foreign cars and for foreign clothes, and in his later years he followed in the footsteps of Goering in Nazi Germany, and plastered his chest with ever more medals.

Once firmly in the seat of power, Brezhnev began to reverse the process of intellectual liberation which had been seeded in Khrushchev's day. Cultural exchanges of groups from the democratic world and the literati of the Soviet Union well and good, but not on any account between them individually and those of the outside world. It was unwise to chafe out loud or to write or to circulate critical and dissenting articles. You were liable to be prosecuted and punished to years of imprisonment, or sent to a mental home. It was politic for fellow members of the intelligentsia to concur with the governing powers in condemning such individuals.

On one occasion in 1966, when we were lunching with Mme Achmanova in her communal flat, the doorbell clanged whilst we were eating and a man came in with a document, handed it to Mme Achmanova and asked her to sign it. She read it through quickly and signed with a great flourish of her pen, saying, 'There you are,' and handed the document back to the man, who then departed. She turned to us and said, 'The document asked for my agreement, together with that of a number of other people, that Yuri Daniel and Andrei Simoneski should be brought to trial.' She added, with a little laugh, 'Of course, I had to agree!'

The two men in question were dissident writers who had fallen foul of the ruling hierarchy. They were condemned to years of detention and not released until Brezhnev's death in 1982. They then emigrated to the United States. Our friendship with Mme Achmanova is described in the section 'Encounters with Russians'.

Leisure and Exercise

Accommodation and meals out at Zavidova were not exorbitant, but they were not exactly cheap, and the eighty miles from Moscow were a good two hours' drive, so only the more senior members of our embassy staff made use of it and they probably only visited it once during their tour.

Perlovka, where we had spent happy summer months in 1948, was now no more, the lease having expired. The embassy now rented a small dacha with a garden in the outer suburbs of Moscow which could be booked for a weekend or even a week by members of staff to come out to for a breath of fresh air or an escape from their flats in the large apartment blocks of the city. Families with young children especially enjoyed this amenity. Also available now was a club and bar set up after office hours in part of a building in the city which housed our commercial section. There was space here for a cinema and a badminton court which doubled as a venue for occasional Scottish reels.

Those members who had cars could now drive out for Sunday picnics and walks within the permitted radius of fifty kilometres. Also, for those who, like ourselves, were interested in visiting ancient monasteries and other places of interest which were beyond this limit, permits could always be obtained. Equally, visits to some of the old cities, which involved a night away from Moscow, could be arranged.

Skiing on Sundays was now a regular activity enjoyed by foreigners and Russians alike during the long winter months. Apart from the slopes through trees on the Lenin Hills, there now existed an area unbeknown to us in Stalin days, which offered a couple of treeless slopes long enough to exercise one's turns—but once down, you had to laboriously climb up again. This was pretty exhausting.

A couple of times each winter, on a sunny Sunday we would drive out to Tzaritzina, Catherine the Great's hunting lodge where my young boys had first tried out their skis. Now we enjoyed skiing gently through the woods and onto the iced and snow-covered lake. It was a very beautiful area, but I found walking on skis on the lake a desperately cold experience. Not only was the air very cold, but the ice below the snow sent a great chill up one's legs and body. A good tot of vodka in the car on the way home to a warming lunch was the answer. The Russians had now constructed a medium-sized ski jump on the Lenin Hills, and it was fun watching the young men practising their jumps.

For us ladies of the diplomatic missions, exercise, other than Sunday skiing, was a morning ballet class three times a week. There was also a weekly evening folk and country dancing class and both these classes were set up by the

LEISURE AND EXERCISE

Russians. As an evening class was incompatible for me, I very apprehensively opted to join the morning ballet classes. Following is the letter I wrote to my family:

Don't laugh: I am now going to a ballet class! Three times a week. This is a specially organised activity for the dip. ladies. We used to have a very enjoyable and excellent class in the old days, with a wonderful elderly ballet mistress from the Bolshoi. We now have a rather portly gentleman called Mischa, also ex Bolshoi, who all the dip. ladies think is absolutely the cat's whiskers. He is a born mimic and I must say is very expressive and funny when demonstrating how we look attempting to perform. It's wonderful exercise and fun but I am always utterly exhausted when I return home.

You should see some of the shapes in their black, very tight tights and figure hugging vests! A not altogether becoming costume for all and sundry! I don't possess this get up as yet. 17 years ago we all wore skirts, but obviously if one wishes to be 'with it', black tights and vests it will have to be. I have ordered the costume. (NB— we do not rise onto our tippy-tippy toes!)

Encounters with Russians

Contacts

Although now in the sixties we did breathe freer air than in 1947–1949, nevertheless, except with one individual during our three years in Moscow, we were unable to strike up a friendship with any other Russians. This was sad, for by and large Russians and Anglo-Saxons get on very well together. Our joint sense of humour is very akin, far more so than with Germans. It was one of the frustrations of life that one might meet an individual at some reception with whom one clicked, but it was impossible to further this brief acquaintance.

I did, however, have very amicable relationships with the wives of members of the governing hierarchy who were always extremely friendly whenever we met. I was invited annually by them together with all the other wives of Heads of Mission, as well as a large number of Russian ladies—wives of government officials and distinguished ladies in their own right, like the astronaut Valentina Tereshkova—to a splendid afternoon of entertainment to celebrate International Women's Day in early March. Following is what I wrote to my mother:

At the beginning of this week I was busily helping the Russians to celebrate 'Women's Day'. This 'glorious' day falls on March 8th and a terrific do is made of it. On the eve, the Heads of Mission wives are invited by the ladies of the government, Mrs Brezhnev, Mrs Gromyko, and all their colleagues to a 'Tea party'. No tea is produced, but plenty of wines and spirits and a cold buffet, all this at 3pm. Also hot Blinis (pancakes) with caviar and smoked salmon. All rather difficult when one has only recently finished lunch, but one has to partake or they would be offended. After various speeches saying how splendid we women all were and after drinking each other's health we then moved into a vast room where there was a five piece orchestra and proceeded to dance. It was just like being back at school, all the ladies dancing with each other. There was quite a lot of what I call ring-a-ring-a-roses business and chanting of Russian folksongs. All very matey and extremely funny. The funniest item was a modern dance known as 'Bunny hops', any of the younger generation can explain to you what this is, but seeing all these vast bosomed and posteriored Russian ladies with the ladies of the dip corps sandwiched between them solemnly 'bunny-hopping' round the room is one of the funniest things I've ever had to do—it was quite hilarious. The afternoon ended with a 'Koncert', and we were all bidden to a small theatre auditorium in the basement of this special banqueting house and had about an hour's variety programme, singers, dancers, jugglers and so on, ending with a short film of the circus on ice. An excellent little film taken last winter at the circus here, where all the turns were in fact performed 'on ice'. Ladies swung on the flying trapeze with skates on! And large brown bears played ice hockey. They were most amusing.

Politically, owing to the Cold War situation, the relationship between the Soviet government and the western world was strained, but like a mirror—one side blank, unresponsive, the other side luminous and responsive. Away from politics, the Soviets expressed friendliness to us foreign diplomats and obviously made efforts to compensate for the restrictions that were in force. Thus they set up our dancing classes, formal ballet type and folk-dancing type. Hence, also Zavidova, for a breath of real Russian country air on the banks of the Great Volga River, and hence too the permission to visit monasteries and cities of interest beyond the fifty-kilometre limit around Moscow.

Musical encounters

Now in the sixties with new people at the helm, they arranged 'cultural evenings'. Their way of expressing this was to introduce us diplomats to the 'Arts of Soviet Russia', so musical evenings and art exhibitions of contemporary painting and sculpture were set up.

The musical evenings were always enjoyable and instructive. Our first experience was an evening to meet

Shostakovich and listen to some of his music. This took place in November 1965, soon after the great parade day.

At that time, although I was aware of a new great internationally acclaimed Russian composer, I had heard little of Shostakovich's music and was totally ignorant of his background and the tribulations of his life, though I knew that Leningrad was his home town. So I was disturbed and moved to see such a thin, fragile man with such an air of misery and unhappiness on his face.

The concert took place in a handsome nineteenth-century or early twentieth-century house, of the same period as our embassy, and which the Russians used rather as we do Lancaster House in London. The concert took place in a large handsome drawing room which just about held all the heads of mission and their wives and a handful of Russians. We were all seated on comfortable armchairs.

The evening opened with a short lecture given by a man called 'the secretary of the Academy of Music'. He talked about Shostakovich's music in general and told us the evening's programme: a selection of the 24 preludes and fugues Shostakovich had written for the bicentenary of Bach's death (this should have been celebrated in 1950, but as the war had only just ended it was celebrated in 1955). These would be played by the well-known pianist (to Russians only at that time), Tatiana Nikolaeva. This would be followed by some songs sung by a mezzo-soprano, and finally two musicians would play a piano and cello sonata. At the end of the concert we would have the opportunity of meeting all the artists concerned. Shostakovich now came into the room escorted by a Russian and was seated in the middle of the front row. We were seated a little to his left, but I was able to glance at him quite easily. I learned that evening that he had been an excellent pianist and at the age of 21 had competed in the international Chopin competition in Warsaw and had won 'honourable mention'. Now, owing to some nervous disease, he could no longer play the piano. 'I imagine this must be extremely distressing for him. He looks at least 10 years older than his years' is what I wrote to my mother. He would be sixty the following year.

Tatiana Nikolaeva now entered the room, gave a little bow to Shostakovich, sat down at the piano, gathered her thoughts together and began to play. She played extremely well in a very authoritative manner, as I think Bach should be played and as these preludes and fugues of Shostakovich should equally be tackled. I liked all the selection chosen bar one which was loud and thumpy; I liked her playing very much.

A mezzo-soprano followed Tatiana Nikolaeva and sang a number of songs from a cycle Shostakovich had written. They lacked the charm of Schubert songs, but were perfectly pleasing and she sang them well.

Finally, a cellist and pianist played a cello and piano sonata. The pianist was extremely young but obviously very competent and had a fiendish last movement to play. I don't know how many wrong notes he may have struck, but I don't think it really mattered.

At the end of the concert we were offered a glass of wine and light refreshments and were introduced to the partaking artists. All through the concert, Shostakovich had sat immobile with a look of intense concentration. When we were introduced to him, as we were unable to speak Russian and he knows no word of any foreign language, we didn't tarry over our meeting. Apart from what the French would call 'les politesses', we did not want to inflict ourselves on him. Anyway, he is extremely shy and meeting us foreigners must have been an ordeal.

We liked Nikolaeva. She had visited Germany and could speak a little German—she had given concerts in Berlin, but she only visited Great Britain in the nineties, when she had a great success. Her husband was a charming man, older than herself. He spoke quite good French and told us he had been a violinist in the Bolshoi Orchestra. He had retired two or three years previously as he had found it too exacting as he got older. Our evening had been very interesting and enjoyable.

We enjoyed two further 'musical evenings' under the auspices of the protocol department of the Russian Foreign Office. The first of these was to meet Kachaturian, composer of various genres of music. He was an exuberant Armenian, born in Tbilisi. Initially a cellist, who studied in Moscow and who then switched to composing music. His film music and extracts from his ballet *Spartacus* could often be heard on Russian radio.

A selection from his works were then played to us, thumpy piano solos which I did not like, then some rather attractive songs and finally some extracts from ballets including some from *Spartacus* played either on piano and violin or on two pianos.

At the end of the concert we met Kachaturian, who speaks no foreign language but cleverly managed to more or less understand our very inaccurate and bad Russian. It was a pleasant evening.

Our final musical evening, which I recall as 'the evening of the angels and their harps', took place in 1967. When we were ushered into our concert room in the house called 'Spiridonka', there in a semi-circle were some twenty harps, each one with a gilt chair beside it. Presently in trooped a corps of angels (minus wings!) but all dressed in long white robes—some slim, some large. They sat down and proceeded to play. The music was unfamiliar to me but like a mixed choir of voices, soprano, alto and bass, they all harmonised together and the result was very pleasurable. Never before nor since that evening have I heard music performed in this manner.

Alas the 'angels' did not join us at the end of the concert to drink a glass of wine or partake of light refreshments. Years later I have from time to time received a Christmas card depicting angels with wings and lyre rather than harps, which always remind me of that evening in Moscow. In a small room in the National Gallery, lo and behold there is the original, a 'primitive' all blue and gold from the Sienna school of painting. I warm to it and my memory travels back in time.

Only one individual crossed the portals of the British Embassy to join us for an intimate lunch for six people. The individual was the great cellist Mitislav Rostropovich. He was permitted to come, for one of his pupils at the Conservatoire of Music was Elizabeth Wilson. Her father, our ambassador in Belgrade, had come to visit her and was staying for two or three days with us. Rostropovich had met Sir Duncan Wilson when he visited Belgrade on a concert tour. Sir Duncan had mentioned to him that his daughter Elizabeth showed promise as a cellist. 'Oh, let her play for me,' was Rostropovich's immediate riposte. What a terrifying ordeal this must have been for Elizabeth, but she evidently carried it off splendidly, for Rostropovich invited her to come as his pupil at the Moscow conservatory. We found Elizabeth in Moscow when we arrived in September 1965. In the New Year, Jacqueline du Pré joined her, equally to study for a term with the great master. They both lived in a student hostel but the British Embassy was their post office and both of them came to collect and send their letters. We saw Elizabeth quite often and her intimate knowledge of what was going on in the musical world was always of great interest. It was through her that I was able to attend, together with my sister-in-law, the end-of-year concert given by the students of the conservatoire in which Jacqueline du Pré was a shining star. She played the recently discovered Haydn Cello Concerto with the conservatoire's student orchestra under the baton of Rostropovich. I have never heard a more inspired concert than this one. There seemed to be an electric current between Jacqueline and Mitislav which communicated itself to audience and orchestra alike. It was an unforgettable afternoon and the applause at the end was fantastic.

Elizabeth also obtained tickets for my husband and myself in a box at the Bolshoi overlooking the orchestra when a closed performance of Tchaikovsky's great opera *Eugene Onegin* was being given. It was a very special occasion. Not only was Vishnevskaya (translated as 'cherry blossom'), a great soprano, taking the leading role of Tatiana, but her husband, Mitislav Rostropovich, was undergoing his baptism of fire as a conductor, for he now took up the conductor's baton for the first time to conduct a great opera. It was a very thrilling occasion. All the leading personalities of Moscow cultural life were present. At the end of the opera the Bolshoi went wild with enthusiasm. Rostropovich was greatly admired as a superb cellist but could he conduct? And, heavens above, he was presuming to conduct his own wife in this great opera!

It was a great privilege for us to have been given these seats. My eyes danced restlessly between stage and the conductor.

Vishnevskaya and Rostropovich took repeated curtain calls. Finally the lights dimmed and an unforgettable evening came to a close.

Living Conditions

Associating with groups of Soviet citizens was on a different plane to individual contacts, other than for just a superficial and passing encounter. So a ban on any close links between their citizens and foreigners was the overruling fact. Maybe this was partly due to the poor and cramped housing conditions of their people. The less these people saw and understood the way of life of foreigners, the better. It might engender feelings of envy and disquiet and unwelcome questioning on their part.

Although the dearth of accommodation in Moscow had eased considerably by the sixties compared with the post-war decade, no one had surplus accommodation. No room in a three- or four-roomed flat would be free of a bed occupied by some family member except probably in a flat allocated to a senior government official. In George Orwell's satire *Animal Farm* he had the USSR clearly in his sight when he wrote, 'All animals are equal but some animals are more equal than others'. This exemplified the housing situation in Moscow in the mid-sixties.

Communal flats, where a family would share kitchen and bathroom with one, two or even three other families, was still very much the order of the day. Even a citizen who had reached a certain status in his profession, entitling him to a flat of his own incorporating kitchen and bathroom, would very likely be sharing it with other members of his family: a married daughter with husband and child, a teenage son, an unmarried daughter, perhaps an aged grandmother as well. Obviously it was quite impossible for Russians to ever entertain in their own home. The most favoured people would be able to acquire a dacha of their own in the countryside. They would occupy it on Sundays and holidays. (In the sixties, it was still a six-day working week for Soviet citizens.) For government officials and people in top jobs, this would be a perk which went with the job. These dachas would be situated within a large wooded compound surrounded by a security fence and there would be an armed guard at the gate.

Madame Achmanova

There were now, however, a very few selected individuals who were permitted to have friendly association with foreigners. Thus we had a very friendly and enjoyable contact with the head of the English department of linguistics at

Moscow University, Madame Achmanova. She refused ever herself to come to the embassy, but she did entertain us on several occasions in her communal flat in Moscow, where she had just one room divided by a thin partition into her bed-sitting room and her dining room. Toilet and kitchen facilities she shared with three other occupants. But she also had a two-roomed dacha surrounded by an orchard on the fringe of a forest in the countryside outside Moscow and would invite us there on a Sunday.

A couple lived here all the year round but we never met them. When the professor had guests they would retire to the kitchen-living room. Here there was a large Russian stove on top of which you could spread your bedding to keep warm in winter. Toilet facilities were in a hut outside the back door leading into the kitchen.

Madame Achmanova had a shower erected in a small shed in the garden of the dacha. It consisted of an amalgam of bucket, basin and a jug with the rose of a watering can attached, fitted up with a system of Meccano-type pulleys. A Heath Robinson contraption, but it was effective and very ingenious.

In the summer, beneath an apple tree, the whole scene reminiscent of Turgenev's play *A Month in the Country*, is where we would gather and partake of an al fresco meal and jabber away for hours on end with her and a small handful of her friends, mature students from her English department at the university. When my cousin, married to a Cambridge professor, came to stay with us for a week in the summer of 1967, we took them for an al fresco lunch to Mme Achmanova's dacha. She was a charming hostess. This was a bonus to their visit to us and they too recognised the Turgenev-like setting.

In winter we would bring our skis and glide through the nearby pine woods. Through a clearing we espied a cluster of houses and a church with dome and pepper-pot domelets all painted in green and bespattered or sometimes smothered in snow—very picturesque. After a good hour's walk we would return to the dacha and sit around a table and enjoy helpings of borsch and hunks of bread. A glass of vodka warmed the cockles of our heart.

We lunched a number of times with Mme Achmanova in her communal flat situated on the ring boulevard around inner Moscow. The apartment block in which her flat was situated was on the second floor, right opposite the office block of the American embassy. Her assistant at the university and close friend was always present, so it made us just four people, the maximum for her table, and this friend fetched the prepared repast from the communal kitchen at the end of the corridor. She also cleared it all away at the end of the meal.

The Royal Shakespeare Company and the National Theatre

We had been told in London that besides a visit from the BBC Orchestra, with Sir John Barbirolli, we were to expect a visit from the Royal Shakespeare Company, with Sir Laurence Olivier. They duly arrived in December 1966, and on the opening night, Sir Laurence gave a magnificent performance as Othello. It so happened that Jenny Lee, the first Arts Minister in the Wilson Government, had just been spending a week in Moscow, but stayed on for this opening night. We had given a large lunch party for her to meet Russian ministers and other individuals who would be of interest to her. She was a very bubbly and agreeable personality and spoke enthusiastically of her special baby, the Open University.

We invited the Royal Shakespeare Company to supper at the embassy after the performance of Othello, together with Russians from the theatre world. We had been told that Sir

Laurence would require a good forty minutes to remove his make-up, have a shower and get dressed, so we ordered food to be kept back for the Oliviers and the other principals in the play—Billie Whitelaw (Desdemona) and Frank Finlay (Iago), and for ourselves and Jenny Lee.

It was a cold and snowy night, and when the Company arrived, well ahead of the principals, they obviously relished the warmth, the food and the drink. We circulated amongst them and were surprised at the youth of some of them—hardly out of their teens. We too were hungry but had to wait for nearly an hour before the principals finally arrived. When they did, we led them into the small and cosy sitting room with a log fire, which leads out of the ballroom, and we all sank gratefully into comfortable chairs. Mr Moody, the butler, and the Cherub, one of the footmen, brought food and drink which was very welcome. Sir Laurence was visibly exhausted after his demanding role and was not in a mood to chitter-chatter. However, there was no need for this, for Jenny Lee was quite ready to babble away about her week in Moscow, the Open University and her ideas on encouraging the arts as soon as she was back in the UK. We were rather irked by all this, but I dare say some of it was of interest to our guests.

Suddenly we were startled to hear someone with a loud voice calling out, 'Where is the British ambassador?' A man, warmly dressed, appeared in the doorway. My husband leapt to his feet and his private secretary, following close on the heels of this intruder-visitor, explained, 'This is Lord Thomson of Fleet (the Canadian newspaper proprietor and media entrepreneur), who has just arrived in Moscow.' My husband hastily led him into the adjoining sitting room, beckoning the secretary to follow them. Consternation gripped our party. 'Well, I never!' exclaimed Joan Plowright (Lady Olivier). Presently, my husband returned, minus Lord Thomson, who had been escorted back into the lobby. Sir

ROYAL SHAKESPEARE COMPANY AND NATIONAL THEATRE

Laurence, who had been rather silent up till now, growled out, 'Who was that very rude man?'

It appears that Lord Thomson had made his own private arrangements to interview Brezhnev the following day, without any help from the Foreign Office, hence our embassy having no prior knowledge that Lord Thomson was about to visit Moscow.

On his way in from the airport, he learned from his driver that there was a large party at the British embassy that evening.

'Drive me straight there,' he commanded the driver. 'I shall like to see what's going on there.' I think in our hearts we all echoed Lady Olivier's comment: 'Well, I never.'

The second performance of our theatre group was *Hobson's Choice*, which the Russians seemed to enjoy as much as we did. They all wore earphones, which gave them instantaneous translation. It is such an amusing play and for us it was such fun seeing the various actors who we felt we were beginning to know, in such very different roles. The beautiful, innocent, young, golden-haired girl who had been Desdemona now had the leading part as a quite objectionable, scheming spinster in her thirties with a few strands of grey hair and a very sharp tongue, and Iago was equally now in a very entertaining role, very different from that in *Othello*.

The National Theatre, which now incorporated the Royal Shakespeare Company and was performing in London, was producing a number of plays other than just Shakespeare's. It came to Moscow in the second half of September 1967. We were delighted to see its members again and gave a buffet party for them at the Russians' preferred hour of 5 p.m., for them to meet their Russian counterparts—actors, actresses, managers, directors of theatres and critics. The guests all turned up, which was very gratifying.

Monday is the rest day for theatres in Russia and so it was

on a fine sunny Monday that the Russian Ministry of Culture entertained the National Theatre with a stand-up buffet lunch in the vast refreshment hall on the top floor of the great new modern building between the nineteenth-century Imperial Palace and the great churches. This fine building is built of marble, concrete, burnished steel and plate glass. In its core is an auditorium seating 6,000 people. At one end is a vast stage with every possible modern contraption, the whole place illuminated by a changing pattern of lights. Along one side of this great auditorium is a moving staircase, which takes one up to the refreshment hall. This building was primarily designed as a meeting place for the great all-party congress of the USSR. As this only meets once in a blue moon, opera and ballet under the aegis of the Bolshoi and for mixed concert programmes are now staged here. We met very much the same people who had come to our embassy party. I told my mother that the food was nasty but was followed by very friendly speeches—and then a grand tour of the building was laid on for us. This was extremely interesting both for us and for our company. After seeing all the backstage workings we were taken up to the terrace walk, some twenty feet wide, which leads out of the refreshment hall. The views from here are superb, right across the city in all directions, and at eye level, a mere stone's throw away, the golden domes and pepper-pot cupolas of the various Kremlin churches. We were lucky on our day, for just previously we had had three days of unremitting rain.

New Horizons

I had been very reluctant to return to Moscow in 1965 but I found those three years, 1965–1968, not only educative but of extreme interest. I met a huge variety of people, from top-ranking politicians to captains of industry, academics, leading musicians and actors, directors of auction houses, surgeons and zoologists, not only from my own country but their Russian counterparts, though of course the lack of fluency in the language was a great handicap. I learned a lot of Russian history and a great deal about Russian culture. All things Russian have remained of interest to me ever since.

A fundamental difference between the two periods of my Moscow experience, with an interval of eighteen years in between, was that the distance between the UK and Moscow had shrunk. There was now an established link between our two capitals, for both British Airways and Aeroflot flew two flights a week, and they took just four hours. The rail link across Europe was re-established and the sea link by Russian boat between Tilbury Docks and Leningrad provided a slower but agreeable journey, calling at Stockholm and Helsinki on the way. Moreover, although it cost the earth, you could now communicate with family by telephone. The line was not always clear and you had to book it well in advance. Christmas Day was a great day to communicate.

It was now twenty years since the end of the war which had so devastated the country and it was not surprising that in the early post-war years, foreigners were not welcome in Russia. For one thing, there was no accommodation for them. However, by the mid-sixties, circumstances had changed and now, as I have already indicated, Moscow was welcoming foreign groups who brought prized foreign currency. Individuals could also now obtain visas without due difficulty.

So it was that each spring (never mind the slush!) we had a fairly constant stream of family members and friends, which was fun. On their first morning, I would take them for a tramp through the Kremlin. Then, in the afternoon perhaps a visit to one or other monastery on the outskirts of Moscow, or to picturesque Kolomenskoe, a few miles up the Moscow River, where there was an extremely interesting great church and a palace which had been resurrected in the eighteenth century from its predecessor, burned down by fire. The original was all timber built, but its replacement had a certain amount of stone work incorporated. It was now a museum. It was a very picturesque and peaceful area along the banks of the river—a very favourite spot of mine. Museums and galleries and the churches of the Kremlin I left our visitors to explore on their own. On a number of weekends, together with my husband, we would take them to destinations further afield. This, together with visits to Russian opera and ballet, greatly enhanced my knowledge of Russian culture.

The Russian hierarchy appeared to be keen that we diplomats in Moscow should learn and absorb a little of the rich heritage of their country. Hence, they allowed us to visit Russian cities and regions (having obtained the necessary permit to do so) and they invited us as their guests to visit Siberia. Moreover, they also invited us to various cultural opportunities, like meeting leading musicians, and invited us now and again to attend one of their great historical operas, magnificently staged in the great new theatre-cum-congress hall in the Kremlin. So, I would read up the history beforehand (and glean quite a deal of other related history as well). We also attended, as their guests, a couple of minor operas by Tchaikovsky, as well as ballets like *The Corsair*. All these were excellently produced at a smaller theatre than the Bolshoi, and all very enjoyable.

Return to Leningrad, February 1966

The first event of cultural interest in 1966 was the coming of the Royal Shakespeare Company, described in an earlier section.

In mid-February our Prime Minister, Harold Wilson, accompanied by his wife Mary and his personal secretary Marcia Williams and a large following of Foreign Office officials, arrived on a turbulent day of sleet. The next three to four days were days of great hustle-bustle and it was a relief when this cohort had all gone. This visit is also described earlier.

When calm once more returned, and the hard frosts were over, we decided to give ourselves a break. Leningrad called us. We so very much wanted to see the unbelievable: the resurrection of the great palaces, some fifteen miles from Leningrad, which we had seen in such sad ruins in 1948.

We were told that Peterhof was now completely restored and that the restoration of the great palace built by the Tzarina Elizabeth, and embellished and enlarged by her daughter-in-law, Catherine the Great, with a splendid garden and a sculpture gallery all designed by a Scotsman, Cameron, and always known as the Cameron Gallery, was almost completed. So, as of yore the night train from Moscow deposited us at 7.15 a.m. in Leningrad and we were once again having breakfast at the Astoria Hotel.

We were truly amazed at what we found. Not only were these palaces once more grand and impressive, but Leningrad now had such a different aspect. No longer was it a grey, sad and silent city, practically bereft of traffic on its streets. Now there were buses and cars and plenty of pedestrians, and the Nevski Prospect, the main artery from the banks of the Neva to the railway station, the distance between Marble Arch and the British Museum, was a bustling thoroughfare.

Hardly had we returned from Leningrad, than my brother and sister-in-law came to stay for a ten-day visit. It was just ahead of the great spring thaw. On the last weekend of February we took them for a weekend to Yaroslav, an ancient town on the Volga, about 150 miles north-east of Moscow, the road taking one through Zagorsk.

Yaroslav

Our plan was to sightsee in Yaroslav in the afternoon of our arrival, then on the return journey, on the Sunday, to stop off at Zagorsk—a must for all visitors to Moscow, if they can spare the day.

An agreement was signed between Queen Elizabeth I and Ivan the Terrible (in the mid-sixteenth century) to found a trading centre in Yaroslav, and soon ships, plying up and down the Volga and via various lakes into the gulf of Finland, carried merchandise between England into the very heart of Russia and on beyond to the east and down into Persia. Peter the Great allowed British shipwrights to build ships here to enable them to carry on this trade. Thus a link was formed between St Petersburg and Yaroslav which was manifest in giving the town an eighteenth-century St Petersburg architectural flavour. The most interesting building is the old theatre built in this epoch and still in use when we visited the town. It is reputed to be the oldest playhouse in Russia.

My recollections of Yaroslav are rather hazy, but the blizzard we encountered in the late Saturday afternoon remains quite vivid in my mind. As large flakes of snow fell upon us, ever more intensively, my brother and my husband, who were deep in conversation, strode out on their long legs, never glancing back to see if we were there. They arrived back at our hotel a good hour before my poor, by now rather unhappy, sister-in-law and I did. With snowflakes relentlessly falling into my eyes I became completely disorientated. Usually I had a quite good bump of locality, but on this occasion it eluded me completely and we were soon lost, as lost as the babes in the wood. We floundered on. There were few people out and about and those that were, were hurrying for the shelter of their homes. When I did manage to stop someone and mentioned the name of our hotel, he/she seemed not to understand, and hurried on. Well, eventually we did get back to our hotel. Our stress gave way to fury when we found our men sitting back comfortably in chairs and sipping tea, apparently quite unconcerned about us!

'Well, we were a bit surprised you weren't just behind us, but we knew you would turn up sooner or later,' said my husband. 'Didn't you worry about us?' asked my sister-in-law. 'No, we didn't worry at all.' The callousness of these men—unbelievable!! 'Well, there you are dear,' said my sister-in-law, 'that's typical male chauvinist piggery.'

Hot tea gradually revived us and we simmered down. Copious, excellent Georgian wine with our dinners enabled us to joke about our experience.

On our Sunday drive back to Moscow, we found the whole countryside under a blanket of fresh snow. It took us a good hour longer to reach Zagorsk because of the snow on the road—only short stretches of road had been partially cleared. The great monastery was magnificent to behold, dominating the snowy landscape, and we all enjoyed our two hours there. It being Sunday, a service was in progress in the main church. Our guide ushered us in and we listened for a while to the deep resonant singing of some of the monks. It was impressive. For my brother Robbie, this week was a deeply satisfying experience. He was well read in Russian literature. This winter experience in the forested region of Russia, together with the experience he and I had had together many decades previously, travelling in a slow train between Moscow and Baku across the endless featureless steppes in the heat of summer, gave him a feeling of empathy with the Russian authors whose characters lived in this vast land.

Then at the end of March, our son Michael spent a three-week holiday with us. 'What do you remember of those three weeks?' I asked him. 'Well, er, waterskiing on the Volga,' he answered. 'In March?!' I exclaimed. 'What did you wear?' 'Can't remember,' was the answer. *'Quelle blague, quelle blague,'* as the French would say. 'Well,' said Michael, 'my colleagues were very impressed when I told them this.' No doubt a good story. Well, we enjoyed plenty of culture during those weeks and they included a long weekend in Kiev, on the banks of the great Dnieper River where we admired the great mother church of all Russian churches, the Cathedral of St Sophia, together with the eighteenth-century church of St Andrew (both now museums) which dominate the town. A second weekend was to Vladimir Suzdal, where the sculptured frieze on the great church of Dimitrovski Sabor is so very reminiscent of that on the cathedral in Kiev. It was on that weekend that we were so captivated by a meadow so full of wild flowers leading to the enchanting little church on the River Nerl.

The monasteries and convents were all of interest and pleasing to the eye, and the Russians were now busy on restoration work, for these buildings had mostly suffered years of neglect since the revolution and during the war years. A number of them were now again in use but for what purposes I do not know. One of them, the largest, a one-time monastery with a magnificent very massive five-storey-high bell tower with the entrance gate way beneath it, is now a penal establishment for women. We could only admire the gate from outside. Another very aesthetically attractive convent was where through the centuries ladies of good birth would find refuge, either willingly or confined there by brothers or bored husbands. Peter the Great confined his forceful sister here when he found her a nuisance and overbearing.

A few days before Michael's departure on a lovely sunny morning, the Kremlin was looking particularly beautiful. A row of lime trees had been planted the length of the terrace in front of the great palace. They were covered in white blossom, which sparkled in the sunshine. 'Let's take a quick walk before lunch,' I said. So out we went. Not only was there blossom on the lime trees, but the terrace was covered with a thick carpet of fallen blooms. It all looked very lovely and the Russian passers-by were delighted. 'Just like snow,' they explained, and Russians all love their snow. It covers all the dirt and mess with a blanket all pristine white.

A few hours later, Michael's eyes and nose were streaming. It was the first onslaught of hayfever which, in late spring and early summer months, has plagued him ever since.

Early Summer 1966

At the end of April, I returned to England for a short visit, as it was my mother's 80th birthday and it gave me the opportunity to visit my daughter. I remember a turbulent evening and night crossing to Stockholm during which I felt queasy, but survived. The North Sea was also fairly rough but I had found my sea legs by then. On the return journey I was accompanied by my husband's sister, who was coming to Moscow for a three-week visit.

We shared a comfortable cabin, and enjoyed good weather throughout the journey through the Kiel Canal and on to Stockholm and Helsinki and finally the lovely early morning sail into the estuary of the Neva and the final tie up at the quayside in the heart of Leningrad. The trip brought back memories of nineteen years earlier when I was accompanied by two small boys. But there was an innovation—to our indignation, on our first morning on board we were roused at 7 a.m., while still fast asleep, when a disembodied voice told us in Russian, 'Time to wake up and do your exercises. They will start in ten minutes.' This was followed by the singing of patriotic Soviet songs. In vain did I hunt for a means of switching it off. Later in the day I asked, 'Could we please be spared this early morning rousing?' I am glad to say the intercom was switched off.

I don't think there was a dull moment for Sophie during her three weeks with us. I remember her great thrill when looking out of her bedroom window—there in front of her eyes was the splendid view of the Kremlin.

I had also arranged for us to spend a night in Leningrad before taking the night train to Moscow. This gave Sophie a day and a half to have a quick look around. In the afternoon we just walked around and took in the lovely buildings on the banks of the Neva but as the next day was a lovely day, I thought, well, let's go out to Peterhof and let's do it on our own, by boat. Earlier in the year, when my husband and I returned to Leningrad after nineteen years' absence, a guide had taken us by taxi to see Peterhof and Catherine the Great's palace at Tzarskoe Selo but we returned to Leningrad by boat directly from the jetty at Peterhof. I learned then where to find the correct quayside, the cost of return trips and the frequency of the boats. It was already in my mind's eye that this would be something nice to do with Sophie. And so it was, and my Russian was up to the occasion. We had a lovely day and we were lucky to find the famous fountains at Peterhof had now been turned on. This was something new for me too, and we both enjoyed our trip enormously.

My sister-in-law's visit coincided with the busiest six weeks imaginable. On the day of our arrival in Moscow at 7.15 a.m., back from our boat journey from England to Leningrad, my husband told us that at 5.30 that afternoon an arts council group, the Georgian Society, would be invading us for drinks. A similar group the previous week had been entertained by my husband and a third group would be coming the following week. Each group consisted of about thirty members. We had received a number of introductions about individual members but two dukes had picked up their pens before leaving their homes and written directly to my husband saying they would like to call on him when in Moscow. The dukes in question were the Duke of Wellington and the Duke of Bedford. They were in separate groups and each received an invitation to lunch with us. These were accepted and they missed out on their respective scheduled programme for the afternoon.

Our two dukes were full of interest. The Duke of Wellington was 84 and he told us that he had been the most junior third Secretary at our embassy in St Petersburg between 1908 and 1912 and that he had not only known, but had actually flirted with one of the two daughters of the sugar king who had built our present house in Moscow. He had visited the family on each visit he paid to Moscow, so not unnaturally he was extremely interested in seeing the house again. Our dining room where we entertained him had been the library. He was a charming man and so full of stories. We would have loved to have seen more of him, but his programme did not allow for further time.

The Duke of Bedford had opened Woburn Abbey to the public and introduced a zoo and amusement park in the grounds some four years previously. We had actually visited it and were extremely interested in all that the duke and his French wife, Nicole, told us about this great enterprise. He was the first stately home owner to start a zoo. The Marquis of Bath followed suit and went one better by introducing lions at Longleat. Different breeds of deer and other non-ferocious animals were Woburn's speciality. The Bedfords were a very entertaining couple and we were saddened six years later to learn that the duke had made over the entire estate to his son and heir. This was so that the estate should be spared crippling inheritance tax on his death. He himself had had such a struggle when he had inherited Woburn, which had been allowed to become utterly run down and had been sorely neglected. In Moscow he and his wife were particularly interested in visiting the two palaces, now museums, which had belonged to the Sheremetiev family, the greatest of the aristocratic family in Tsarist days. They were Ostankino, on the very boundary of Moscow, and Kuskovo, in the countryside outside. The latter now houses a fabulous collection of china. They both still have some good pieces of furniture and statuary but the majority of the great collection of pictures owned by the family were now in galleries in Moscow and Leningrad.

The three weeks spent by my sister-in-law in Moscow with us were of very varied interest, culture and fun. Three or four visits into the Kremlin complex, together with visits to other interesting sights in the city and in its immediate vicinity, peppered the three weeks. We paid a visit to the horse-trotting races, where the horse trots, pulling the driver in a small seat attached by long reins to his harness some 15 feet behind. Very attractive and entertaining to watch. Then there was a visit to a stud farm—this of special interest to Sophie, who loved horses. Not only did beautiful horses parade in front of us, but we also saw a large group of mares with their foals out in the open. The farm was about thirty miles distant from Moscow. After seeing the horses we were taken for a troika ride, which was most exciting. Full out they go, these horses—we were told at 30 kms per hour. One has to keep one's eyes half closed or tighter as there is a good deal of dust and bits of mud flung back from the horses' hooves. There were two troikas laid on for us, GWH and Sophie were in one, whilst I was in the other with the arm of the director tightly clasped round my waist as we thundered along. The rest of the party—there were around a dozen of us from our embassy—then had their turn. In a troika the two outside horses gallop whilst the middle one trots. Trotters are a special breed, very strong and powerful. This expedition had been laid on for us by the protocol department. In an invitation we had been asked to choose a suitable date, so we made a point to fit this in during Sophie's stay.

One morning I took my sister-in-law to the zoo to visit the two pandas, Chi-Chi and Anan—such enticing creatures. Anan was half as large again as Chi-Chi and about twice her bulk. Both animals were being fed when we arrived. Anan had a bowl of porridge and looked so funny sitting heavily and squarely on his vast backside with the bowl on the floor between his legs and dribbling porridge all down his chin, and then doubling himself into a large black and white ball to get at the porridge with his mouth. Chi-Chi had already had her porridge—she was being fed with sheaves of grass through the bars and was most photogenic as she put out her paw and took some in and then sat back on her haunches, propping herself up comfortably against a great log whilst she nibbled away. The hope was that these animals would mate in September. We did not think that the housing arrangements were at all propitious for this—their outdoor runs were at opposite ends of the little stable where they slept. Here their two pens were adjacent but with only a grill in the dividing wall through which they could eye each other. 'Perhaps as the weather warms they will be given adjacent outdoor runs and can then see each other all day—and fall in love?' I wrote to my mother. Desmond Morris came out to Moscow especially to see them. He came and lunched with us and was a most interesting guest.

For culture the prime event was the four-yearly Tchaikovsky music competition in June (John Ogden had won the piano competition four years earlier). In these contests, competitors always have a gruelling time. We were interested in the piano and violin sections. Here the candidates had to compete their way through two phases; the first always included something by Bach but of their own choosing. In the second phase, if they had got through the first one, they would present two pieces of their own choice but dissimilar in style. Two finalists would now emerge to compete against each other playing the respective Tchaikovsky concerto with full orchestra. The international judges had sat through the entire competition, judging each phase. How they came to their final unanimous conclusion, I have no idea. To us the young male and female contestants all played so brilliantly. Harriet Cohen, one of the English judges for the piano competition, lunched with us.

BACK TO MOSCOW, 1965–1968

My sister-in-law and I spent two long afternoons at the competition, held in Moscow's concert hall. These afternoons were open to the public. The first afternoon that we attended was phase two of the piano competition. The second afternoon we sat through two successive renderings of the violin concerto with a half-hour interval between. We were exhausted at the end; it had been a little too much for us. Which was the better rendering? I don't know. It seemed to both of us that the second contestant must have an inestimable advantage over the first.

Two evenings later we went to the end-of-year concert of the conservatoire. This was not open to the public, but we managed to get tickets for it through the good offices of Elizabeth Wilson. This was the concert in which Jacqueline du Pré played the newly discovered Haydn cello concerto with her master, Rostropovich, conducting. It gave all who attended it such a thrill.

Earlier in the week Sophie and I went to a production of Benjamin Britten's *War Requiem*. This was the first time it had been given in Russia. I was particularly interested in going to this concert and noting how the Russians staged it as I had seen and heard it in the Albert Hall. It was a very impressive performance and quite differently staged to that in the Albert Hall. Now the chamber orchestra, together with the solo tenor and the solo baritone, were seated in one of the galleries above the main stage of the Tchaikovsky Concert Hall, and the boys' choir was in the opposite gallery. The solo soprano, all dressed in glittering white, stood on a pedestal right at the back of the main stage between the men's and women's choir. This was a very effective arrangement and I thought far better than lumping everyone together. At the Albert Hall only the boys' choir was separated—they were right up in the gods. As I had a book of the words, I was able to follow it all very well.

The Queen's Birthday Party

During the two and a half weeks after returning to Moscow, an ongoing activity whenever there was time to fit it in was gardening, for on 9 June we would be celebrating the Queen's official birthday and on that date a vast cohort of people would descend upon our garden to drink her health in tea, beer and soft drinks. Looking down onto the garden from our upstairs sitting room window I was astonished to note the transformation that had taken place during my absence. No trace now of squelchy slush and expanses of brown earth. From a green carpet rose clumps of tulips, a few lupins, masses of forget-me-nots and a few other flowers and it all made an attractive picture. 'How nice,' one thought, but a walk in the garden revealed a different picture. The tulips were in full bloom but would be over in two weeks and the forget-me-nots were already looking straggly and the carpet of green was compounded of weeds and little self-sown seedlings from last year's plants. How could we make the garden look tidy and attractive within two weeks?

On contract with the botanical gardens in Moscow a lady gardener would come from time to time, do a little gardening and bring plants for bedding out. She had not yet been this year so I sent for her urgently. Elena was a nice little person who chattered away very fast in incomprehensible Russian. With the help of Brian Fall to interpret, she pointed out that the self-sown seedlings must be super for having survived the long winter and all those severe frosts, and therefore they must be preserved and transplanted. On closer inspection they were mostly orange-coloured marigolds—not my favourite flower!

The only help available for any work in the garden was an ancient dvornik (or sweeper) with a broom and a shovel. He was responsible for keeping the precincts of the embassy clear, swept and tidy. In winter he shovelled snow aside endlessly. In the summer he mowed our lawn and carted away mess. My husband firmly said he had no time for gardening; it was up to me to get it looking tidy! My sister-in-law offered to help. I sent out a circular asking if there were any enthusiastic gardeners, male or female, on the staff who would be willing, after office hours, to put in an hour or two, helping in the garden during the next two weeks. One male responded and spent some three hours all told and did yeoman service. Elena brought several boxes of little plants but I hardly expected them to bloom in time. Shortly before the great day she brought some boxes of large marguerites in bud. I was unenthusiastic; however, Elena said, 'Anyway, they will be in bloom and will look quite gay—we can throw them away afterwards.'

That year, 9 June fell on a Thursday. The past week had been sunny and hot and continued so into Monday and Tuesday. I had had a huge screen of old sheets put up to screen a corner bed full of peonies fully out, to protect them from the sun. Wednesday dawned grey and the air became even more sultry. I took an armful of old *Times* newspapers and made tents to cover some urns I had planted up with pansies, to give them some protection against the rain I feared—and sure enough, at 5 o'clock precisely an almighty thunderstorm with torrential rain broke over our heads. The flimsy protection given the plants did nevertheless give a modicum of protection from the heavy rain. The storm lasted an hour. Shortly after that little Elena turned up with chrysanthemums and double petunias to replace shattered plants and to fill up any vacant spots. So, she and I set to and finished at around 8.30 p.m., whilst Sophie decapitated every dead head in sight. The garden was really looking very tidy and quite colourful from all our efforts. I felt it was OK. But what if on the morrow a similar storm should break at 5 p.m.—the hour of our party?

Well, Thursday morning dawned grey, cold and

forbidding. Our hearts sank, though it was not actually raining. At 10 a.m. we rang the meteorological office at the airport. No encouragement for the afternoon: 'It will probably rain.' So there it was, one could not just go ahead and organise the party in the garden. The decision was taken: the party must be in the house. So, for the rest of the morning all the furniture had to be relocated, carpets taken up and the rooms prepared for about double the number of people than we knew there was room for. The safety element crossed my mind. Could the floors withstand such a horde of people? It was not, however, actually raining and an awning over the terrace out of the ambassador's study was up, so we decided this room should also be prepared with a buffet table. People here at least would be able to see the garden.

Promptly at 5 o'clock the hordes began to file in. My husband and I shook hands with them all at the top of the stairs and in less than no time two hundred people filled up the rooms. But these were not our guests—they were all our own staff, and therefore co-hosts with us on this our national day. And then the guests—up and up the stairs they came, in an unending stream. My jaw ached from the fixed smile, my hand wilted. Presently the senior Russian guest arrived—the Deputy Prime Minister, so according to custom my husband abandoned the receiving line and took this gentleman to the far corner of the dining room which was being reserved for the VIPs. I was really alarmed for the floors. I sent word in that staff must move down to the study and terrace, so out of the ballroom door they began to come, and it became an up-and-down stream on the staircase. Soon the up stream stopped, and I could abandon my post. I plunged into the dining room. Within the next twenty minutes the clouds all disappeared, the sun came out and as the people upstairs could now see others wandering around on the lawn, they naturally wished to join them, so for the second half of our party, it became, after all, a garden party. The rest of the food and drink were carried down by the minions and everyone voted the party a huge success and they all said, 'How lovely the garden is looking!'

Vladimir & Suzdal

When the great thaw arrives (from March to June), it is almost impossible to take any outdoor exercise, so this is the prime time for sightseeing excursions to visit interesting and picturesque monasteries which doubled as fortresses guarding approaches to Moscow. They were mostly to the east of the capital from whence erupted the Tartar hordes. They all had great splendid walls around them, and a visit to them was always enjoyable and full of interest. The spring months were also good for trips further afield to interesting towns which would involve a night away from Moscow. Amongst these were Vladimir and Suzdal, separated by about thirty miles. Unfortunately they were situated on the further side of a no-go zone for foreigners, so to reach them one had to take the train to Vladimir. The journey took around three hours. Permission for the trip had first to be obtained from the Russians who would then lay on a car and an Intourist guide to meet one and guide one around. We visited these towns twice and always found something new of interest. The first time we spent one night in Suzdal, and then overnighted in Vladimir so that we might visit a little gem of a church on the outskirts of the town before boarding our train later in the morning for the return journey to Moscow.

On the second trip our chauffeur Triatsin was allowed to drive our own Rover to meet us in Vladimir and drive us here and there preceded by our allotted guide in an Intourist car.

Vladimir and Suzdal occupy a distinctive slot in the history of Russian art—the architectural simplicity of form and style built of limestone quarried in the region made for a very individual harmonious entity. They were built on a square plan with a single cupola above an elevated drum, which was very restful and pleasing to the eye.

There are two large churches in Vladimir and a number of interesting smaller ones all built in the early twelfth century and all conforming to the same basic design. The exception to this is the great Uspenski Sabor on a hilltop dominating the town below (like Lincoln Cathedral does), above the Kliasma River. The entire hill top is encircled by a mediaeval wall with a splendid picturesque gateway leading down to the town. The original building was burned to the ground by a great fire in 1183, and when immediately rebuilt had a great new spire added to the original design. It now also had four domes built around the central dome, the usual design of Russian churches, signifying the four evangelists around Christ. It is a splendid building but my preference was for the second great church of Dimitrievski Sabor. Its exterior is one of the most beautiful I know in its pristine simplicity, yet richly ornamented with small carved figures of saints and demons, animals, fishes and flowers galore, but nothing protruding, all recessed, giving the impression that someone had thrown a great patterned lace shawl over the entire building.

The little gem we visited on our last beautiful morning in Vladimir is a miniature replica of the Dimitrievski Sabor, minus carvings. It stands on a hillock overlooking the Nerl River. To reach it one had to traverse a meadow the like of which I have never seen again since that early sunny spring morning. An unsullied expanse of every imaginable wild flower in all shades of the rainbow lay like a wonderful carpet, that one hesitated to tread on, between us and the little gem that stood above it: 'Lily-like, lovely and serene, lovely but no one now prays within its precincts, serene because the purity of its lines is not complicated by carvings.' This is how Lady Kelly describes it in her book *Pictures of Russia*, published in the early fifties. It stands out prominently in my gallery of photos lodged in a recess of my gallery of memorable moments as I recall my past decades.

Suzdal is always bracketed with Vladimir, for its churches of the twelfth century and succeeding two to three centuries were built on a square plan with a single dome and a spire rising above it, but like all cities in the path of the Tartar hordes, it suffered much depredation, and rebuilding would be more in the Muscovy style.

In my recollection, Suzdal was now a village, rather than a town, at the core of an area of hills and dales with a number of one-time convents and monasteries strewn amongst them. It was an area that percolated peace and charm with trees and greenery in the dips with possibly a small pond and little stream and birds flitting around. A peculiar feature of the village itself was a row of churches built in a straight line along the top of a ridge. They were built in pairs; big brother and little brother. Big brother was airy, and worship was celebrated there in the summer months. Little brother was where the congregation assembled in winter. It was small and could be heated with a great stove, and the worshippers could huddle together and keep warm. These churches were simple and unadorned and of no particular artistic merit. Their interest lay in the fact that they were built in pairs. But why so many pairs so close together and in a straight line? I never got a satisfactory answer to this question.

Visit of the BBC Orchestra, January 1967

In January 1967 the BBC Orchestra, under the leadership of Sir John Barbirolli as their guest conductor, visited Moscow and Leningrad for a series of concerts. A number of distinguished soloists accompanied them: John Ogden, who had won the Moscow piano competition four years earlier; Jacqueline du Pré, the budding young cellist who had studied

VISIT OF THE BBC ORCHESTRA, JANUARY 1967

with Rostropovich the previous winter; Heather Harper, the well-known soprano singer; and the French composer and conductor, Pierre Boulez. This was the first foreign orchestra to come to Moscow for several decades and these musicians had a riotous success in both cities. Although the Russian public were very familiar with their own modern Soviet music, they had not had the opportunity of hearing foreign modern music nor of hearing foreign artists other than from the satellite countries. The programmes chosen by Sir John Barbirolli and the BBC were all of twentieth-century music, apart from Tchaikovsky's piano concerto, that John Ogden played in Leningrad and which had won him first prize in the Moscow piano competition. We attended two concerts in each city. On the opening night in Moscow, first something by Schönberg was played (to me unmemorable), then came Jacqueline du Pré, playing Elgar's cello concerto. This was of special interest to us as we knew Jacqueline, as she had studied for a few months with Rostropovich during our first year in Moscow. She played it brilliantly, to great acclaim.

During the interval an assortment of instruments were placed on the stage—two pianos, one grand and the other a diminutive piano, a mandolin, a balalaika, various bells and gongs, clappers and symbols. Pierre Boulez and a posse of musicians now appeared, and we were regaled with a medley of contrapuntal sounds, as the dynamic young Frenchman conducted his own composition 'Les Eclats' (the flashes). It was fun but not music as I understand it. It was greeted with enormous enthusiasm by the largely youthful audience and by modern Soviet composers of this era. I gathered that Boulez always attracted youth and 'avant-gardes' and as he looked like a young Napoleon, when the latter was just 'le general Bonaparte' he appealed quite particularly to the girls and young ladies, just as in contemporary England, the Beatles appealed to young females. After 'Les Eclats', the medley of instruments disappeared, the full orchestra returned and Pierre Boulez now proceeded to conduct Debussy's 'La Mer'. The applause at the end was so tremendous that an encore was given—the Prélude 'l'Après-midi d'un faune'. Perhaps the fact that both the composer and the conductor were Frenchmen is the answer to their brilliant and exquisite performance.

Both my husband and I had enjoyed this concert enormously and I described it in detail in a letter to my mother. Of the second concert, only two comments to my mother were made. The first was that John Ogden had played a concerto by Bliss, which we found utterly uninspiring, but we were looking forward to hearing him play the Tchaikovsky in Leningrad at the weekend. The second comment was that Heather Harper now took the stage and sang a series of songs, first from the opera Wozzeck by the Austrian composer Alvan Berg, and then songs by Webern. I was surprised that I enjoyed both series very much. I had only heard music by these composers on the radio and had not enjoyed what I heard at all. Heather Harper has a lovely voice and sang these songs beautifully.

Unfortunately my husband now succumbed to the three-day flu, prevalent in Moscow at the time. We had been scheduled to accompany the orchestra to Leningrad when they travelled up by the Thursday night train, but owing to the flu, we had to delay this by twenty-four hours, turning the Saturday into an extremely hectic day. Arrangements had been made for my husband to pay courtesy calls on the mayor of Leningrad and other city dignitaries on that morning before hosting a lunch party at the Astoria Hotel for these worthies, together with their wives, to meet the leading members of the orchestra, the relevant soloists (bar Jacqueline du Pré, who had to return to London as she had prior engagements there), and of course Sir John and Lady Barbirolli (a distinguished oboist in her own right) and Pierre

VISIT OF THE BBC ORCHESTRA, JANUARY 1967

Boulez. Leading musical personalities in Leningrad plus the director of the Hermitage were also to be our guests.

So, on that Saturday morning, instead of a leisurely breakfast after emerging from our train at 7.15, my husband had a great rush to shave, wash, and get changed into suitable tidy clothes before his first 10 o'clock appointment.

I was left to freeze in our grand suite—it was snowing outside and Leningrad was just as bitterly cold in mid-January 1966 as it had been eighteen years earlier.

I now quote part of the letter I wrote to my mother about this Leningrad weekend:

We had a very satisfactory Leningrad visit. All went according to plan. In spite of it all being so soon after the flu, GWH was none the worse, all the invited NOBS of Leningrad turned up to our lunch party. In fact they 'over fulfilled' the PLAN (this is a stock expression which appears regularly in the Soviet press to describe how splendid some worker is for he/she having completed more work than had been expected of them), an extra deputy Mayor asking if he might come too to our lunch party and bring his wife. The BBC concerts were a huge success, and Leningrad looked beautiful in its winter covering of snow and ice. It was icy too—I haven't felt so cold all winter. The reason for this though was partly because our rooms were inadequately insulated against the weather, and we had icy blasts whistling in through the joints of our double windows. They required to be sealed up, and a good stuffing of cotton wool put between them at the bottom. Also the radiators were too small. We had expected to be over hot in the hotel so were surprised and unprepared jersey-wise for such iciness. However, when I complained, the hotel did produce an antediluvian electric fire. It was not very efficient, but certainly helped. On the Saturday when we arrived there was a snow storm all day long with an icy wind and it all came straight at our windows. GWH was making official calls so I was left to freeze or go out in the snow storm. As it remained pitch dark until 9.30am and full daylight didn't seem to be there until an hour later there was no inducement to rush out immediately. So I froze until just on 11, and then smothered myself in clothing and bravely went out into the snow storm. I felt I could not be colder if I went out, in fact might feel warmer subsequently. This was indeed so, and by walking the minimum amount facing into the storm it was quite bearable, and those lovely buildings looked so beautiful with snow falling that one forgot that it wasn't really very pleasant walking abroad.

But the walk gave me a lovely glow and a good appetite for our luncheon due in an hour's time. On Sunday the weather had cheered up and there was even a little hazy sun.

My husband very much wanted to see the view down the river Neva, just as I had done on the Saturday morning in the snow storm, so having had lunch and recovered from our three-hour tour of the Hermitage with its director, we sallied forth. The wind had been so biting on the Saturday that I had not tarried long. This time we walked onto the bridge linking the two branches of the Neva, via Vasilevski Island, on which is built the superb Admiralty building with its golden dome and golden spire. We drank in the superb view: to the right is the green and white palace, now the Hermitage Museum, and across the great wide expanse of the frozen and snow-covered Neva is the Peter and Paul fortress with its golden darning-like needle piercing the sky above the royal chapel, the mausoleum of the Tsars.

This walk had taken over half an hour. The doctor had told my husband not to go out in the cold on the Saturday and one felt the temperature was now dropping, so we made our way back to the Astoria. However, I very much wanted

VISIT OF THE BBC ORCHESTRA, JANUARY 1967

to walk along the Fontanka Canal, some ten minutes' walk inland from our hotel. It was lovely—great icicles were dripping down from the eaves of the grand houses on either side of the canal and beautiful little bridges span it at intervals. Cars can drive down on either side but there were very few of these and one was some distance away from the Nevski Prospect, the main artery of the city. As dusk fell the lights all came on and it all seemed lovelier than ever—I felt I must return to the banks of the Neva to look at the panorama now that it was all illuminated. In fact I walked back onto the bridge.

There are a number of superb panoramas of cities around the world, but I am sure that in wintertime, no other city can offer this ethereal fairy-like beauty of Leningrad, now once more St Petersburg.

The Leningrad Concerts

On both evenings we went to the BBC concerts given in the beautiful Leningrad Concert Hall. On the Saturday evening we had John Ogden playing the Tchaikovsky concerto. He was given a great ovation for an excellent performance, which inspired the orchestra to play superbly. However, the director of the Leningrad Conservatoire of Music said, 'Yes, a fine performance but not Tchaikovsky, all John Ogden' and became quite eloquent on this theme. Quite interesting, as he had been on the jury when John Ogden had been awarded first prize at the Moscow competition four years earlier.

After the interval, Pierre Boulez took the rostrum and we had a repeat of 'Les Éclats' with its cornucopia of instruments, as in Moscow. I really enjoyed hearing it a second time. Pierre Boulez now conducted Debussy's 'Les Images'. The evening was enjoyable and the Russian audience was very enthusiastic.

BACK TO MOSCOW, 1965–1968

At the Sunday evening concert, John Ogden thumped out a Bartok concerto—loud and untuneful—it left me cold. I have no particular recollection of the rest of the programme except that the last item was Elgar's second symphony, which both my husband and I found long and tedious, but which was evidently a great favourite of Sir John Barbirolli's. One saw this reflected in his face as he was conducting it. At the end of the concert it was rather amusing. We were talking to him and to Lady B and he was still steeped in this music and saying, 'Isn't it beautiful? And that lovely coda, and it so epitomises the end of an era, and didn't they love it?' and Lady B very briskly and in a down-to-earth voice said, 'Yes John, I think they took it remarkably well.' 'My husband still chuckles when he thinks of it,' I wrote to my mother. 'Lady B is such a nice person, I liked her immensely.' In Moscow I had taken her and Heather Harper shopping for fur hats at a 'commission shop' where one paid in foreign currency. The shop was next to the Nova Devichi Monastery on the great bend of the Moskva River.

We first did a sightseeing tour of the monastery and of its churchyard where most distinguished Russians are buried and which has some very interesting headstones, some very elaborate, and we then proceeded to the commission shop. Lady Barbirolli bought one fur hat, Heather Harper three.

After the concert we bundled up into our warm clothing, collected our luggage from the hotel and caught the night train back to Moscow. 'A very bumpy, rather sleepless journey,' I reported to my mother. The BBC Orchestra and soloists were also on our train and they were all catching a plane back to London later the same day.

The following day the embassy received a message from the orchestra to say that a double bass was missing; 'Could the embassy please make enquiries?' 'How very strange,' was the Russian comment, 'after all, a double bass is not a mouth organ.' Some Russians really do have a sense of humour. The

VISIT OF THE BBC ORCHESTRA, JANUARY 1967

double bass was located—left behind at the Leningrad railway station.

This is what I wrote to my mother:

John Ogden gave three solo concerts in Moscow, after the departure of the BBC Orchestra. What a strange man he is. Huge, like a great ungainly bear, yet with the softest voice imaginable, extremely shy with a diffident manner. In his playing he seems to have two personalities—with an orchestra he plays authoritatively and with zest. His solo playing is quite different. The great chromatic Fantasia and Fugue of Bach seemed curiously emasculated and a Beethoven sonata (op. 29) was equally unimpressive. (However, I had never heard that sonata before.) Then he played some Debussy and Ravel and a Chopin valse as an encore. These were all enjoyable. He has a remarkably light touch as a solo player—this does not particularly suit Bach or Beethoven. I am sure he is a very kindly and gentle person. He is only aged 28 or 29 but looks at least 10 years older.

Tour of the Hermitage, January 1967

When we returned to Moscow in 1965, we looked forward to revisiting Leningrad. We had been told that the wonderful palaces along the Gulf of Finland, belonging to the Tsars, Tsarinas and other members of the royal family, were all gradually being restored. Peterhof, Peter the Great's palace, had been the first to be tackled and its restoration was now completed. At Tzarskoe Selo, Queen Elizabeth and Catherine the Great's palace with its Scottish designed garden and park, had equally been restored bar a few of the stately rooms. One by one the other palaces were being tackled. It was incredible to us that this could be so, having seen in 1948 the devastation and ruin that the German armies had wrought in the war. We waited until the summer of 1966 to travel up to Leningrad for a weekend of sightseeing and marvelled at what we saw.

Now, in January 1967, we were once more in Leningrad, this time for the two evenings of concerts given by the BBC with Sir John Barbirolli and as it turned out for a never-to-be-forgotten tour of the Hermitage, with its charismatic director. At our lunch party on the Saturday we had put him next to Sir John Barbirolli—the two men clicked as we had thought they might. The director then asked Sir John, 'Do you know the Hermitage?' 'Alas no,' was the reply, 'this is my first visit to Leningrad.' 'In that case,' said the director, 'let me be your guide to the splendours of our collection. Please come at ten tomorrow morning, with Lady Barbirolli and six other guests from our party here.' 'Sadly I must refuse for I have to take a rehearsal for tomorrow evening's concert,' was Sir John's reply. 'But Lady Barbirolli will come?' suggested the director. 'Also no,' Lady Barbirolli hastily replied, 'you see, I always like to be present at my husband's rehearsal.' Momentarily crestfallen, the director then rallied and said, 'Well, what about the Harrisons and six others, to make a maximum of 8?' We accepted with alacrity. Accompanied by Simon Hemans, who had succeeded Brian Fall as private secretary to my husband and who could act as interpreter for us, and six other members of the BBC contingent who were not involved in the Sunday evening concert, we all turned up at the Hermitage at 10 a.m. the next morning for this tour of the Hermitage.

Imagine Buckingham Palace, the British Museum, the National and Portrait Galleries, together with the Victoria and Albert Museum in one linked great assemblage of art in all its splendour and manifestations—well, that is the Hermitage.

The director first led us to the 'Golden Treasury', housed

TOUR OF THE HERMITAGE, JANUARY 1967

in the upper basement. We had visited the Scythian treasures and the Imperial jewels eighteen years previously, having first obtained a special government permit to do so. This time, led by the director, no special permit was required, nor did he have to give the day's password to the guards sitting by the great steel doors which confronted us. As soon as we appeared, the doors were unlocked and we walked into a brilliantly lit chamber, where, in display cabinets, some on the walls others on tables, were the Scythian treasures—daggers, hunting horns, goblets, bracelets, rings and emblems galore. The Scythians were superb craftsmen who had crossed the Black Sea and had ruled the northern shores of the sea and settled in the southern steppes of Russia between the eighth and fifth centuries BC. They had links with both the Chinese and the Greeks, so I presume the Silk Road was already extant as a trading route. In 1948 I had been a complete ignoramus concerning 'Scythes', but now I was much more clued in. Moreover, having recently lived in Iran and enjoyed the rich artistic heritage there, I now appreciated very much more the beautiful objects of the Scythian treasures. An archway led through into the chamber of the Imperial treasures. Here were fabulous jewels and wonderful trinkets, Easter eggs and little boxes fashioned by that master craftsman Fabergé. Here were also lovely trinkets and 'objets d'art' presented to the Imperial family by foreign potentates. Our director pointed out special items of beauty and interest. I would have loved to spend longer in these two wonderful rooms, but it was a question of 'onwards'.

Now we plunged into the dark gloom of the lower basement where it was jolly cold. Here we saw a prehistoric mammoth, complete with great tusks! Also the oldest carpet (fifth century BC) both dug out of the permafrost of the Altai mountains of western China and on the frontier with Siberia.

I wrote to my mother: 'It is a rug about 5ft square with delicate fading colouring with a sort of Turkmenian elephant's foot pattern with a lovely silky sheen which gives it the appearance of being woven in silk, but no, it was wool. It was quite intact and one marvelled that it could have survived throughout so many centuries—some 2500 years!'

From here we went up to the private apartments of Catherine the Great, glancing briefly through open doors at the grand throne room and at other ornate state rooms, and on through rooms hung with tapestries and furnished according to style and provenance, with examples of ceramic or majolica wares on top of them.

The director would dally for a few moments here and there, recounting stories about this and that, until finally we found ourselves in a long corridor with closed doors on either side. About halfway along, the director stopped at a certain door and ushered us into a long room. The sound of shuttlecocks being driven back and forth reverberated. There were a number of looms weaving rich brocades and other furnishing materials. At the end of the room were rows of sewing machines—a large table divided this area from the looms. It was a hive of activity. The newly woven materials were being cut out. The sewing machines sewed them up for re-covering sofas and chairs, or making into curtains. The seamstresses and embroiderers were under the supervision of a professor of needlework and soft furnishing and in a small annex was her office, where we found chairs awaiting us and tea and sweetmeats. We sank gratefully into our chairs and sipped our tea whilst the professor told us in French, Italian, a little English but chiefly German, for those of us who understood it, how she and her colleagues in charge of the soft furnishings of the great palaces outside Leningrad before the war had managed to salvage samples of curtains by cutting sufficiently large pieces of material from the bottom of the curtains and it was these samples, stowed away in a safe location during the war, which could be and were now copied for the weaving of new material for making up into

TOUR OF THE HERMITAGE, JANUARY 1967

replacement curtains and so forth exactly like the originals. The taking of samples from the curtains was done as the German guns approached ever nearer!

With this background knowledge, it made summer visits to the restored palaces all the more interesting. Further, the director explained that the furniture, tapestries, china and glassware were all brought into other sections of these workshops for restoration and there was equally a restoration department for pictures.

Feeling refreshed and rested, we now tackled the picture galleries. We had a whiz-bang tour lasting an hour. We were allowed to tarry a few minutes in front of those masterpieces especially loved and selected by our director. And so we marched from the Italian Botticellis, Bellinis and Leonardos to the Dutch galleries with their huge number of Rembrandts.

The director chose three of these for our special attention. Then, as we were all Brits, he took us through the British galleries, again stopping briefly by one or two selected pictures. The same treatment for the French and German galleries. And so our tour ended. We did not visit the extensive oriental department or the sculpture and statuary. We were exhausted but elated—we had had enough.

Visitors and Travels, Winter to Summer 1967

I remember 1967 as a year of memorable and enjoyable occasions. A year of sunshine—actual and in its figurative sense. A year of educative culture, travel and welcome visits from family members and friends. A year with a happy April wedding back in England, when I acquired a daughter-in-law. The year started off fiendishly cold in spite of lovely sunshine, but before the onslaught of the following winter, we enjoyed a fantastic sunny autumn, the sun shining right into November and no snow until after all the celebrations of

BACK TO MOSCOW, 1965–1968

7 November marking the 50th anniversary of the 1917 revolution, the start of Soviet rule, were well and truly over.

A letter of 27 January to my mother says:

For 3 weeks the thermometer outside our sunny sitting room window has registered a constant $-16°$ centigrade, often down to $-20°$ and on one day skidaddling down to $-28°$. The great outdoors makes me feel positively sick, but I like to take a breath of fresh air each day, so walk briskly once round the little park behind our Embassy with my woolly scarf covering my mouth like everyone else one sees. My teacher has taught me how to breathe: 'Never open your mouth—breathe in slowly, count 5 slowly and let your breath out. This way you protect your lungs'. I have decided that Siberia would certainly not be for me and I am not surprised that the Bishop of Fulham, who has been staying for the inside of a week, should have decided that in future he would only visit the northern countries of his vast parish in the summer months.

A bare week after dispatching this letter, lo and behold an invitation addressed to the British Ambassador arrived at the Embassy: the Protocol Department of the Russian Foreign Office were organising a four-day visit to Siberia, centred on Irkutsk (the capital). Besides Irkutsk, Lake Baikal and the new town of Bratsk would be on the itinerary. The British ambassador and his lady were cordially invited to join other heads of mission for this excursion.

Siberia in February! We shuddered with the anticipated cold, but we accepted the invitation. So there we were a week later winging our way to Siberia, landing for refuelling at Omsk, flying over Tomsk, towns I remembered figured prominently in Jules Verne's book *Michel Stroganoff* which I had much enjoyed reading as a schoolgirl, when a pupil at the French Lycée in Tangiers.

See later for a description of this memorable trip; I will just say here that it was four days of sunshine without a cloud in the sky.

The Bishop of Fulham, who stayed with us during that frantically cold January, looked every inch a bishop. A large imposing man, very benign and friendly, who loved to chatter away, quite particularly on the charms of Mauritius where he had been chaplain for two years before becoming a bishop. The Rev. Masters, chaplain of the Anglican Church in Helsinki, was also a huge man. He came to Moscow periodically to minister to his flock there and would stay with us. Disaster befell on the first occasion. He lowered his bulk into one of our imitation Chippendale chairs, when crack, crack, crackle reverberated in the room and there sprawling on the floor was the poor reverend. Two chair legs had broken. We rushed to his help, but I had to ring for assistance—he was too heavy for my husband and I was quite useless. Mindful of this disaster, as soon as I met the bishop I insisted on finding a good solid chair for him to sit on.

Three weeks after our return from Siberia, we were in for an extremely busy month, socially and culturally.

Our son Bruce arrived a week ahead of my husband's sister Isabel and her schoolmaster husband Mat. They came for a two-week visit. They were all three of them lucky, for during those three weeks what I would call the cream of Russian ballet and opera figured on the Bolshoi spring programme.

For opera, the fare was *The Queen of Spades*, a whodunit in operatic form (Pushkin and Tchaikovsky), *Eugene Onegin*, a Tchaikovsky romantic opera, and *Boris Godunov*, the great historical opera by Mussorgsky. The latter was produced on the vast stage of the new Congress Hall in the Kremlin. The crowd scene at the coronation of Boris, as he emerges from the great cathedral church, was very realistically transposed onto the stage from the actual setting a mere few yards away. For ballet, we had *Swan Lake* and *Romeo and Juliet*, with the exquisite prima ballerina Ulanova in the title role. She had been Margot Fonteyn's inspiration, who then, in her turn, equalled Ulanova in the same roles. The third lovely ballet that our visitors had the luck to enjoy was *Bakchisarai Fontan*, a ballet about the goings-on in the Tartar Khan's harem in the Crimea.

My afternoons were largely taken up sightseeing around and about Moscow with our guests, leaving them to visit museums and galleries in the mornings on their own.

On their first morning I would take my visitors on a walk through the Kremlin past the great White Palace, through the cathedral square and out onto Red Square. On taking my husband's sister and her schoolmaster husband on their first Kremlin visit, I was highly amused when Mat took over being 'the guide'. He loved holding forth and considered that everyone around was a pupil to be instructed. He had read up all about Moscow before his visit to us, so he pointed out to us the three great churches, naming them correctly, and gave us a little lesson about each of them. As we emerged through the Troitsky gateway onto the drawbridge linking Red Square with the Kremlin: 'Ah, Red Square!' he exclaimed, stopping still and taking a deep breath. 'Now turn your eyes to the right and there you will see St Basil's' and he began to hold forth about Ivan the Terrible and his victory over the Tartars at Kazan and hence the building of this extraordinary church in commemoration of that victory and as a thanks offering. 'Now look at those Turkish style turbans as cupolas, and what fantastic colours.' Mat waved his arms around; the guards on duty were transfixed with astonishment. Passers-by in Red Square stopped and stared. Suddenly there was a loud toot from a car which was coming through the archway of the Troitsky Gate. The guards jumped to attention. We were hastily shoved into the square, and the car full of important Russians sailed through. Mat fell silent, but Isabel and I thought the incident very funny and laughed, and I now said, 'Now turn your eyes to the left and there you will see Lenin's tomb where Stalin has been laid beside him, you can visit that on your own if you wish and are prepared to queue.' There was a long queue of people, stretching the length of Red Square on the left, all waiting their turn to walk past the open coffins of Lenin and Stalin, side by side in the holy of holies in the very centre of the mausoleum.

One weekend we took our visitors off to visit Vladimir and Suzdal (as already described). Unlike the previous year when Michael was with us and the trees were in fresh green leaf, and wild flowers were blooming, in 1967 there was still much snow around and no sign of spring. We had had such a very severe and long winter. Suzdal now looked quite different, sparkling with snow, and we visited other nunneries and monasteries we had not previously seen. We all enjoyed our weekend very much and the weather was fine.

The Palace of Weddings

One event was a visit to a 'Palace of Weddings', described as follows in a letter to my mother:

> *Yesterday morning I joined ladies of our Embassy for an organised visit to a 'Palace of Weddings'. There are two such palaces in Moscow. It was most interesting. Only ladies conduct the ceremony. It was explained to us by one of the 28 ladies connected with the establishment, that only first marriages take place in a 'Palace'. If one partner has already been married then the couple must go to an ordinary registry office. After telling us a little about the ceremony we then assisted at one of the marriages. We stood each side of a hall and presently bride and groom, she in a 1 inch above the knee white wedding frock, with white veil and long white gloves and accompanied by mothers and fathers and a brother and about four other*

people marched in, two by two. They halted in front of huge double doors, and a lady all in black with a little white collar appeared through the door which closed behind her. She then said 'Welcome to our wedding ceremony', the doors opened wide and the opening bars of Tchaikowski's piano concerto came loudly over the loud speaker. There was a huge desk at the far end of the room behind which stood two other females in the same black dresses with white lace collars. We all filed in and stood on either side by the wall. The groom and bride about 10 paces from the desk, and the guiding lady joined her companions behind the desk. The music was switched off and the lady in black in the centre then made a solemn little oration, asked each of the protagonists if they wished to marry t'other, to which they answered 'Da' (Yes). They then each signed a large book, and again stood at their allotted place. Music was again switched on, more softly. This time it was from 'Nutcracker'. I think the Sugar Plum Fairy's dance. 'Now kiss each other' commanded the lady in black. Then one of her companions came up to the couple with a little bowl in which were two rings. The bride took off her glove and, with difficulty (I think the ring was too small), the groom popped a ring on her finger and she did ditto by his. But here in Russia they wear their rings on their right hand. The director of ceremonies then followed up with a little sermon, which included the exhortation 'Not to forget their parents, who had done so much for them'. She then wished them every happiness and good luck and a 'good life together' and that was the end. Grand kissing all round with all the relatives, and then they processed out to the strains of the march from Romeo and Juliet.

We then joined the wedding group in the 'champagne room' and they invited us to drink with them. So we countered by saying we would like to do this but would like to present them with two bottles of champagne. Mrs Williams and I also agreed it would be nice to 'bunch' the bride, so Mrs W went to buy a bunch from the kiosk in the hall, all ready there for the purpose, and her small daughter then went up to the bride and presented the bunch with a very deep curtsey. This was a huge success.

Our lady guide then took us into the 'Bride's Room', where we found four prospective brides waiting for their turn with mothers fussily arranging the veils. The whole of one side of the room was one huge mirror. I think there was a 'Groom's Room' somewhere, but we were not shown it. But we were then taken to the 'Present' shop, where there was a display of jewellery, as well as vases and little trays. This is where the participants could buy gifts for the occasion, including, of course, the rings.

It was all very interesting, and conducted with due solemnity and ceremony. Ceremony lasted about 20 minutes.

More Travels

In April we briefly returned to England for our son John's wedding, but in May and June we were back in harness. For the Queen's birthday party in June we had a glorious day and so it was again in 1968, so no crisis weather-wise as we had had in 1966. Successors of ours were able to have a marquee in the garden in case of rain, but finance for this was not available in our day. In July I returned to the UK to spend two weeks with my mother ahead of my husband's leave in August and in the first week of September we returned to Dubrovnik for a week there. We had such happy memories of our holiday in 1938 when we were stationed in Berlin and booked into the same hotel, but we were saddened and astonished to find it was now utterly different: doubled in size and quite impersonal. However, we still had the amusing and attractive view of the old harbour with fishing boats chugging in and out and rowing boats crossing to the little island which was beyond my swimming reach. No speedboats to disturb the peace, a few sailing boats, always a picturesque sight, and the swimming was still a joy.

From Dubrovnik we flew to Istanbul, where we joined a Russian boat for a five-day journey around the northern coast of the Black Sea before landing at Sukhumi in Georgia, where Simon Hemans, my husband's current private secretary, met us in an embassy touring car, driven by our own nice chauffeur, Triatsin. We were to spend two memorable weeks in Armenia and Georgia. It was a wonderful trip, full of interest, both for the people we met and for the very varied scenery. See later for an account of this trip.

Siberia, February 1967

Lake Baikal

Our three-day tour to Siberia was based on Irkutsk, more or less plumb centre between the Ural Mountains and the China Sea. The month was February, the year 1967, and all the cities of Russia were in the grip of ice and snow.

I have never felt so cold before or since this trip, yet on all those three days the sun shone down on us out of a clear blue sky. I think I had visualised non-stop blizzards.

At 8 a.m. on our second day we drove some fifty miles to the shores of Lake Baikal following the course of the Angara River, the only river to flow out of Lake Baikal though it is fed by a great number of small rivers and streams. About half way along we stopped to visit a dam built across the river with hydraulic works along its top which generate electricity for Irkutsk and its district.

From the top of the dam one looked on one side at a

frozen expanse of man-made lake, while on the other side, way down below us, was the frozen-over river wending its way to Irkutsk and then on for a further nearly 1,000 miles to the Yenisey, one of the great rivers of Siberia.

For the first few miles above the lake the Angara was frozen over, but curiously it then flowed freely in an ever-widening channel between banks of broken ice until, for the final twelve miles or so, to Lake Baikal, the water now ran quite freely. Here there were myriad birds, ducks mostly, but also some geese flying around and swimming, diving and preening themselves and obviously enjoying life hugely. There were plenty of fish to assuage their hunger. It was strange to see this extraordinary sight in ice- and snow-bound Siberia in February.

It was explained to us that at the very end of Lake Baikal there were a number of hot springs and as a result, as we would presently see, the Angara flows freely from beneath a roof of ice for some twelve miles. Straggling birch trees and bushes adorned the bank sides and we then reached the source of the river, Lake Baikal. We were utterly astonished to find ourselves at the base of a 20-foot-high waterfall with an 8-foot wall of ice on top, stretching in an absolute straight line from one great rock cliff to another, marking the end of the lake and the outlet for the river Angara.

Pedestrians and the occasional car and truck could be seen walking and trundling across from one bank to the other. They looked like figures in a Lowry picture. The whole scene was fantastically beautiful and in the lovely sunshine the world sparkled like a diamond. The snow along the branches of the trees and bushes, the sparkle of the river, the snow all around and about and the spray from the waterfall all combined to make it a never-to-be-forgotten scene.

We now clambered back into our coach and zigzagged our way up to the shore of Lake Baikal. Our coach stopped some fifty yards from the edge of the ice wall we had seen from the front of the waterfall. Now we were on the shore of this great lake—before us was a pristine sheet of ice, covered with snow, and stretching and fusing into the distant horizon, hemmed in between hills and even higher mountains. As we had seen from below, people and the occasional truck and car were crossing the frozen lake at its narrowest point just above the ice wall.

Not far from the shore we saw three little wigwams set up on the ice. Within each sat a man on a little stool, tremendously wrapped up in padded clothing and hood and holding a line which dangled down into a hole deep through the ice to the waters below. They were fishing for omul, a unique Lake Baikal fish—in taste not dissimilar to sea trout. We savoured some, and delicious it was too, grilled, threaded on 2-foot long wooden spits propped up round a bonfire right by the lakeshore. There were logs strewn around and members of a welcoming committee invited us to take a seat on these. Presently, hunks of local fresh bread with freshly grilled omul on top were handed around, together with tooth mugs full of vodka! We all decided that the great Siberian outdoors was quite tolerable with sun overhead, a bonfire to huddle around every so often, the warm glow generated by the vodka inside us, and beautiful scenery to enchant us.

Nestling among the pine trees on the hillside behind us were a cluster of little villa-type houses built of rounded planks of timber painted in different colours. In the centre of this complex was a large Swiss-type chalet housing a restaurant, cinema and rest rooms. The whole complex was what the Russians call a sanatorium and this was where we were housed for our one night by Lake Baikal.

An hour was allocated for lunch and rest before setting out for the Letimological Institute some 3km along the lake. On the way we stopped and the more stalwart of us climbed to the top of a hill from where we had a splendid view of the lake. Sadly the higher mountains were lost in mist, and it was extremely cold. Soon we were taken to the institute, where we

SIBERIA, FEBRUARY 1967

were given a lecture on Lake Baikal, the most beautiful, the deepest, the cleanest, the richest and generally the most wonderful lake in the world. We were invited to look at stuffed fish and all sorts of diagrams.

Back at our village cinema we were shown some excellent documentaries on the wild life, vegetation and scenery of the district. The forests, we were told, abound in bears and sable and there were good pictures of both.

A very enjoyable day ended with what the Russians called a 'communal supper' (the term actually printed on our programme). This consisted of a banqueting table all laid out for us 37-odd diplomats plus a drove of journalists who had accompanied us from Moscow, plus a squad of the leading Russian personalities of the region—people like the president of the regional council, the mayor of Irkutsk and other dignitaries who had driven the fifty miles from Irkutsk for the occasion, accompanied of course, by their wives.

A good time was had by all. There was lots of food (three courses of omul, smoked, poached, and enclosed in pastry), lots of drink and finally dancing to a very good band from Irkutsk and so to bed around midnight with a 7 a.m. wake-up for another long day.

In 1967 Lake Baikal had no industrial development of any sort along its shores. The waters were completely unpolluted, extremely pure and very blue. I have read that by 2003, a few factories have been erected and that in consequence the waters are no longer unpolluted. Sad!

I shall always remember Lake Baikal—pure enjoyment. I am just sorry I never had the chance of seeing it in summertime.

Irkutsk

Our trip to Lake Baikal was sandwiched between two days of endless lectures liberally laced with statistics which only our

Luxembourg colleague diligently scribbled down. The rest of us would sit glassy-eyed on hard chairs. My husband usually had his eyes firmly closed—after all, if required, these figures could all be obtained back in Moscow—could they not?

On our first Siberian morning we were taken for an hour's tour of Irkutsk. We were all charmed by our delightful guide in her beautiful white fox-fur hat which framed her pretty face. She spoke good English although she had never travelled outside the Soviet Union—she was born and bred and now married in Irkutsk.

We liked Irkutsk. In 1967 there were streets which still had traditional timber houses, the wood all now mellowed to an attractive dark honey colour. The eaves and the surrounds of the windows had elaborately carved fretwork edging, painted sky blue. There were also avenues of eighteenth- and early nineteenth-century buildings of white stucco, all very pleasing, with icicles dripping down from snow-covered roofs— and everything glinted in the lovely sunshine. Redevelopment had not yet seriously taken over here in Irkutsk and as yet there were no high-rise buildings. Forty years on I expect this has changed. The embankment along the Angara River, all frozen over with ice floes, all lumpy, bumpy, was attractively laid out. There were also a number of churches with traditional domes and pepper pot cupolas some painted gold, or covered in gold leaf, others painted green or blue. Sadly, Sonia our guide explained to us, as we had to be at the district regional offices at 10 sharp to meet the Irkutsk and regional worthies there would not be time for us to visit any of these churches, so presently we found ourselves shaking hands with a number of gentlemen and two large ladies who invited us to take our seats around an oblong table and we were then subjected to a lecture on the industrial output and the potentialities of Siberia. Proceedings were greatly lengthened as everything was translated, first into English, then into French. Our two interpreters were sorely tried as

SIBERIA, FEBRUARY 1967

they struggled with our respective vocabularies and we were amused when the French chap not infrequently was stuck for a word, and would finally inject 'enfin' as a substitute. Endless statistics were quoted as we got ever more restive on our hard chairs. Only the Luxembourg colleague scribbled on. At last it all came to an end with tea and sweetmeats.

Now at last came the moment to experience Siberia as we had all pictured it since childhood—Siberia was synonymous with intense cold—how true! I had never felt so cold as during the next couple of hours, when we visited an aluminium factory. We were driven some ten miles into a featureless expanse of white country to a complex of ugly buildings all connected with the production of aluminium. As we emerged from our coach we encountered a wall of intense cold, such as none of us had yet experienced: −28°C. We were led to a 300-yard long shed with great boilers atop hissing, spitting noisy furnaces set at regular intervals down each side of the interior of the shed with an 18-foot-wide walkway down the middle. The shed was open at each end and an icy draught blew all the way down, turning this walk into a horrible experience—unbelievably cold in spite of these great hissing boilers down each side. There were miles of pipes and tubes everywhere, and although there was a chap accompanying us and presumably explaining what was happening, it was so noisy his voice was quite lost in the din. Our group became ever more straggly, everyone going at his/her own pace to get through this inferno as fast as possible. The men won easily, and the women grumbled at being abandoned but it was a case of each for him/herself. The cold, whistling draught blew in our faces as we struggled in our heavy boots and thick clothing to increase our pace. But at last this taste of purgatory came to an end and we were able to flop down on chairs as we reached the haven of the warm admin building. It was then we realised that two ladies—the wives of the Syrian and Tunisian ambassadors respectively—

were in great distress, with tears rolling down their cheeks. One of them complained of her frozen fingers in spite of wearing two pairs of gloves, but the other much more seriously of her legs. The poor dear, instead of wearing warm trousers like the rest of us, had donned her silk stockings (perhaps to impress the gents of the town council?) and these stockings had actually frozen onto her legs. Luckily excellent first-aid was forthcoming and the two ladies (great friends) were then tucked up in sheepskin rugs and driven back to Irkutsk in a car.

Due maybe to the unhappy mishap to two of our ladies and the obvious non-enjoyment of the rest of the party, I think the management decided the sooner they were rid of us the better, so I remain ignorant as ever as to the components of aluminium or the process of making it prior to turning it into pots and pans.

By the evening the little Syrian lady's fingers had thawed out and she was her usual gay self at dinner followed by an evening at the circus. But the Tunisian lady did not re-emerge until 8 the following morning as we climbed into our bus to take us to Lake Baikal.

After lunch we deviated off our road to Irkutsk to visit a large experimental farm, experimenting in growing cereals, fruit and vegetables that could mature in double-quick time in the short summer season and which could also withstand a certain amount of frost. Obviously with the entire country under deep snow, there was nothing for us to see, so we were subjected to another lengthy lecture (three times over, Russian, English and French). Many of us nodded off—we had had a long morning. However, eventually we were plied with glasses full of delicious milk or smetana (soured cream) and sticky buns accompanied by hard-boiled eggs. As it was not long since lunch, only a handful of people succumbed to these. And now we were taken on a tour of immensely long cowsheds full of splendid-looking black-and-white cows—all of them linked up to the most up-to-date automatic milking machine. The sheds were spotlessly clean, sluiced down at frequent intervals. We were duly impressed. We understood that only for some two months in the summer were the cows let out into fields when the grass was lush. Apparently the region is extremely fertile and responded well to the various experiments.

On our return to the hotel, my husband and I felt in dire need of stretching our limbs. A church on the far side of the square beckoned us—so we set off. Sadly, the Siberian winter defeated us. It was so excruciatingly cold we only managed to walk halfway across then turned back; the temperature was now about $-30°C$ and it hurt to breathe in such cold air. One required training for this. My Russian teacher had taught me the technique which revolves around counting to the number five three times over very slowly—breathe in and hold it, and breathe out. The object is to warm the air you breathe in so that the lungs should not suffer shock from icy air.

That evening after supper we all went to the circus. A circus is a must in every Soviet town; Russians love the strong men who toss each other around and the ladies on the flying trapeze, and of course the clowns make constant quips on current affairs and decisions and are always greeted with great guffaws of joyous laughter. The 'pièce de resistance' at this circus was a troop of polar bears who were hilarious as they repeatedly climbed to the top of a slide to slither down sometimes on their bums, sometimes on their tummies to end up with a great splash in the pool provided for them. Their look of complete enjoyment was such fun to see. We were told that Irkutsk was the only city where you could see performing polar bears.

And so ended our first day in Siberia.

BACK TO MOSCOW, 1965-1968

Bratsk

Bratsk is situated about 500 miles north of Irkutsk in very wild and lonely forest country known as the 'Taiga', which stretches right across the northern half of Siberia. This is permafrost country. In 1966, we were told the last frost was on 3 July and the next first frost was on 21 August. Throughout the year we were told the mean temperature had been −7°C. In summer the top 3 feet of ground thaws out, but beneath that for at least 6 feet it remains solidly frozen. What is so surprising is that Bratsk is no further north than Edinburgh (in latitude) and is slightly south of Moscow (Northumberland for us) yet it is so perishingly frigid.

During the fifties the Russians decided to build a second dam across the Angara River with hydroelectric turbines across it which would generate not only sufficient power for a new industrial complex in the area, but there would be enough surplus electricity to be transported to the very heart of the Russian steppes in the motherland. The spur to the project was the fact that this region was very rich in minerals.

The Russians are very proud of this dam—'the biggest in the world,' they said. It certainly was impressive, not least its situation in this lonely wild country. On the day of our visit the temperature was −28°C. We hastily transferred ourselves from plane to coach and on to the warm haven of the lengthy enclosed corridor on top of the dam connecting the two banks of the Angara River, here four times wider than in Irkutsk.

Huge turbines lined one side, gently and hypnotically humming in the background. It was all spotlessly clean and in this harsh world it was very soothing. Cups of tea and sweetmeats were handed around as we gazed out at the extraordinary view on either side of our corridor (there were windows between the turbines). On one side was the great snow-covered frozen lake, and on the other a most awe-inspiring view of a vast horizon with dense Taiga bisected by what appeared to be an enormous boulder-strewn glacier disappearing into the mists of the far distance; it was *not* a glacier, however, but the river Angara on its journey to the Yenisey.

After our visit to the dam we were driven through the district and saw something of the various housing projects—tenements to house the workforce for the industrial development, together with housing, schools, library and 'gastronomes' for the planners, architects and engineers—the latter were accommodated in attractive chalets, painted in various colours and divided into eight apartments, many with an outlook onto the lake. Alongside these were small individual houses each with a small plot of ground fenced in and with a garage and outhouse at the rear. All this development was well planned and well designed. Pine trees were everywhere; obviously many trees had had to be felled, but this had been carefully and sensitively carried out.

Our lunch had been organised in a central community house and here we met the boss and the man responsible for the whole project of this new town since its very inception eleven years earlier. He was a charismatic individual and after our meal he gave us a short and interesting talk—then back to our bus, plane and finally once more back in our hotel in Irkutsk.

Our visit to this town buried in the Taiga and miles from civilisation had been an exceptional experience for us. It was interesting to note that because of its isolation and the harshness of its climate, Bratsk had to offer amenities not available elsewhere to attract top-grade personnel to come and live and work there.

And so ended our three-day trip to Siberia—a unique experience.

I do wonder how Bratsk has developed in the years that have elapsed since this visit. As it is not on the tourist route, it would be quite difficult to discover.

The Black Sea, Autumn 1967

Having sailed from Istanbul to Trebizond along the southern coast of the Black Sea on a Turkish cargo boat (room for a few passengers) in 1960, it was extremely interesting seven years later to sail along the north coast on a Russian passenger steamer. On both trips our on-board accommodation was good and comfortable. Our food was OK, though not always entirely to our liking. Service was prompt and personnel were courteous. Russian restaurants are not famous for promptitude or courteousness. However, on Russian passenger boats, either in the north between London and Leningrad or in the south between Istanbul and the eastern ports of the Black Sea, we never found ground for complaint and we enjoyed both our trips enormously.

On the first trip in 1960, we were motoring all the way from London to Teheran, which included a ten-day stopover in Greece. In 1967, this journey took up a slice of my husband's annual leave, which ended as soon as we reached Russian soil in Odessa.

Our Turkish cargo boat paused briefly just outside innumerable little ports, loading and unloading all manner of cargo, from goats to quantities of upright cane chairs. Everything was dangled from the ship's crane to be lowered into a waiting barge below. The long-suffering goats did not enjoy the experience very much, but we found the changing scenario fascinating to watch from our deck just below the bridge overlooking the ship's hold.

On our Russian boat we just sat back in deck chairs and enjoyed the changing panorama from the mountainous and rugged coast of the Crimea to the lush green coast beyond and at the further end an occasional glimpse of the Caucasus mountains.

THE BLACK SEA, AUTUMN 1967

Varna

On our trip along the western and northern coast of the Black Sea, we steamed by night and called at a different port each day.

On leaving Istanbul we hugged the coast westwards, past the estuary of the Danube, until we reached Varna in Bulgaria. Varna has lovely beaches to its north which were being developed as a tourist playground. We joined a sightseeing tour which took us to this area of 'golden sands' as described in our little brochure, and indeed they were truly golden with the special attraction that lovely trees grew right to the edge of the beach. Beyond them, modern skyscraper hotels had been built with plenty of attractively laid out gardens between them. My husband enjoyed a lovely swim whilst I, feeling extremely frustrated, watched him, blowing my nose every other second, having caught a cold on our last day in Istanbul.

Our tour included a stop at a souvenir shop full of a variety of junk, though some quite attractive needlework, but everything exorbitantly expensive. We bought nothing in spite of our guide doing her best to encourage us. However, a party of Japanese tourists who were fellow passengers fell upon these 'souvenirs' with great earnestness, hissing and exclamations of '*ah-sodeska*'. They amused us very much, for we knew that back in their homeland they could purchase similar merchandise far more cheaply, but of course they would not then be souvenirs of their holiday.

Apart from this Japanese group there were few other passengers until we reached Odessa, but from here on our boat was full of Russian trippers.

BACK TO MOSCOW, 1965–1968

Odessa

Before leaving Moscow at the end of July for our holiday leave, my husband had informed the foreign ministry of our projected plans of touring Russian-controlled territories and gave them our itinerary, asking for arrangements to be made for a local Intourist guide to meet us at our various stopovers along the coast and then in Georgia and Armenia to guide us around. What was our surprise to find when we reached Odessa that we were met not only by an Intourist guide but also by a young professor of English and two members of the town council, one of whom presented me with a bunch of roses and said, 'Welcome back to Russia'—a very kindly gesture but poor roses. They were even worse for wear after a hot afternoon of touring the sights of Odessa, clutched by me.

Odessa is a large and busy seaport, but the commercial harbour with its consequent mess is well away from the passenger harbour. The city is built along the top of a high cliff with a great wide promenade along the seafront, reminiscent of the great promenade in the French city of Pau with its splendid view of the Pyrenees. A great and wide staircase descends from this promenade down to the passenger harbour and it was at the top of these that our two worthies from the town council bade us farewell and we proceeded on our tour. This great staircase has been made famous as it figures in Eisenstein's great film, *Battleship Potemkin* when either the sailors fire on the proletariat as they descend the steps or vice versa and a great massacre on these steps ensues. I never saw the film, which was produced in 1925 and which had a huge success in cinemas throughout Europe and made Eisenstein famous as a foremost film director.

Odessa has many tree-lined avenues, an older, picturesque corner, and also a handsome opera house.

Yalta

The following morning we spent a very pleasant two hours sitting up on deck and steaming around the bulge of the Crimea to Yalta. The scenery is wild and beautiful with rather stark mountains falling steeply into the sea. As we steamed along the shore my husband tried to identify the palaces he knew from the 1944 Yalta conference, but so many new massive 'sanatoria' have been built in the intervening years that he wasn't too sure about it. We were met by a very slim blonde woman with heavily made-up eyes, high dagger heels and a Zis black car. She took us for a lovely drive right along the coast, a nostalgic trip for GWH. We walked around the Livadia Palace and glued our noses to the windows, peering into the great dining hall which had been the conference room and is now the dining room of the sanatorium which is lodged there. We also peered into what had been Roosevelt's bedroom, now a little sitting room. We looked into a rather pretty little cloistered courtyard and we admired the splendid view. Blondie told us that soon the sanatorium would be giving up the historical rooms which would then become a museum. There was a plaque on the wall by the main door stating the fact about the Yalta conference having taken place there. We then motored some further eight miles to the Vorontsov Palace where the British delegation with Churchill had stayed, but en route we stopped and called in on a new, modern sanatorium where the current American ambassador in Moscow and family had spent a fortnight recently. What the Russians call a sanatorium is not quite what we understand by this term. For them it means primarily a convalescent home with various medical facilities, but it also means a super holiday rest home where, under doctor's orders, you can avail yourself of the medical facilities, or if you don't require anything specific you can just sit back and enjoy the amenities. To be able to stay in a sanatorium somewhere is obviously the ultimate in luxury for the Soviet citizen, but I think you have to be a well-favoured citizen or else have the means of some pretty astute wire pulling to get a 'propusk' (or entry pass) for a sanatorium and in this society where some are very obviously more equal than others, the big shots manage to get themselves to the best and most modern of these establishments. The authorities will also arrange for distinguished foreigners to stay in such establishments if they wish to spend a holiday period in one of the resorts. The suite occupied by the American ambassador, up on the fourth floor with a balcony, was a corner suite with a wonderful view and all comforts. Even the bathroom looked quite good! Sanatoria all have their own private beaches, and on this coast where the cliffs are steep many of them have their own lifts to take you up and down. This particular sanatorium had a separate and extremely nice building for its restaurant and recreation rooms, a semi-circular building with great plate-glass windows and a balcony set with dining tables.

The Vorontsov Palace is a museum. It is pure Scottish baronial, set in a very beautiful park. The Prince Vorontso responsible for it had been Russia's ambassador at the Court of St James, and he imported both a Scottish architect and some other Britisher (history doesn't relate whether English or Scottish) to lay out the park. The house is of course ugly and rather absurd, but with a noble oak staircase and some lovely panelling and some good English furniture—a very suitable place for the British delegation. Blondie was very impressed that GWH seemed to know his way around better than she did!

Before setting out on this tour GWH told Blondie he would like a swim, so she now took us to the Intourist beach, and oh what a horrid place it was! A small pebble beach entirely covered by more or less naked bodies stretched out on raised wooden slabs. At one end a concrete platform had been built with a roof over it, and the slabs with their humanity were arranged in serried rows, all cheek by jowl touching each other. Along the beach were some four iron erections looking just like French 'urinoires', where with half your legs visible you could change. This Intourist beach was separated from the ordinary plebs' beach by a six-foot wire fence. The only good thing to be said for this beach is that it was only half as crowded as the plebs' beach. However, there was nothing wrong with the water, and GWH enjoyed his swim. I sat on a wooden slab and again sniffled.

Blondie parked us on a bench for us to eat our lunch and bade us farewell. After lunch, consisting of a slice of bread, each with a slab of cheese, some biscuits and some fruit we had brought along from our breakfast on the boat, we now set off on foot to explore the actual little town of Yalta, and came to the conclusion that it was a jolly scruffy place, no worse than a popular seaside resort in England, but just about as tasteless. We had hoped to find some nice postcards but unfortunately this is something the Soviets just haven't bothered about. Resort postcards are all the same: the local Lenin Square, the gates into the local park of culture, the local workers' club, and perhaps one very poor specimen of a local view. We were delighted to return to our ship and view Yalta's lovely background from our deck.

Sochi

The following morning we docked in Sochi. This was the favourite resort of the hierarchy—many of whom had villas here financed by the government. It gave a quite different impression from that of Yalta. The Crimea's stark mountain grandeur had given way to soft green hills and valleys and small bays with streams running into them. The air was warmer, softer and more humid. We were met this time by an earnest young man who spoke excellent English and combined being a teacher in the local language school with being an Intourist guide, but like most over-earnest young men, he was completely devoid of humour.

A visit to a sanatorium had been arranged for 12 noon so there was time for a little tour around. Believe it or not, the first place he took us to was the railway station, designed by some famous Soviet architect or other. It was monumental; it was pillared; there were statues. We parked on a dusty crescent. 'Would you like to get out and walk about?' asked our earnest young man. 'No, I think we can see the station quite well from here,' replied my husband politely. Next stopping place was the Pioneer's Palace and park, which looked totally uninteresting. 'Would you like to get out here and walk in the park?' asked our young man, and without thinking I just said, 'No, not a bit.' It was rather rude really, and poor chap, he looked rather startled. 'Well, I will now take you to our famous park with its famous trees and ponds.' Here we did get out, and indeed there were nice trees and shrubs, and we were also amused by driftwood statues of birds and animals standing in small ponds, which with the minimum of carving were extraordinarily lifelike. After this it was time to go to the sanatorium, a grand and sumptuous building with two semi-circular wings all built on top of a hill.

A vigorous, good-looking director with a deep scar below one eye—a war wound—met us and took us to his office where he gave us a little talk on his sanatorium. This one apparently specialised in cardio-vascular and respiratory tract diseases, for which conditions the special sulphur hydrochloride water of Sochi are especially indicated: you bathe in it or just immerse parts of your anatomy (this is difficult to understand!), you inhale it in different strengths, you drink it, finally you place your head under a running tap to prevent premature baldness. In fact later we watched a youngish man doing just that. The director then went on to explain to us why the Black Sea is called 'Black'—not because of storms and mountainous seas but because of this chemical which bubbles up from springs in the nether depths of the sea at the eastern end. It turned the metal anchors of ancient mariners black when they hoicked them up and so they named the sea 'Black'.

There was a spring in a nearby valley which bubbled up this special water. A clinic had been built beside it and patients were taken there for their prescribed treatment.

The director now took us on a tour of his establishment. We marvelled at the number and variety of imposing electrical machines set up on the ground floor of one of the wings. Here a row of separate cubicles had been installed, each with its specialised apparatus. 'Are these all Russian machines?' asked my husband. 'Some are, but others come from the USA, some from Italy, France, Czechoslovakia and East Germany,' was the reply. 'But where are the patients?' I enquired. 'Some may be swimming in the sea, some may be at the mineral spring clinic,' answered the director. 'Some just relaxing.'

We also saw a highly modern and well-equipped dentist's room with a lady dentist ready to perform. But when we looked in she was unemployed.

'Each patient comes here for 26 days and this sanatorium has room for four hundred. There is a daily turnover of eighteen people. But not everyone comes here for medical treatment. Costs are defrayed by their union, but some people pay their own expenses!'

The director now took us upstairs to the great central dining room, three floors up—no lift! I could not help wondering how good this could be for people who really suffered from cardio-vascular or respiratory tract diseases! But it was a lovely airy room, spotlessly clean, with separate small tables all set for lunch. 'Is Georgian wine part of the cure?' asked my husband. 'Certainly not,' replied the director. 'No alcohol is drunk here by patients. However,' he added with a twinkle,

'I should be very pleased to offer you a glass of some excellent wine which I have; just a minute,' and he went off and had a chat with someone. 'It will be ready in five minutes.'

Meanwhile, he took us to see one of the suites—they were all similar. They were either two- or three-bedded, well furnished and all leading on to a balcony, and each room had its own bathroom (pretty good one by Soviet standards). The view from the balconies was lovely. Apparently a private bus took patients down to a private beach and brought them home again. 'Strictly regulated sun and air baths as well as sea baths are all part of our therapy,' said the director.

And now we returned to the dining hall and sat at one of the tables. The special wine, Number 11, was brought along and the director made quite a to-do of how very special this was and difficult to obtain. It was rather good, fairly sweet, a little like a light dessert wine. Slivers of cheese were offered with it, and the director said, 'And what would you like to eat now?' We demurred, said we must be off, but the director would have none of it and sent for the chef. Full of bows and smiles, he suggested we might care for a little chicken. This seemed an excellent suggestion, so finally, not having expected lunch here, we did in fact have a very nice lunch. Not too much of it, nicely cooked and served. We ended our meal with delicious fruit. At ten to two, the director got up abruptly and said we must leave, for the patients would be coming for their meal at two. I think he was keen they shouldn't see our empty bottle of wine!

To round off the visit to the sanatorium, we paid a fleeting visit to the mineral spring and the clinic built there. The director himself showed us round, though there was nothing very different from any other similar spa establishment.

We felt it was now time for some beach life. Our guide insisted that we go to the beach of the Intourist hotel out of town, so we dropped him off in the centre of Sochi and proceeded with the driver to the Intourist hotel. This is a finely situated edifice, and could be made into a lovely deluxe hotel. It has a beautiful terrace and nice grounds down to the sea, but it made a deplorable impression on us. The restaurant had thick calico curtains close to the windows which excluded the view. There were no comfortable chairs on the terrace, no sun umbrellas, just a few rather grubby tables with dirty cloths and rusty-looking chairs. As for the ladies' cloakroom, it was disgusting beyond belief! The beach, however, was better than at Yalta. In particular there were fewer bods. We were given some nice lilos which we put on two contiguous wooden slabs and enjoyed a peaceful forty winks. GWH then bathed. Although my sniffle had gone, I was left with rather a cough, so thought it wiser not to swim, though I longed to. Our guide had told us that we could easily order a taxi to take us back to town, so we had let him go off with the car. However, up at the hotel they said a taxi would take at least forty minutes to appear, so we firmly went out into the road and took the bus back. Taking a bus in the Soviet Union was a new experience for my husband, though I was quite familiar with the procedure. You climb in at the back of the bus and out in the front. There were both a conductor and an automatic ticket dispenser in this Soviet bus. You popped your five kopeks in and he twiddled a handle and you pulled off a length of ticket. However, if you had no change, your money was handed up the bus from passenger to passenger till it reached the driver. He kept a box with change in his cubby hole, and in due course back came the change all the way down again to be handed back to one by the conductor! This elaborate system was several times in operation.

Batumi

That night we sailed for Batumi, the last Soviet/Georgian port at the eastern end of the Black Sea. Like Odessa, Batumi is both a naval and a commercial port; it is also a frontier town. There were no Russians on holiday here—military as well as naval personnel were very much in evidence, however.

We were met by Irina, an English-speaking Intourist guide. She was married to a military man—whether officer or other rank, we never discovered. They had a six-year-old son and they lived in a one-room flat. At the time, the boy still attended a pre-school kindergarten where they looked after him until his mother was due to fetch him home, but the following year, at the age of seven, he would start school, and there would be no one to tend to him after school hours. There was no room in her flat for any extra person, so Irina would have to give up her job to look after the boy. She was obviously very distressed by this situation. She disliked living in Batumi and pined for Kuibishev and Moscow, where her mother and relatives lived.

She took us on a tour of the old town, which had much charm. The one- or two-storeyed houses, all with deep verandahs, were built of stone and stucco and had vines growing up the pillars of the verandahs, trained to make a tunnel of greenery, a very attractive feature. We saw quite a few bunches of grapes dangling down, but just out of reach. Several of the streets also had flowering trees, apparently pink Indian lilac in full bloom interspersed with twelve-to-fifteen-foot-high trees with glossy green leaves. However, one of the streets had been incongruously planted with silvery conifers. I imagine Russians must have been responsible for these to remind them of home—they looked quite out of place!

That night, our boat doubled back to Sukhumi, about three-quarters of the way back to Sochi. We had called into Sukhumi briefly after Sochi to drop off Russians, but we were keen to visit Batumi, which we had heard was attractive, so we stayed on board, sailed on to Batumi for our day there, and now spent a further night on the boat back to Sukhumi.

Here we were met by Simon Hemans, my husband's

private secretary and successor to Brian Fall, and an equally fluent Russian speaker. He was now going to tour Armenia and Georgia and travel along the Georgian military highway through the heart of the Caucasus with us. The plan had been to take a plane back to Moscow once we had reached the Russian side. We had heard that heavy storms at the end of August had washed away part of the road, so this would no doubt mean a change of plan; we would learn more when we reached Tbilisi (previously known by its Turkish name of Tiflis). Simon had driven down from Moscow, sharing the long drive with our own chauffeur and with an embassy couple who were going to spend a few days here and then fly back to Moscow.

Simon had spent the night in a hotel in Sukhumi and reported that it was the worst he had yet encountered in the Soviet Union (he had not yet experienced Bukhara!). It was dirty, expensive, had no hot water and surly personnel. Luckily we ourselves did not have to stay there. The lovely weather we had enjoyed for our Black Sea cruise and our day in Batumi had now given way to rain, so we did not tarry in Sukhumi, but set off immediately for Tshaltuba, where we thought arrangements had been made for us to stay in a sanatorium.

During the first part of the journey we were interested to see stone houses raised up on stilts. They all had deep verandahs which could double as an extra room. We were reminded of similar type houses along the Iran–Caspian coast.

Sukhumi to Tbilisi

We spent three days between Sukhumi and Tbilisi and two nights in Kutaisi, the second most industrial town in Georgia. All I remember of it was a large vegetable and fruit market where we stocked up with peaches and grapes.

We had intended spending our first night at Tshaltuba, a very attractive spa with a number of sanatoria. It had had a great write-up in a book of reminiscences by Sir William Hayter, one of our Moscow predecessors. However, when we arrived at a very attractive-looking sanatorium, where we had understood that Intourist had arranged for our stay of one night, we were very disconcerted to discover that the director had never received any intimation of ourselves and our hope of spending a night in his sanatorium. He was very sorry but he had no free rooms, though he could turn someone out. 'Certainly not,' said my husband, 'we will go to the hotel.' 'There is no hotel,' said the flustered director. 'A hotel is being built and will be ready next year.' As it was raining, we wasted no further time in Tshaltuba but motored some 16 kilometres on to Kutaisi. How lucky we were to have Simon with us, though he was surprised and quite put out to find that Russian was very much a second language—Georgian was what the population of Kutaisi spoke, and though some public notices were in both languages, many were only in Georgian.

On our second night, we had planned to stay in Gori, Stalin's birthplace, but again we were thwarted. This time it was due to the closure of the road between a famous ancient monastery we were visiting, which dominated a hill, and Gori. A recent storm in the mountains had swollen the river to the extent that it was unfordable, so back to Kutaisi we drove. My memory is a blank as to what this hotel was like! Indeed as I recorded nothing about these three days, they have rather faded into the mists of time. I do, however, remember that the drive on our third day from Kutaisi to Gori was exceptionally lovely. The sun was shining and our road twisting up and around flanks of Caucasus mountains gave us some beautiful views, with the autumn colouring just beginning to manifest itself on trees.

Gori itself was disappointing. Although there was a huge

statue of Stalin in the main square and a monumental museum, the latter had been stripped of memorabilia which might have been interesting to see. There were no photos of him as a boy or young seminary student. Not a single photo of family—only pictures and objects connected with him together with Lenin and subsequently as the great man and leader of Russia. We learned later that anything pertaining to his family had been removed three months earlier when his daughter Alliluyeva defected. Gori itself was an ugly little town with matchbox flat development. Triatsin, our chauffeur, muttered that things would have been different in his day!

We did get the impression, however, that local pride in Joseph Dzhugashvili, known to us all as Joseph Stalin, was very strong here and to a certain extent throughout Georgia. He was their most famous son.

And so on to Tbilisi for one night before embarking on our trip to Armenia. We were in the same hotel we had stayed in nineteen years earlier!

Armenia, Autumn 1967

Between the lush green seaboard of the eastern Black Sea, with its warm moist air and Tbilisi, the countryside taken as a whole has left the impression with me that this must be the vineyard of Georgia, from whence come the excellent wines. Besides vines galore, however, plenty of other fruit and vegetables of all sorts are grown: citrus trees and pomegranates, aubergines and melons and even plantations of tea. Closer to Tbilisi one became aware that the wide plain at Batumi was giving way to land hemmed in by the high Caucasus mountains to the north and the uplands of eastern Turkey and the southern hills of Georgia to the south, and on their far side was mountainous Armenia.

On our last enjoyable day in Tbilisi nineteen years earlier, when we walked with sandwiches and a bottle of Georgian wine in our knapsack along the ever rising ridge to the south of Tbilisi, I felt if we could just walk on along the ridge, would we not reach Armenia? Yes indeed, is the answer, but a long way on. It took us two hours to motor up and down ridges and finally to zigzag the flanks of a high hill above a gorge to reach the top of a pass around 8,000 feet, and there below us was desolate Lake Sevan and Armenia.

But after all Lake Sevan was not that desolate, for the shores were now being developed as a resort. We stopped for lunch at the Intourist restaurant and ate 'Ishkan' (the Prince of Fish) a speciality of Lake Sevan, not that different from 'Omul', the speciality of Lake Baikal.

A further two hours' drive brought us to Yerevan and our first sight of Mount Ararat rising straight up from the banks of the Araxes. It towered high above the flanking mountains and made an indelible impression on all of us—not least on Triatsin, who had never before encountered a mountain.

Nestling beside big brother Mount Ararat is the perfect little cone of Little Ararat. The majesty of this famous biblical mountain took us by surprise, for we had seen it from the Turkish side when we motored to Teheran nine years earlier and we had been very disappointed to find it quite unimpressive.

As a city, I found Yerevan unattractive. It is built of red tufa stone, the colour of unmellowed red brick, and the first impression it made was of unwelcoming coldness. However, its inhabitants are friendly and well disposed towards strangers. Our hotel in Lenin Circle (name not yet changed), though not luxurious, was clean and adequate, but its restaurant fare was not very palatable. 'No soup after 7.30' and only spiced rissoles on offer for our supper. 'Let's try some Armenian brandy,' suggested my husband. 'Winston loved it at Yalta.' I was hesitant, didn't think I liked brandy, but urged by my husband I agreed to take a little sip from his glass. 'Hm, yes—OK! Well give me a little,' I murmured, and every evening after that I enjoyed it. Before leaving Yerevan, my husband bought two bottles! We noticed with some surprise that our fellow hotel guests had a bottle of it on their breakfast table.

When our Intourist guide appeared the next morning—a handsome black-haired girl with large black liquid eyes, the prototype of Armenian womanhood—we asked her why the hotel was full of Armenians and so many more crowding round the entrance and in the lobby the previous evening?

'Armenia', as we nick-named our guide, told us that throughout the year there was a continual throng like this, of Armenians who returned to view their homeland not only out of curiosity, but also to look up relatives and in many cases to find work and resettle in Armenia. On telling this to our American colleague in Moscow, he said there was also a continual stream of Armenians wishing to emigrate to the States.

Echmiadzin

'Armenia' took us on a morning tour of Yerevan. We visited the historical museum, where we found a large wall map of the world on which were clearly indicated the centres of Armenian population, however small, and we were told that a lively correspondence was kept up between the mother country and those wildly scattered communities.

The Matenadaran library was another port of call. It houses the largest collection of Armenian manuscripts, some of them extremely ancient, amongst them the 'Echmiadzin Gospels', a source of enormous interest to scholars of early Christianity.

'Armenia' told us that an appointment had been made for my husband to pay a courtesy visit to His Holiness the

Catholicos, the head cleric of the Armenian church, that afternoon. My husband had asked for such an appointment months earlier from the Ministry of Foreign Affairs in Moscow. So that first afternoon in Yerevan, we motored to Echmiadzin, some 18 kilometres west, but as at Tshaltuba three days earlier, found we were totally unexpected. Never mind, in due course we were ushered into his presence.

Echmiadzin has been the centre of Armenian Christianity from earliest times. It has a number of very ancient churches. The Catholicos lived in a large magnificently furnished palace in the grounds of the cathedral close with a well-stocked vegetable and fruit garden.

We found we were not the only people seeking an audience that afternoon. When we were finally ushered into His Holiness's presence we found two Armenians accompanied by a priest in the audience chamber. One was Italian, the other Lebanese. We were all introduced to each other and then sat down. The Catholicos was an impressive-looking man in his fifties with brushed back greying hair. He was wearing a very smart grey cassock with a beautifully worked silver cross dangling from a chain on his bosom. He sat behind a desk with a fine cream-coloured rug hanging on the wall behind him. It had the Armenian cross worked in colours in the centre with a border of mythical animals round its edge. My husband was invited to sit at the side of the desk, whilst the rest of us sat on either side of an oblong table placed in front of the desk.

The Catholicos spoke fluent French and explained that his English was not very good. Poor 'Armenia', who had insisted on accompanying us into the presence, knew not a word of French. However, no sparkling conversation ensued. His Holiness introduced no subjects and tended to answer only in monosyllables the various topics my husband attempted to raise, from the Lambeth conference in London two years previously, which the Catholicos had attended, to the

Echmiadzin Gospels we had seen in the library that morning, and to our projected visit the following day to Gekhard where there was a complex of old cave churches hewn out of the rocks. We had been told that the morrow was a special Sunday which we would find very interesting. No special comments from His Holiness, so after fifteen minutes with smiles and bows, we withdrew.

Before going into the precincts of the cathedral, we had a quick walk around the well-tended garden. A large area was planted up with rows of different varieties of grapes, Muscat amongst them, with their names clearly written on labels.

We found the old church very interesting and well kept. What we did not appreciate was very loud potted music over a loud speaker, both inside and outside the church. This was in accompaniment to some small service that was taking place in one of the chapels. What interested us in the precincts was a little group of father, mother, two children and a sheep walking solemnly round and round the church. Armenia explained to us that the following day, a Sunday, was some special feast day, and that it was customary amongst the devout if they had some special request to make to the Almighty, or as thanks offering for the granting of some wish, to sacrifice a sheep. The poor animal is processed three times round the church, then has an ear nicked and the sign of the cross is made on the forehead of those making the sacrifice. He is then led away just outside the precincts and slaughtered and the meat is distributed to any passers-by.

We had occasion to see several sacrificial sheep the next day when we went to visit Gekhard, at the end of an impressive gorge in the mountains east of Yerevan. As we rounded the last bend in the road, a most astonishing sight greeted our eyes. There were innumerable picnic parties, Persian style, complete with carpet and table cloth and a tremendous spread of foods and bottles of drink, on every available flat piece of ground. Close to each little group was a barbecue, and a tripod with a huge cauldron dangling over the fire. A tremendous smell of shashlik pervaded the air, and everyone seemed to be having a very merry time. Instruments were twanged, and a dance, akin to an eightsome reel, was being danced by one very gay party. It was all very Persian and very colourful indeed.

Cars and lorries blocked the road beyond this picnic party, but we passed many more as we wended our way on foot for the next 200–300 yards to the main church, leaving Triatsin to find somewhere to park.

Gekhard is a monastery but its complex is most curious. There is a main and very fine early-twelfth-century church with a wealth of intricate carved stone decoration, but attached to this church are three further ones directly hewn out of the rock face. They are not just caves but complete little churches with elaborate doorways and pillars and an altar all carved out of the rock. Entering the main church, one could barely distinguish anything. We had come from bright sunlight into deep gloom. Gradually one's vision adjusted, helped by the light of candles placed around and about, even in niches carved out of the stone high up on walls and pillars. It was extremely crowded inside and we were immediately aware of much noise, in particular of screaming babies. We made our way towards this hullabaloo and found ourselves in the sanctuary where there was a large font. Babies were being baptised. Completely naked, they were held by an elderly priest with a large white beard and straggly hair. He dipped them, immersing them completely in very murky-looking water before handing them back to their parents. Now they were struggled back into their clothes. No wonder they wailed so vociferously. Father, mother, granny, brothers, sisters, godparents, uncle and aunts—a whole cohort of relatives assisted each baptism. We moved on to view the three rock churches. Finally we were once again in the little courtyard outside the entrance to the main church, but we were still within the precincts and I was slightly appalled to see the 'sacrificial' butcher in operation. I hurried hastily by and watched instead the local photographer dressing up a handsome young Armenian in a traditional costume of a mountain warrior, with bandoliers, pistols and embroidered slots for his bullets. With a fine great sheepskin hat on his head, he then struck a theatrical attitude and click went the camera. There was quite a queue of people waiting for their turn.

Further on there was a very large and gay picnic party having their feast right up against the wall of the church. As we walked by they warmly invited us to come and join them. We encouraged Simon to do so, ourselves rather pusillanimously retreating with much bowing and smiling. Simon had to gobble down some unknown bit of sheep from the vast cauldron sandwiched between a folded bit of typical Persian bread. Washing this down gratefully with a large tumbler full of sticky sweet wine, he then beat a hasty retreat, but not before he was given yet more sheep enfolded in bread and wrapped for good measure in a sheet of Pravda. This was meant to be for us! We thought it would be fun to see our Russian chauffeur Triatsin's reaction if Simon gave it to him. However, luckily for him, as we made our way back to our car, we passed an old beggar woman, and I hope Simon gained merit by being able to hand over the Pravda sacrificial parcel into her grateful hands. Triatsin had turned the car and we soon found a spot for our own picnic.

Our third and last day in Yerevan was a Monday and we had planned to visit a seventh-century fortress, perched up on a promontory, high up in the massif of mountains north-west of Yerevan. But first of all my husband was to pay a courtesy visit to the Minister of Foreign Affairs. When the Minister heard of our intention to sightsee Amberd fortress he said, 'In that case you must visit the Byurakan observatory,' and he immediately asked his secretary to put a phone call through to the observatory to see if it would be convenient for us to call in. The answer came back that the director would be delighted to receive us and show us around his observatory.

Byurakan is the ultimate village on the road to Amberd fortress, which is some 10 kilometres beyond. Byurakan lies high on the mountain slope of Mount Aragata, only slightly less high than Mount Ararat. We ourselves were not all that enthusiastic about visiting the observatory, but after our visit we were delighted to have had this opportunity to do so. It was not only extremely interesting but also very instructive and Mr Mirzoan, its director, was charming and very lucid in explaining and showing us his immense astro-physical telescope for studying the structure and matter of stars. He then offered us the sweetest and most delicious peaches I have ever eaten. 'Sunshine is the answer to the sweetness of fruit—they absorb it throughout the day and lose some of it during the hours of darkness. So they are at their very best in the evening. This part of Armenia is amongst the sunniest in the world. We are also blessed with plenty of rain,' explained the director.

After this visit we continued up the road to where it came to a full stop. A five-mile walk now lay ahead of us. We followed a rough track which at a certain point divided. We took the wrong one. No signpost visible. Our track took us to the edge of a ravine. The fortress was on the far side. It was now 4 p.m. and it would have taken a good hour to clamber down the gorge and up the other side. So we never reached Amberd fortress. But we had a splendid view of it and on turning round the whole of Armenia seemed to be at our feet, with Mount Ararat majestic and splendid in the background.

Next day, back to Tbilisi and Georgia.

Georgia, Autumn 1967

Following our three interesting and enjoyable days in Armenia, we now spent five days in Georgia, the first two non-stop breathless days based in Tbilisi, followed by three days in Passanaouri, a village up the Georgian military highway, in the Caucasus. Back in Tbilisi we were now VIPs, not just trippers taking a week's holiday away from Moscow life, as we were nineteen years earlier, and so for these two days, Georgian hospitality was lavished upon us.

At 9.45 on our first morning, the Deputy Minister for Foreign Affairs, who doubled as Professor of History at the university, picked us up in a Ministry car and took us to call on the Minister himself, who gave us a short discourse on Georgian economy which included the fact that Georgia had been given the task of providing 95 per cent of the tea for the whole of the USSR. Later in the afternoon we visited a tea plantation where we were shown a leaf-picking machine, invented by Georgian engineers and now exported to other tea-growing areas of the world.

After this visit we went to call on the Prime Minister, a jovial gentleman who had been in London earlier in the year as a member of the Soviet delegation led by Kosygin, and had met GWH there and greeted him now like an old buddy.

He received us in a vast great palace—marble staircase, columns, vaulted ceilings—built since we were there nineteen years earlier. He offered us a green fizzy drink tasting like cough medicine.

After that the professor took charge, whisking us off at dangerous speed in the Prime Ministerial car to Mtscheta. Following are extracts from the letter which I wrote to my mother about our whole trip:

Mtscheta was the first capital of Georgia, about 25 km away up the river that runs through Tiflis. It is surrounded by mountains. We first visited the splendid 11th century cathedral here and found the bishop in splendid cope and richly decorated orthodox onion shaped hat taking a small service—lots of incense. Don't quite know why there was a service. There seemed to be no locals present—just a busload of mixed jovial Georgians & Russians apparently just sightseeing, like ourselves. Anyway the service presently came to an end and we were able to look around—wonderful carving on tombs on the floor—all Georgian Kings were buried here. The church stands on a green sward surrounded by an old mediaeval wall. When we came out a photographer insisted on taking group photos of ourselves together with this busload of cheerful trippers—I think he probably belonged to them.

After that we were taken to a local restaurant newly built in 'old fashioned' style supposed to imitate an old Georgian peasant house, with a domed ceiling built rather as you would roof a house of playing cards; one card overlapping the other all the way round till there is only a round hole left in the centre. Here the overlapping tiles were planks of wood and the centre was glassed over. We sat on low wooden stools around a wooden table and the cooking was done in one corner—we had an excellent Georgian meal—all sorts of the usual hors d'oeuvres: cold little cutlets of suckling pig; kidney beans in some savoury sauce; sliced tomatoes and raw onion peppered with a herb out of which our fizzy lemonade tasting like cough medicine had been made, also slabs of cheese. This was followed by shashlik covered by unsweetened gooseberry jam, which surprisingly went very well with it—all washed down by a local wine which was drawn from great barrels along one wall of the room. In Georgia you may only drink when the host proposes a toast—you can't just sip when you like. I was sternly reprimanded by our host, who explained the Georgian custom, when I started sipping my wine. You can *propose a toast but first ask permission from the host. Naturally toasts are legion—we drank one to you and any other parents of those round the table.*

After the meal we all staggered out into the sunshine feeling decidedly tipsy and our host said in French, 'I am sure we all want to visit the toilet, follow me.' So we all followed, winding our way towards an obvious hut. After that, a visit to another 11th century church with a tiny little 4th century chapel in the grounds and then a drive up to an old church perched high up on top of a crag overlooking Mtscheta. We had a wonderful view from here of wild mountain country—but the big peaks have not shown themselves since we've been here. Then back to Tiflis [Tbilisi], first to visit a tea plantation area where we were shown the leaf-picking machine then on to a 'palace of weddings' where we assisted at a wedding—much less ceremonial than in Moscow and to the accompaniment of dreadful raucous music. Then a drive all around an entirely new part of Tiflis—very nice indeed, followed by a short ride in the new metro, a quick visit to two museums where we had no time to look and appreciate anything. Onwards, to a tour of a champagne factory where 7 varieties of champagne are produced, one of them pink. We sampled 5 of them! Finally, back to the hotel for an hour's welcome, wash and brush-up before going to the opera where the Foreign Secretary joined us. It was a Georgian comic operetta, reminiscent of Strauss and Rossini, called Koto and Koti. It was great fun with some splendid Georgian dancing. At last, back to the hotel and bed, utterly exhausted!

After breakfast on the following morning one of our young local guides who rejoiced in the name of 'Hamlet' (his father having been an actor) took us to the local market, where we were very impressed by the variety and quality of both vegetables and fruit. We stocked up on fruit for our forthcoming three days in the Caucasus mountains.

After this we motored some 8 kilometres west of Tbilisi to the central administrative offices of not only the wine industry but also of a number of farms devoted to the growing of fruit and vegetables for the local market in Tbilisi which we had just visited. After a brief tour of the vineyards and one farm, the director of the whole complex gave us a short and interesting talk about the aims and economics of it all. By now it was almost 2 p.m. and we were very ready to be entertained by the Prime Minister himself who had driven out for this purpose.

For the next three hours we feasted and toasted each other again as on the previous day. Our menu consisted of a series of tasty little dishes, some delicious cutlets of suckling pig amongst others. It was all very convivial but I found it exhausting. Simon missed the 'satisfying centrepiece of a substantial main course', a remark he makes in his report of our entire trip, which amused us. Simon, a generation younger than ourselves, obviously required more sustenance. Finally, back to Tbilisi for a visit to the 'House of Tea' and we sipped Georgian tea. A quick brush-up at our hotel and off to the circus for the evening.

After these two hectic days we looked forward to three days in the mountains. Sadly we would not be able to drive right through the mountains as storms had brought rock falls which closed the Georgian military highway for some three miles, so new plans had to be made.

The next day I wrote the following:

We are now in Passanaouri—a little village on the Georgian military highway—the road across the Caucasus. We are staying in quite the most civilised hotel since Istanbul! It is new—small, slightly different in design from the usual Soviet hotel—but above all it is SPOTLESS—and much

GEORGIA, AUTUMN 1967

cosier—and the bathroom works from A–Z—and well finished off. Such a surprise—so we think Passanaouri very cute—actually scenically it is also rather attractive— about 2 hours drive from Tbilisi—so after clocking in, and as it was a gorgeous day, we drove on up the road and had a lovely picnic right up near the pass on a green alpine meadow with bushes of wild azalea which had turned glorious shades of red. All the mountains visible. After picnic, drove across pass to Kasbek—down in the valley, and at the foot of the 2nd highest peak of the Caucasus, Mt Kasbek—quite clear. We had a lovely walk.

After a good night's rest in this nice alpine hotel, a second glorious day tramping around the mountains. Marvellous autumn colouring of trees and azalea clumps and the delicious smell of hay-making in alpine pastures (late crop?) and where the scythes had not yet reached we were thrilled to see masses of blue gentians. In early summer, the wild flowers must be wonderful up here. The air was delicious, crisp, sweet-smelling but the sun was very burning. Only the cow bells of Austria and Switzerland were missing.

The next day it was back to Tbilisi to drop my husband off at the airport, for him to catch a plane back to Moscow, and for Simon and me to drive to Rostov-on-Don around the flanks of the Caucasus. To have driven from Tbilisi all the way back to Moscow would have been too far for Triatsin to do solo. So Simon was to share the driving with him as far as Rostov and the rule was no member of the embassy must travel anywhere in the Soviet Union on their own—hence my doing this drive to Rostov-on-Don. Simon drove the first part. I was pleased about this for we had found that Triatsin was not very good at mountain roads. He had not had any experience of them until this trip. He relied entirely on his brakes on downhill stretches, however steep. In fact, at an early stage after leaving Passanaouri on our drive back to Tbilisi, my husband asked Simon to take over the driving, as Triatsin's reliance on his brakes was too dangerous.

We spent one night on the way. I wrote of our final day the following in a letter to my mother:

On our last day of motoring, from Krasnador to Rostov, we traversed black earth country. Never have I seen anything like as flat or a road quite so straight. Distances are endless, the cultivated areas are boundless. Every so often there were windbreaks of trees. The landscape seemed empty of all life. The country was all ploughed up except close to Rostov. There had been recent heavy rain and the sides of the road and the occasional country lane were thick with gooey mud. I was glad I did not live in that part of the world.

The Central Asiatic Republic of Uzbekistan, 1966–1994

Both my husband and I were keen to visit the Asiatic republics of the Soviet Union. The legendary cities of Bukhara and Samarkand drew us like a magnet. The imaginations of people have been fascinated over the centuries by the mere mention of these two names. So, in October 1966, together with my husband's private secretary, who would be able to interpret for us, we set off for those central Asian regions. Having spent the best part of five years in Iran prior to our return to Moscow, we were particularly interested in this region, culturally so very close to Iran. Twenty-eight years later, I returned as a mere tourist to the same region. I was a member of the Royal Society for Asian Affairs who organised an eighteen-day tour of Uzbekistan in May 1994. In 1966 we visited the two legendary cities plus an extra one, Khiva, a city I had never heard of. In 1994, these three cities were on our tour, but in addition we spent three days in the lovely Fergana Valley, hemmed in by the Altai mountain range, part of the Pamirs, north of the Hindu Kush.

It was extremely interesting for me to revisit these legendary cities and to note how they had developed through the intervening twenty-eight years. No high-rise buildings in 1966, when Bukhara was an entirely oriental city, almost totally enclosed by a wall. In 1994 only a small part of the wall remained and a veneer of western civilisation had crept in, and it was evident that areas demolished with attendant mess in 1966 had been redeveloped, but obviously further demolition was going on in 1994. However, high-rise buildings did not yet pierce the skyline.

Samarkand was different. It had the aura of a capital city as it nestled in the rich agricultural land, watered by the Amu Darya (Oxus) and its tributaries. Indeed there had been an administrative centre here over the millennia. Nearby to Samarkand were the ruins of Soghdia, a city with close links with Greek civilisation. A contingent of Alexander the Great's army settled here after Alexander had defeated the rebellious tribes who were harassing his army in Persia and whose stronghold was Soghdia. Alexander then marched on to the banks of the Indus to the south east after crossing the Hindu Kush.

The silk road linking China and Europe wended its way through Soghdia in the second century BC but Soghdia was then superseded by Samarkand which now became the chief entrepôt town for the trade which flowed both ways along this famous trade route—the Golden Road. The Mongol invasion took place in the thirteenth and fourteenth centuries, with first Genghis Khan and then Tamerlane, who both destroyed all before them as they headed relentlessly ever westwards with their hordes. But Tamerlane was born in the smiling Zervashan Valley, in a town a little to the east of Samarkand, and he never lost his love of the area. On his return from the shores of the Mediterranean he temporarily laid down his arms and settled in Samarkand, making it his capital, and it now became a great cultural centre.

Ulug Beg, his son, became a learned scholar rather than a warrior like his father. His special interest was astronomy. The first of the three great mosques-cum-madrasses, which form what is known as the Registan, was built by him and bears his name. The other two, also mosques/madrasses, were built in the course of the next century and a further number of madrassehs were built. Tamerlane himself had a vast mosque built, the Bibi Khanum, in memory of his favourite wife. It is thought it was built in too much of a hurry and with too large a dome. In 1966 restoration was in progress and was still in progress twenty-eight years later, but it still gave the impression of a propped-up ruin.

Bukhara had been utterly devastated by the two Mongol invasions. It had already been a great centre of learning for several centuries, even before the Arabs had brought Islam to it. In the fourteenth, fifteenth and sixteenth centuries, as in Samarkand, mosques/madrassehs were built, and learning was revived.

The Russians in Central Asia

During the nineteenth century the Russians were aware that Britain, France, the Dutch and the Portuguese all had overseas colonies in Asia and in Africa, which greatly enriched their economies, and decided that the time had come for them too to expand. The Asian territories beyond the Volga and the Caspian Sea were an obvious area for this purpose. As the century progressed, region by region of central Asia fell under Russian rule.

The Khanates of Bukhara and Khiva became vassal states. The emir of the first and the khan of the second were finally swept away in the Russian revolution of 1917.

THE CENTRAL ASIATIC REPUBLIC OF UZBEKISTAN, 1966–1994

When the Russians conquered Samarkand, it became their southern administrative centre and capital with a strong military presence. However, the centre of the town, with its mosques, madrassehs, mausoleums and markets, was not in any way disturbed by the pre-revolutionary Russians—they were perfectly tolerant of Islam. A cantonment for their troops was built on the fringe of the old town and soon this area took on the aspect of a Russian provincial town with typical well-proportioned whitewashed houses along tree-lined avenues for the many Russians with commercial and business interests who now came to Samarkand. This historic city now took on a new lease of life for, since trade along the Silk Road had dried up some three to four centuries earlier, it had fallen into serious and sad neglect.

In Bukhara, where the Emir had complete despotic jurisdiction over its citizens, the Russians built an army cantonment ten miles to the south of the city, and Bukhara remained oriental, unaffected by any taint of western civilisation.

Samarkand

Samarkand cast its spell on us from the moment we touched down on the morning of 6 October 1966. It was a lovely autumn day and we were full of eagerness and anticipation.

Our hotel was on one of the leafy avenues in the Russian enclave. It was a quiet and peaceful road with hardly any traffic along it. We were given a warm welcome and although our accommodation merited no stars—it was very basic and had a dreadful bathroom (rusty old bath, no plug for the basin) and we were momentarily put out—the friendliness of the restaurant personnel and a good tasty meal ending with some superb local fruit quickly restored our spirits. In the next couple of days we discovered that the restaurant manager was an Armenian who much enjoyed food himself and saw to it that his guests in his restaurant should be given local produce and served with politeness and without an untimely delay. We had never met this kind of service in any other Russian restaurant up to then and indeed we never would again.

We arranged with Brian, my husband's private secretary, that we should gather for an afternoon's sightseeing in half an hour's time, and he was to make the necessary arrangements with the Intourist guide.

When the time came for our outing, there was no Brian. Where was he? 'Oh, he went out for a little walk, he should be back now.' We waited some ten minutes and then decided to set off on our own with the guide. On our return some three hours later, there was Brian in the hotel lobby looking rather sheepish. It appears he had been arrested and marched off to militia headquarters for taking a photograph of a donkey with a beturbaned Usbeki aloft. 'How picturesque,' thought Brian. Hardly had he taken his snap, than two young militiamen wrenched the camera out of his hands and marched him off to the militia station. The young militia men, eager to impress their superiors, thought they had caught a spy red-handed, for behind the donkey there was an army barrack and they could not believe that anyone should bother to take a photo of a donkey without having a sinister ulterior motive. Luckily Brian had both his passport and his Russian identity card in his pocket, so after having the almost-new film confiscated and being given a cautionary reprimand on the iniquities of spying, he was allowed to go free.

On our group tour in May 1994 we spent four nights in Samarkand. One glorious morning, our bus took us up to the top of the pass of the mountain ridge which forms the backdrop to Samarkand. From here a wonderful panoramic view was spread out before our eyes; from the distant Pamirs way east to the outposts of the Hindu Kush across a wide fertile valley to the south and to the south-west were the mountain ridges which separated us from Afghanistan.

We stretched our legs on an hour's lovely walk along our ridge. The ground was carpeted with wild flowers, the air was fresh and invigorating and I was strongly reminded of Iran. We all wished we could have spent the entire day up here with a picnic lunch. Two museum visits had been arranged for the afternoon with invited experts to explain the exhibits to us, however, so back to our hotel in Samarkand for lunch.

Shakhrisabz

The whole of the following day was spent visiting Shakhrisabz, Tamerlane's birthplace. It was a long and tiring drive, for our road took us around a rather arid rocky landscape similar to the mountain ridge we had walked along the previous morning. In Tamerlane's day, the distance would have been halved as he would have ridden on horseback over the ridge and down into the green bowl where Shakhrisabz nestled.

The impression left with me of Shakhrisabz was of a green city with avenues with double rows of trees planted along channels of water and with many rose beds, the flowers scenting the air, a feature we had encountered in the cities of the Fergana Valley.

We had come to see the ruins of the vast palace Tamerlane had ordered to be built here. It was not yet completed twenty-three years later when Tamerlane died, and all that remains of the palace now is an immense high entrance arch, considerably restored, but this does have wonderful coloured mosaic tiling enhanced with gold-leaf decoration high up in the arch itself—'out of reach of robbers,' volunteered Inez, our guide. The ruins of this vast palace were on a par with the ruins of the Bibi Kharum mosque in Samarkand which Tamerlane erected (also unfinished) in memory of his beloved wife. The pair are good examples of what the French would term 'folie de la grandeur'. Sadly on this outing, the day was so very hot and sultry, so different from its predecessor, that I at least found it very tiring. The following morning it was pouring with rain.

Sightseeing in Samarkand and sightseeing in Isfahan in Iran are very rewarding experiences. The colour blue springs to mind immediately: blue domes, blue ceramic sheen on expanses of mosaic tiling on walls—this all standing out against a dun background, and over all a blue sky.

As Tamerlane swept though Persia with his hordes, he was presumably struck with appreciation of the buildings he saw. He sent architects, artisans and artists of all sorts back to Samarkand, for the idea of eventually settling there must already have germinated in his mind. It is therefore not surprising to find a channel of Persian culture running from Persia into what is today the southern rim of Uzbekistan.

Three pictures are forever stored in a cubbyhole of my mind as I switch on the relevant button of memory. These are: the interior of the Lutfullah mosque on the Great Maidan of Isfahan; the Gur Emir mausoleum of Tamerlane in Samarkand—the whole of its exterior, but specifically the interior; and finally, the pristine white marble mausoleum, known as the Taj Mahal in India. All three perfect in their proportions, their simplicity and their beauty.

We did not visit the Gur Emir on that first afternoon of sightseeing, in 1966 as it is some way away from the centre of the city, but the next day when we did, I was tremendously struck by its beauty. To my delight, twenty-four years later when visiting the region, our twelve-storey-high hotel was a mere five minutes' walk away. I delighted visiting it on each of the three out of four early mornings that our tour spent in Samarkand and the light was perfect before breakfast. Then there was the tour visit to it with the guide. On our last morning, to everyone's surprise, it was pouring with rain, which did not desist on our bus trip back to Tashkent, so no visit that last morning to the Gur Emir, but a brief stopover to visit Ulug Beg's observatory on our road.

On our last afternoon in Samarkand in 1966, our guide drove us some twenty minutes out from the centre of the city to a small rocky hill out in the desert. Here, under an archway, steps led down, down, down into a cavern below. Our guide told us how, with a huge sextant and an astrolabe mounted on rails beside it, Ulug Beg had plotted the entire solar system and discovered over 1,000 stars with amazing precision. Telescopes did not yet exist in his day. A copy of his *Catalogue of the Stars* was discovered in 1648 in Oxford's Bodleian Library, but the whereabouts of his observatory was only unearthed in 1908 by a Russian amateur archaeologist/one-time army officer. Our guide invited us to plunge down the steps to view a portion of the arc of the vast sextant, built so far down in its rocky cavern to minimise the shock of earthquakes. The upper portion had protruded above the ground and a two-storey observatory had stood at this spot. I refused to go down, but my husband did and found it interesting. The story of Ulug Beg has put him on a par with Copernicus and Galileo.

Twenty-eight years later a small museum had been built here with appropriate photos and explanations. Our tour that year (1994) spent a bare fifteen minutes here on our way back to Tashkent from Samarkand—and it poured with rain!

A visit to a Kolkhoz (a collective farm) on the outskirts of Samarkand was also inserted into our itinerary in 1966. The Kolkhoz was very large and included both dairy and agricultural sections, but no cotton was grown here. There was, however, a section devoted to the growing of grapes. It was now October and the grapes had all been harvested and the plants pruned. We watched trenches being dug along the rows and it was explained that the plants would be bent over into the trenches, then buried under lots of earth, this to protect them from the often very severe winter frosts and snow caked into blocks of ice. We had never heard of this procedure elsewhere. About 1,200 families worked the farm. They lived largely in separate cottages. We found this visit interesting and impressive and we liked the director who entertained us in his office before showing us around.

Now, on to Bukhara.

Bukhara

Bukhara was enveloped in a dust storm during the two days we spent there in 1966, so whereas Samarkand had given us the impression of a smiling, colourful and engaging city, Bukhara wafted an impression of doom, dust and death.

Our hotel, with dreadful accommodation and food and with surly personnel, was in the old city by a site of demolition, the dust of which mingled with the stinging sand of the Turkestan deserts It was not far from the Ark (palace, fortress, centre of government in the Emir's days) and the infamous deep pit at the bottom of which our countrymen Connolly and Stoddart struggled to survive amongst nasty creepy crawlies until they were executed and buried in front of the Ark nearby—a horrible event which took place in 1842. The two famous great mosques, one of them a madrasseh and actually still working as such, were a short walk away. They face each other with great entrance portals, all tiled. But the swirling dust was such that their colouring and the turquoise blue of the domes of the mosques did not stand out at all. Close by the Kalgan mosque stands the 43-metre-high brick minaret. The Emir's prisoners would be made to climb the many steps up to the top in order to be pushed over the parapet to their death. This minaret dates back to the eleventh century and Tamerlane spared it on his conquering drive through Bukhara for he so admired the fantastic bands of intricate patterned brickwork fashioned out of small bricks and alternating with bands of kufic

THE CENTRAL ASIATIC REPUBLIC OF UZBEKISTAN, 1966–1994

writing, picked out in similar small bricks. But for us, the swirling dust was too much to linger and admire anything. It was not until twenty-four years later that I was able to admire and enjoy my sightseeing in Bukhara. And then in 1994 our group did marvel, as Tamerlane did, as we stood at the foot of this minaret, at how artisans could have put together this wonderful patterned brickwork up and up and up. On this occasion we also visited a tenth-century mausoleum which had been buried by sandstorms over the centuries and only discovered in 1930 by the Russians as they laid out a park by an adjoining spring and pool. We had only driven past it in 1966, but now we stopped and admired the similar intricate brickwork as in the minaret and I was able to recall to members of our group who had been to Isfahan, how in the most ancient part of the oldest mosque in that city, the Friday mosque, very similar brickwork can be admired and that too is of the tenth century. So there was an obvious link between the two cities.

Bukhara is an oasis city, watered by the Zeravshan River, like Samarkand, but there are also a number of springs here and pools had formed around them, but these became the source of much disease for which Bukhara, for all its learning, became notorious. When the Russians conquered Bukhara in the nineteenth century they drained most of the pools and saw to it that the drinking water for the inhabitants should be clean and safe. Adjacent to the once-buried mausoleum is a small museum, with photos and diagrams of the nasty worms which had infested the pool and showing what they did to the human inside—I spent no time looking at these!

At the end of a hot and exhausting morning of sightseeing in 1994 around the minaret and the mosques, our group were led to a café beside the Lyab-y-khauz, a large pool in the centre of the old city. Here we sat and sipped green tea or a cool fizzy drink akin to Coca-Cola. Our café companions were a number of elderly, bearded and beturbaned Uzbekis in local Uzbeki dress and we all watched with amusement a number of young boys, who with shrieks and loud splashes, jumped into the muddy-looking pool from the overhanging branches of a mulberry tree. We sat back in our chairs and enjoyed the spectacle and our interval of relaxation.

Later we visited the summer palace of the emirs. It was an airy building of the early nineteenth century with high-ceilinged rooms with walls painted with flower pictures on a background of light colours. There was much coloured glass which helped to diffuse the strong light from the outdoors. The palace was situated in a tree-shaded garden and must have been an agreeable haven away from the heat of the city.

On one of our afternoons in 1994 we also enjoyed an Uzbeki dress show. We were taken to a house with a long room which had a raised platform along one side and pretty girls paraded down it dressed in old traditional Uzbeki dress—very colourful. The director of the show then asked if there were any men in our group who would be prepared to don Uzbeki male costume and parade for us. Two of our men volunteered. Colourful cotton materials were used for men's clothing, but the ladies had wispy silks as well as wispy cottons, all very attractive.

I then remembered that on our first visit to Bukhara, my husband and I were taken to a cotton-growing area on the outskirts of the city. It was our last morning in the region, the dust storm had abated and we were on our way to Samarkand to catch a plane that afternoon for a one-night stopover in Tashkent, before flying on the morrow to Urgench, from where we would sightsee Khiva.

Cotton picking was in full swing, for it was the month of October—harvest time. A cotton picking-cum-baler was busy moving slowly up and down the rows of bushes and deftly plucking what looked like blobs of dirty cotton wool from the bushes and feeding these to the baling machine. Many of

THE CENTRAL ASIATIC REPUBLIC OF UZBEKISTAN, 1966–1994

Bukhara's inhabitants were busily loading lorries with these bales, which would take them to a factory to be processed and spun.

The economy of Uzbekistan is based on its vast gas reserves and its cotton industry. In the second half of the twentieth century, ever greater areas of the country were brought into the production of cotton. This meant ever more water being diverted from both the Amu Darya (Oxus) and the Sin Darya in the north, which meant the gradual shrinking of the Aral Sea and the gradual killing off of the once-thriving fishing industry there.

Khiva

The third city on our itinerary to Uzbekistan in 1966 was Khiva. To visit this city we flew from Tashkent to Urgench—a charmless town, hot, airless and totally unwelcoming. Having dumped our suitcases in a hotel on a par with the one we had encountered in Bukhara, we drove the 28 kilometres to Khiva and parked our car outside the mud-brick city walls and walked through the great mud brick portal into fairyland—for that is what Khiva is—a city straight from the 1001 Arabian Nights. Once upon a time it had been the last oasis stopover for the caravans on the northern silk route from China to Europe, but once the secret of silk production (a tiddly wee worm, a cocoon and quantities of mulberry leaves) was discovered, first by the Venetians, then by the Spaniards and French, the trade in silk along the caravan routes fizzled out. Khiva, however, became a great market for the slave trade, Russian slaves working for Asian masters, Asian slaves working for Russians. This trade, which had greatly enriched the Khans, was finally put an end to by the Russians in the nineteenth century. From now on and gradually over the decades, Khiva became irrelevant. The neighbouring desert town, Urgench, with its modern Russian industry, superseded it, and the citizens of Khiva increasingly found their livelihood there. Khiva had been largely rebuilt by the ruling Khan in the first decades of the nineteenth century. There had been great rivalry between the three cities of Bukhara, Khiva and Kokand in the Fergana Valley. Finally, at the turn of the nineteenth century, the Khan of Khiva managed to wrest his territory away from Bukharan rule. He now rebuilt his city, sat back and thereafter lived a life of hedonistic pleasure within the framework of Islam. Khiva has no great monuments of antiquity and has left no legacy of learning and wisdom, so perhaps it is not so surprising that I had never heard of it before our visit in 1966. Khiva is the complete prototype of a Moslem city, with mosques, madrassehs, minarets, an ark (palace, fortress, dungeon), a further luxurious palace, a caravanserai and a central square with a drinking trough for animals. The Second World War never touched it. So the Russians decided to make it into a museum city and that is how we found it in 1966, though it was not officially designated as such until two years later.

We found Khiva a quite extraordinary experience. It is a little gem of an Asiatic Moslem city, entirely enclosed within its mud-brick walls, and in 1966 completely empty; no one there, or so we thought. Brian was just ahead of us and had turned the corner of our narrow street when he suddenly rushed back to us exclaiming, 'I've met a camel!' We turned the corner and lo and behold there indeed was a camel being led by a man. The pair appeared to be the only living creatures in this city. How very strange. It was difficult not to believe that Khiva was just a dream. Our guide led us to the Khan's palace and in the very centre was his harem, just as replicated on the stage of the Bolshoi in the lovely ballet of *Bakchisarai Fontan*.

My recollection of both visits (for our group in 1994 also spent a day here) is of a courtyard with an arcaded balcony all down one side and the predominant colour was blue: blue sky above blue-tiled walls, blue-tiled floor and blue fountain splashing in the middle and a host of little doors opening onto the courtyard, at ground level and along the balcony above. My imagination peoples it on both occasions with beautifully elegant ladies, children of all ages and pretty maidens in diaphanous clothes, all tripping around, whilst their lord and master sat back comfortably in his chair, smoking his hubble-bubble as he surveyed the scene and decided which of these lovely ladies or maidens should be his companion for the night. His quarters were on the opposite side of the courtyard.

In complete contrast, in 1994 Khiva was alive with people, for it was Veterans' Day, celebrated both in the Soviet era and evidently after as well. It was a public holiday and the veterans of the war donned their best clothes, pinned on their medals, and with their families celebrated their survival with a happy day in Khiva. Amongst them were two wedding groups, the ladies all dressed in their white wedding finery and accompanied with music, while their friends and relatives were parading through the streets, visiting the various mosques and crossing the square every so often. It was a very gay and colourful scene. What a contrast to silent Khiva with its one man and a camel!

We all enjoyed our visit to Khiva, but there was more enjoyment to come, for a romantic member of our group, Hugh Leach, had suggested to our two guides, Inez, who was with us throughout the tour, and young, pretty little Svetlana, our guide for Khiva, that instead of returning directly to Urgench at the end of our day in Khiva, maybe we could visit the banks of the Oxus, some 10 miles north east of Urgench at the spot where the great duel between Rustam and Sohrab had taken place; moreover it was a beautiful day and we could expect a lovely sunset. Our guides agreed it would be possible. This suggestion was put to our group and we all concurred with enthusiasm.

The legendary story of Rustam and Sohrab is one of the great epics of Persian literature as recounted in the poem by their renowned poet Ferdussi. Mathew Arnold has retold the story in his great narrative poem entitled 'Rustam and Sohrab'. They were the foremost generals of the two opposing armies, Persian and Tartar, encamped on either bank of the Oxus river. Rather than a great clash of arms between the two armies it was agreed that a duel should be fought between two chosen warriors. Rustam and Sohrab were chosen. They were father and son, but this relationship was unknown to them until Sohrab's dying moment. A lucky thrust of Rustam's spear pierced Sohrab's heart. It was a very moving story.

It was a memorable expedition. We walked across an 800-metre-long pontoon bridge stretched across the many channels and sand bars of the Oxus river as it slowly wended its sluggish way the last few kilometres to the Aral Sea. It had long since lost its verve as so much of its water had been siphoned off for cotton growing. The Pamir mountains, where it had its turbulent birth, were a long way away.

The horizon was immense, the sun was low in the sky and slowly sinking ever lower, its flowing light reflected off the ripples of the water and sand bars of the river. Many people, like ourselves, were crossing this pontoon bridge. But they hurried past us, smiling and waving their hands in greeting. They were making for home, while we walked in a more leisurely way, savouring the moment. When we reached the far side, Hugh pulled out his bugle and sounded the sunset call (the Retreat). He then suggested that on our walk back across the bridge we stop halfway. We wondered why? Here, he pulled out his copy of the *Golden Treasury* and handed it to Svetlana, open at the relevant page. She had asked to read the passage, for she had studied the poem at school. She began to read but was so overcome by her emotions that Hugh had to finish the reading. It was very romantic and the sky had turned from gold to orange and vermillion, the outer edges into the softer shades of the rainbow. It was a truly magnificent sunset. So ended my visits to Khiva.

The Fergana Valley

Besides the three cities on the tourist trail, Samarkand, Bukhara and Khiva, a two-and-a-half-day trip into the Fergana Valley was added to the tour—very enjoyable but for the three flights in small Uzbeki planes which it involved. Our group all decided that the Uzbeki attitude to flying was dangerously casual. On our flight to Fergana, it was impossible to tighten seatbelts. Three of us could easily have been accommodated within one belt at its tightest. One wondered what the belts were for? On our second flight from Fergana to Urgench, we lacked a sufficiency of fuel and only just made it to Samarkand. After an unscheduled lunch here, we took off in a replacement plane in which unfastened packages, including a hamper with live chickens, were just dumped on the floor, and when three young boys made their way into the cockpit, the alarm bells within our own heads rang—for only a few months previously a fatal accident had occurred in Siberia when young lads had gone into the cockpit. Our boys were greeted with cheers and hand claps and relieved laughter when they re-emerged into our cabin. They looked most surprised at this greeting.

We spent three nights in Fergana and visited the other two cities of the valley from here—Namenjan and Kokand. My memory of all three is of attractive green cities with streets lined with plane, chestnut and mulberry trees, channels of water and many rose beds and with no evidence of modern high-rise buildings. Apart from a scramble over an arid cliff top dominating the Sir Darja (like the Amu Darya Oxus) rising in the Pamir mountains and debouching into the Aral Sea, the scramble was for eager members of our group to pick up shards of pottery, the detritus of an ancient town destroyed by an earthquake centuries earlier. We were led by one of our members, Professor J. Carswell, an enthusiastic archaeologist and expert on china and earthenware. My more vivid memory is of storks peering down on us from high up as we passed. They were sitting on their nests precariously built at the top of telephone posts on the road leading into Namenjan. A delightful mid-morning break was spent sitting under a mulberry tree in the courtyard of a small working madrasseh and sipping green tea, dangling our legs from our perch on top of tahkts (table-cum-bed), a piece of furniture found from Iran and on throughout central Asia in all Tchaekhanes (tea houses), whilst pretty maidens sang and danced for us accompanied by music on local string instruments (a much appreciated interlude to hot sightseeing).

Before this interlude we visited a porcelain workshop. It was divided into separate sections. We were taken to a long airy hall with three long trestle tables and along one side of each sat a line of young women working as a team on one particular production line job. The team I watched were decorating identical small white porcelain bowls. Each girl held a fine paint brush and in front of each was a small pot of single-coloured paint and a small palette. In front of girl number 1 was a tray full of these little white bowls. She took one and delicately painted the sinuous fawn stalk of a flower. She shoved her bowl on to her neighbour. Girl 2 painted two green leaves, girl 3 added four pink petals and girl 4 inserted a blob of gold colour as a centre piece. It was fascinating to watch the speed with which the girls accomplished their allotted task and shoved the bowl on. When the now decorated bowl reached the end of the line, it was placed on a special tray which was then carried away to an adjoining shed for re-firing. I thought then, and still do, that this was a very labour-intensive operation. I presume it kept a large workforce employed and wages would be low.

This workshop produced all manner of porcelain ware—bowls of all sizes, plates and little figurines and grotesques. It was an agreeable centre to work in. The final output was distributed throughout Uzbekistan.

Kokand

Kokand is a centre of silk production. Families around and about are given a small bucket full of wriggly little worms less than half an inch long. These are then spread out on a table in a shed amidst mulberry leaves. When they have chewed up all the leaves and are now one inch long, they are transported to the first of three small rooms, all part of the family home, the members of whom have vacated the rooms for the worm-growing season. The head of the family welcomed us to his home and explained the whole process. The inch-long worms were now smothered in mulberry leaves; *champ, champ, champ*, the worms soon grew to two inches long and were moved to room number 2, with lots more mulberry leaves on top of them. Here they gorged until they could eat no more, so now they moved again. In room number 3 they curled themselves up and began to spin an endless silk thread around and around themselves until they were entirely enclosed in their cocoon. These were now gathered up and taken to the factory to be processed and the family were paid according to the number of cocoons they brought in.

We also imbibed culture by visiting a mosque and the one-time Khan's palace when Kokand was the capital of the province.

BACK TO MOSCOW, 1965–1968

November 1967: Fiftieth Anniversary of the Russian Revolution of 1917

Extract of letter to my mother in Sussex:

It was a great day of celebration in the Soviet Union.
  It has obviously been a wonderfully happy week for the Moscovites. Not only have most of them had a whole week of holiday, which they appreciate as much as anyone, but the weather has been so utterly fantastic. Spring-like sunshine day after day and a cloudless sky. A little touch of frost first thing in the morning, just to give a little crispness to the air, to make everyone feel they are breathing in champagne as well as drinking it. Not for 90 years has there been such a beginning to November. In fact the garden plants are so surprised, that they are all beginning to sprout as though it were spring; poor things. I'm afraid they have another think coming! Anyway it was glorious to have the parade in such weather, and of course it made just all the difference to the 'toiling masses' who had to foregather very early in the morning and march great distances before reaching the Red Square to follow on to the military parade, and wave their banners and flags. Many of them brought accordions and balalaikas, and there was singing and dancing wherever groups stopped and waited before moving on again. I enjoyed the parade very much. It was very colourful. The beginning is always so amusing. There are all the thousands of officers from the three services lined up with their bands on the square, all looking very smart and spick and span, then when all the Big Boys have arrived and taken up their positions on top of Lenin (the Lenin Stalin Mausoleum), two enormously be-tummied generals standing stiffly to attention in their respective field grey, open Ziz cars (like a Cadillac) are driven at a spanking pace at each other,

FIFTIETH ANNIVERSARY OF THE RUSSIAN REVOLUTION

this making them stick out their big tums more than ever to keep balance, and just when one thinks, perhaps it's an optical illusion, that they are going to collide full face into each other, they glide gently past. Then follows lots of barking of orders and presenting of arms and shouting of short staccato 'hurrah, hurrah, hurrah' by all the contingents on the square in turn, then the band plays and one of the generals (I don't know what happens to the second one) joins the 'Boys' up on top of the mausoleum and addresses the armed forces.

This is followed by the national anthem and then the entire square empties itself of all those on parade, to the tunes of rousing marches. After that came a novelty; a historic pageant, with a flashback to the forces of 1917, and all in the uniforms of that period, and I think lots of the men had either grown moustaches especially for the occasion or must have gone round to the theatres and borrowed some and stuck them on. Anyway they looked very handsome and theatrical especially the 'Commissars' in black breeches and long black coats with elaborate frog fastening and huge great furry hats. All this was followed by noisy tanks carrying bigger and better missiles and rockets, but these were all gaily painted and somehow didn't look so sinister. Then came the 'sportsmennies' in bright woolly suits waving red flags and carrying children on their shoulders who at a given moment were lowered on to the ground and then rushed at all our stands with little bunches of carnations done up in cellophane to the accompaniment of much clapping. As we left the Square the toiling masses began marching past, all of them with banners. At four in the afternoon we were bidden to the banquet on the top floor of the newly built great Congress Hall within the Kremlin complex. Three hours of feasting followed by a most spectacular display of fireworks—these we watched from the British Embassy veranda.

BACK TO MOSCOW, 1965–1968

The Kremlin banquet

In previous years it had just been a stand-up affair, but this year we were all specially seated, and like at a Lord Mayor's banquet husbands and wives sat next to each other. We nibbled food intermittently from 4 to ten past 7!!! Russian meals of this kind are curiously unsatisfying, a nibble at this, a nibble of that. Largely meats and birds of different kinds, then hot sturgeon, then hot shashlik, then hot chicken, but never any vegetable or any other accompaniment, and though the last dishes were so-called hot, in fact were very, very lukey. Some people, but not on our side of the table, were offered whole baby cucumbers and whole rather large tomatoes at the start of the meal with all the cold titbits. All through the meal we leapt to our feet in answer to toasts proposed by Brezhnev or Kosygin, or the Minister of Defence and so on. Vodka, brandies, wines and fizzy lemonades adorned the tables. We were 2500 people. As the long meal progressed there was a lot of jumping up and wandering around, as people went to klink glasses with other individuals at other tables, and everyone became jollier and jollier.

We got home just after 7.30, cancelled our supper but asked for soup to be put in a thermos for later on. Then at 9.30, quite a number of Embassy staff, mostly those living in the compound at the back, came in to watch the fireworks from our veranda. There were 50 bangs, and each time salvoes went up all over the town, but mostly concentrated over the Kremlin, and ourselves, just opposite the Kremlin. They had some very pretty fireworks this year, and with all the illuminations it really was quite a sight. But we got showered with large bits rather like halves of coconuts. It really was quite dangerous! Well that's all for today.

1968

The lovely autumn of 1967 was followed by a mild Moscow winter, a great contrast to the previous one, but January and the next three months were stressful for me, for unhappily I sustained a reversed Collis fracture to my right wrist which necessitated my being sent back to London to Bart's Hospital to have it set. The reason for being evacuated to London was that no member of embassy staff was allowed to go into a Russian hospital if it involved having a general anaesthetic—this for security reasons, as the Cold War was very much in evidence, and an unconscious anaesthetised person could, when asked pertinent questions, babble away facts which would be better not divulged to the Soviets. It was a silly accident—on entering our sitting room, I slipped up on Mansion polish spread on the parquet floor. It had not yet been polished in, so I did a ballet pirouette and down I went. I returned to Moscow after five days, my arm in plaster and throbbing painfully and it was not until ten weeks later that I returned to London. The plaster was at last removed, followed by two weeks of daily physiotherapy for my hand. A further month of wax treatment and massage at the Moscow polyclinic for foreigners and at last my fingers were moving once more, but typing newsletters home was now out. I could only scribble brief letters to my mother before my hand felt tired.

Now into 1968 we only had another nine months in Moscow as occupants of the British embassy, for my husband was due to retire at the end of August. Our three-year stint would be over, so once again we would be packing up our bags and finally returning to Great Britain.

I knew that however reluctant I had been to return to Moscow in 1965 for a second term after eighteen years, I would now, come August, leave a little bit of my heart behind, just as I had repeatedly done since leaving Peking in tears at the age of nine. Fate decreed that I should have my home in a number of utterly diverse and distinctive countries until I finally came to roost in the UK at the end of August 1968.

On my return to Moscow from hospital in London after Easter 1968, my life resumed much the same pattern as it had had the previous two years. At last my arm was out of plaster. It was some months, however, before my hand felt more or less normal and my accident meant 'fini' to my strenuous ballet classes. I went and bid a fond farewell to Mischa and we embraced warmly.

During May we were visited by two lots of cousins and it was with first cousins of mine that I visited Zagorsk. It was to be my last visit to this great monastery and it proved to be a very stressful occasion for me.

My Last Visit to Zagorsk—Spring, 1968

A day out to Zagorsk was always enjoyable, no matter what the season. It was roughly a two-and-a-half-hour drive through attractive woodlands once one was clear of the suburbs of Moscow, and to me it always represented the very quintessence of Russia. For visitors staying with us, it was a must if it fitted in with their timetable and I always liked to accompany them if possible.

My last visit to Zagorsk in the spring of 1968 was with a first cousin of mine and his wife. They were both musical and had a knowledge of pictorial art and appreciation of all things of artistic merit. It would have been lovely to have picnicked on the way but for some unfathomable reason we were forbidden to stop and get out of our car until we had reached our destination. So where should we have lunch? Before entering the monastery, I had discovered that it was possible to have a picnic on the grassy bank below the great

MY LAST VISIT TO ZAGORSK—SPRING, 1968

walls, mostly steep, though there was just one little flattish patch where one could spread a rug and sit and enjoy one's picnic. This is what we did, stopping our car, just before reaching the monastery, enjoying our picnic and then clambering back into the car, so as to make a more formal approach to the great gate and porch rather than just walking round from our picnic. My cousins and I reached Zagorsk around 12.30 on a lovely day.

I had become very familiar with this great monastery and its layout. There was a small museum and small picture gallery with a few excellent items, but they were only opened by special request, so before a projected visit to Zagorsk a call would be put through from the embassy to the office of the monastery to say one was coming and could a guide please take one to the museum and gallery. 'Certainly,' was always the answer. The approximate time of our arrival would be given. This visit to Zagorsk with my cousin was to be a very fraught one for me for I felt from the start that we were there under false assumption. The story of this visit follows.

Our chauffeur, Triatsin, rang a clangy bell and a young man appeared and welcomed us. 'Where is the ambassador?' asked the young man in Russian. I understood the question and alarm bells immediately began ringing in my head. *Gosh, was GWH expected? What's this going to mean?* I asked myself. I was soon to find out, as I hastily concocted a fib. 'The ambassador is extremely sorry, he very much wanted to come, but suddenly there was urgent business he had to attend to, so regrettably he was unable to come.' This in execrable and ungrammatical Russian.

The young man looked disconcerted but said, 'Come this way please, the abbot is waiting to greet you.' He led us into a rather dark room just round the corner of the entrance gates.

The abbot in black cassock with a gold cross on his bosom

was a bearded, silver-haired man probably in his sixties. The young man hastily said something to him, no doubt about the non-appearance of my husband. I repeated the apologies I had made earlier to the young man. The abbot nodded and invited us to sit down and proffered tea and biscuits. We each took one, sipped our tea and I tried to make conversation, but with his limited knowledge of English and my bad Russian, this was very difficult. Very soon the abbot stood up and said: 'Brother XYZ will take you to view our beautiful icons.' We stood up, shook hands and bowed and took our leave. I sighed a sigh of relief and said to my cousin, 'Well, that's all OK, easier than I had feared.'

However, when Brother XYZ, obviously a student monk, instead of turning left and past the large church—the way to the little museum—headed instead across the precincts, towards a substantial building on the far side of the monastery, I thought: *Perhaps there are some special icons over there we have not been shown till now.* We walked past the small Zagorsk church with a little golden dome, past the fenced-in well and one or two small shrines dedicated to holy men. There were open spaces between all these which we had seen thronged with pilgrims one Easter eve, and we had been told that at all festival times, the monastery was always crowded, sometimes for up to three days. I subsequently learned that the large building we were about to enter was the private residence of the Metropolitan, the head of the Zagorsk monastery. There are two other great monasteries in Soviet Russia, each in charge of a Metropolitan, the equivalent of an archbishop. Above them is the Patriarch, the head of the Russian Orthodox Church, whose headquarters are in Moscow. But Zagorsk had the only seminary.

We entered a small hall with a staircase. 'The icons are upstairs,' said Brother XYZ. We followed him up and into the first of three medium-sized rooms, the walls of which were all hung with icons, far more of them than in the little picture

MY LAST VISIT TO ZAGORSK—SPRING, 1968

gallery attached to the museum, so I had been right in what I had surmised.

'These icons are special and have not yet been seen by the public.' Brother XYZ only spoke Russian and he now proceeded to give us a little lecture on a few selected ones. I understood less than half of what he said and I struggled as best I could to translate for my cousins, no doubt inventing a good deal as I went along.

Having viewed the three rooms, Brother XYZ led us back down to the entrance hall and on towards a closed door. This he opened and as he ushered us in he said: 'Before meeting our head, Metropolitan so & so (I have forgotten his name), for luncheon; I thought you would like to come here.' It was a cloakroom with a basin and two separate toilets. We were truly grateful. How very thoughtful of the brother. But luncheon! Alarm bells now rang furiously in my head. We had eaten a substantial picnic lunch not long before. How could we possibly eat again so soon?

Three men stood in line waiting to greet us. Brother XYZ bowed low as he ushered us into the presence. I bowed and my cousins bowed. The Metropolitan stepped forward and proffered his hand. He had obviously been alerted that my husband was not present as he expressed his regrets in hesitant English, apologising for not being fluent. Once again I expressed my husband's deep regrets and the fact that at the last minute he had been withheld from accompanying us.

The Metropolitan was a 5 feet 10 inches tall good-looking dark-haired man with a neat, well-trimmed beard, probably in his mid-fifties. I felt immediately that this was a man with a strong personality. He was very friendly and introduced his two companions to us. All three men wore black cassocks and had crosses dangling from their necks. We were offered small glasses of something liquid, whether bland or alcoholic, I do not recall. Presently the Metropolitan said, 'You must be hungry, let us eat.' My cousins and I exchanged meaningful glances.

The dining hall was quite large. A narrow table had been prepared for us. The Metropolitan sat at the head with us ladies on either side of him. One of his companions sat beside me, the other between my two cousins. What the status of these two men was, I never discovered. The one next to me and opposite my cousin AJ spoke good German and so did AJ, who was never at a loss for words and could always fill a gap in a conversation. The chap opposite me only spoke when spoken to. I have forgotten whether in fact he knew any language other than Russian. Ildica, on the Metropolitan's left, was naturally shy and was feeling as uncomfortable as myself at the prospect of having to eat a second lunch so soon after the first one. I cannot recall anything of our menu except for the ultimate biscuit, but the recollection of that luncheon has left an indelible mark on my mind.

As we sat down, I placed my handbag on my lap and opened it just a little. I spread a Kleenex tissue in such a way as to cover any other contents. As lunch proceeded, helping myself to a minimal amount of each course, I would surreptitiously drop morsels into my open bag, hoping to escape the eye of the Metropolitan and the chap opposite. Whether I was successful or not, I shall never know. At last a cup of tea and some biscuits were handed round. I refused. 'Oh,' said the Metropolitan, 'you must have one of these, they are delicious.' He spoke Russian. He had done so off and on during our meal, having discovered that I knew about as much Russian as he knew English. Reluctantly I took one. It was as hard as a dog biscuit. I managed to chew a piece off, and the rest went into my bag. The plate of biscuits made the round of the table. Finally the plate reached Ildica, and she refused. In a moment of utter wickedness I said, 'You must have one, Ildica, they melt in the mouth!' Ildica took one, and like me had difficulty biting it. We caught each other's eyes

MY LAST VISIT TO ZAGORSK—SPRING, 1968

and spontaneously exploded into irrepressible schoolgirl giggles. Oh, that dreadful moment, trying to control myself. And the Metropolitan? Did he notice? Had he deliberately teased me and was enjoying the joke? I didn't dare look at him and will never know.

How did that visit to Zagorsk end? I remember nothing. Did Brother XYZ escort us back to our car? Did my cousins sightsee the churches? I imagine they did. For me this last visit to the great Monastery of Zagorsk was very stressful.

On my return to Moscow, I at once told my husband about this visit to the monastery. He immediately sent for John Kerr, Simon Hemans' successor as private secretary, and asked him if he could explain why the office of the Zagorsk monastery had been misled into thinking that the British ambassador was planning a visit on the following day. It appears that John had mistakenly thought that a guide to unlock the museum door was more likely to be provided if he said the ambassador wished to come rather than just his wife and two cousins. John was most distressed when he learned the outcome of his untruth. My husband told him that he must now draft a letter of apology in Russian and get it checked by the head of the Russian secretariat before bringing it back for my husband's signature. It was a very unfortunate incident which has remained etched on my mind for ever. It remains one of my most vivid recollections of my Moscow days.

Novgorod, June 1968

Apart from Leningrad, the north of Russia was unknown territory and we very much wanted to visit it. My husband also greatly desired to visit the three Baltic States, Estonia, Latvia and Lithuania, which formed part of the Russian empire in Tsarist days but which had gained their independence in 1918 and were thriving until the Russian armies invaded them in 1940 and they were then incorporated into the USSR as member republics. Not all European countries, nor the USA, had recognised and accepted this annexation. We also had a great desire to visit Karelia, the lake district east of Leningrad so loved by Peter the Great. Apart from the regions, we had also managed to visit a few of the not-too-distant cities of interest from Moscow over long weekends. But within this category there was one important lacuna—the city of Novgorod, which, with Kiev and Vladimir-Suzdal, forms such an important role in the cultural history of Russia. It had suffered badly in the war, its great cathedral of St Sophia largely destroyed by the evacuating German troops and Novgorod's many other lovely churches were equally badly damaged.

Novgorod lies south-east of Leningrad and can be reached by car, by turning east off the Moscow–Leningrad highway about two-thirds of the way from Moscow. As my husband had a week's local leave due to him before retirement at the end of August, we decided to spend it visiting Novgorod and the Baltic States.

There had been no incentive to visit Novgorod earlier in its ruined state but we knew that since the early 1960s the Russians, deeply conscious of their heritage, had begun to resurrect it, so in June Triatsin drove us in our own car first to Novgorod and then on to Leningrad. From here we flew for a day's visit to each of the Baltic states, spending a night each in Tallinn, Riga and Vilnius and then flying directly from Vilnius (Lithuania) back to Moscow. Triatsin meanwhile drove the car back to Moscow, a distance roughly equivalent to driving from London to Edinburgh.

As I have no written record of this trip it has become rather blurred in the mists of time, but reading up about Novgorod, my memory of our day and a half spent there has been refreshed.

NOVGOROD, JUNE 1968

At the end of the war Novogorod was a ruined wreck with its two great cathedrals and numerous other churches all destroyed by the Germans. It was not until the beginning of the sixties that the Russians began to resurrect it, rebuilding the cathedrals and many of the other churches. In the same way as the great palaces along the Gulf of Finland, Novogorod rose new-born like the legendary phoenix. Although in 1968 Novogorod was not yet on the tourist trail, it could now be visited, and we spent a strenuous day and a half tramping from one interesting church to another.

The two great cathedrals built in the eleventh century were famous. The one within the Kremlin on top of the hill dominating the town was pure Byzantine in concept. The other at the bottom of the hill was pure Russian and was to become the prototype for all future Russian churches with a great central dome surrounded by four pepperpot cupolas representing the four evangelists around our Lord.

Novogorod not only gave birth to the design of Russian churches, it was also the spring-head for Russian pictorial art, in particular icon painting. The great master of this genre was Rublev who has attained world renown with his very sensitive and beautiful icon pictures.

Leningrad: The Astoria Restaurant and the Arrival of Fluency

Weary but satisfied with our day and a half of sightseeing in Novgorod, we arrived at the Astoria Hotel in Leningrad in the late afternoon. A shower, a change of clothing, a glass of whisky in our hands, we relaxed in the comfortable chairs of the suite we had been given. Soon after eight we descended to the restaurant which had opened at seven. Hungry, we were looking forward to our evening meal.

We were surprised to find the restaurant submerged in near

obscurity. The oval dance floor at one end was flanked by two rows of parallel deep-shaded standard lamps which just shed a little light on each table beneath them. These were all occupied, as were the tables in the gloom. However, we espied a little posse of tables laid out ready in one corner. Each table had little flag staffs with a national flag attached to it standing on it. There was no British flag, but equally there was no other free table other than one nearby with the detritus of a meal on it.

We firmly sat ourselves down at a table with a Dutch and Danish flag. My husband moved these to an adjoining table which already had a couple of flags on it. We waited. No one approached us. Finally a youngish-looking waitress, carrying a loaded tray, passed us, threw us a glance and barked out, 'The table you are sitting at is reserved.' We took no notice. Having unloaded her tray, as she passed by she repeated herself, and replaced the two flags. When she had gone, my husband picked up the flags a second time and firmly put them back on to the neighbouring table. We waited.

Presently a seedy-looking old waiter came up to us, replaced the flags and asked us to move. 'Where to?' asked my husband. The waiter indicated the table with dirty glass and crockery. 'No, we will not move there,' said my husband firmly. 'You cannot remain here,' riposted the waiter, 'these tables are all reserved for important guests of the hotel.' 'There is no other table properly laid,' said my husband, 'we shall remain here.' 'I am very sorry but these tables are all reserved for a special international delegation. They will be arriving at any moment. You cannot sit here, please move.' 'Fiddlesticks,' said my husband in Russian, his temper thoroughly roused. 'I too am a VIP—very important person—I am the British ambassador and my wife and I are staying at the Astoria Hotel and we want our dinner.'

Never before had I heard his Russian pour out in such a fluent and spontaneous stream.

The waiter looked worried and hurried away. I saw him talking to two females, one dressed in brown, the other a big-bosomed female wearing the usual black skirt and white blouse of authority. We waited patiently. It was now forty-five minutes since we had entered the restaurant.

The seedy waiter now returned, cleared the nearby table of dirty glasses and crockery, spread a clean table cloth and with extreme politeness begged us to move as he was expecting the arrival of the delegates at any minute. He went on to say that he would not be able to attend to us personally, but he would see that we were quickly served. The young waitress was an excellent girl, she would bring us the menu and we would be well looked after. We graciously moved. Smiles and bows all round, and the waitress did immediately bring us the menu. 'What would be quickly available?' we asked. 'Bouillon and boeuf Stroganov' was the reply. 'Right, let's have that, followed by ice cream and bring us a bottle of good Georgian wine.' This was standard Russian fare but the Stroganov could vary a great deal.

I noticed that a foreign couple at a neighbouring table had watched our comedy throughout and gave us an encouraging smile. I doubt that they had understood the interchange between my husband and the waiter. Our meal arrived quite promptly, ahead in fact of the meal ordered some while back by this couple. They began looking alternately at us and at their watches with an expression of slight despair. I felt for them, but happily their meal did presently arrive.

It appeared to be fried steak of some sort. I caught my husband's eye as he gave an amused little tilt of his head in the direction of the couple. I glanced across at them—the gentleman was vainly trying to cut his steak. He sawed this way, he sawed that way. It might have been a lump of stone. Relieved of our own tension, suppressed giggles on our part had to be drowned in wine.

A couple now came along looking for a free table. There

was none, but this couple who were Dutch espied their national flag and sat down at the table we had vacated. The Danish flag they laid flat on the table. To our huge amusement the whole drama repeated itself. The Dutchman was no more inclined to move than my husband had been but he was at great disadvantage, being unable to understand what the seedy old waiter was saying to him. In despair the waiter came to our table and asked my husband if he would very kindly explain to the Dutch couple why they could not remain at that table and there was now a free table elsewhere in the room. Please, please would they move there. My husband obliged and explained to the couple how we had had the same experience. Smiles and bows all round, and the couple moved. The distinguished delegates arrived and were soon served with caviar. But surprisingly the disputed table remained free—a missing couple had not turned up. Before we had finished our meal, a young Russian couple, an ugly gold-toothy young man and his girl, came to sit at that table. They were left in peace.

We spent two nights in Leningrad giving us a final day to visit the last of the great Imperial Palaces to be restored, close to the Gulf of Finland. It was Pavlovsk, built on Catherine the Great's orders by her Scottish architect and garden designer, Charles Cameron, for her unfortunate son, Paul I. Pavlovsk, reminiscent of the style of Adam, the renowned British architect and designer of the eighteenth century, was a handsome building which we admired.

Next morning it was goodbye to Leningrad and we flew off to Estonia for our three-day trip to the Baltic republics.

The Baltic States June 1968

It was a feast day in Tallinn. There was dancing on the streets and many people had donned their national dress. We were met by an Intourist guide, but although it was an enjoyable day. I do not recall seeing anything very memorable. One night here and we flew on to Riga the next morning. Again an Intourist guide showed us around the attractive city and in the afternoon we visited the shores of the Baltic with a lovely expanse of sandy beach. Although it was July, there was a cold nip in the air. The beach was deserted and we did not feel like a swim in the sea.

The following day a short flight brought us to Vilnius. Here the skies were dull and Vilnius the city seemed grey with a Teutonic feel. No Slav influence here, nor indeed had there been any in Riga, but in Lithuania we felt a strong Prussian prevalence and that the yoke of Russian communism weighed heavily on this country. All three Baltic States chafed under Soviet rule, which they had to endure for a further 25 years. After one night we flew back to Moscow. In the meantime, Triatsin had driven our car back from Leningrad.

Karelia, July 1968

Our last expedition in the Soviet Union was undertaken over a weekend in July 1968. It was to Karelia, the northern province of Russia, lake-studded, joined by rivers and streams to the east of Leningrad, a region much loved by Peter the Great. The region had been under the suzerainty of Novgorod. Settlements were established along the shores of a number of lakes. The colonists chopped down trees and brought agriculture to the region. Only a relatively small area was cultivated; otherwise, it is forests that prevail.

Apart from agriculture, the Novgorodians also brought Christianity to the region. A religious community established itself on the island of Kizhi on Lake Onega. There they built ever larger churches to replace ones burnt down in ever-recurring fires. Wood was the only medium available for each and every building, whether house, barn or church, and the amazing fact is that neither nails nor other metal ties were used, such was the skill of their carpentry. The style of church building is reminiscent of that found in Novgorod. A twenty-two-domed Church of the Transfiguration was built in 1714; this amazing construction was followed in 1764 by the building of the nine-domed Church of the Intercession nearby. It was not until a century later that a tall, free-standing campanile was erected between the two churches, thus completing this unique harmony in wood.

In the sixties, the Soviets dismantled a number of timber-built buildings from other parts of Karelia and re-erected them on the island of Kizhi, turning the entire island into a museum. Peter the Great's house from somewhere in the region was dismantled and re-erected at Kolomenskoye, close to Moscow.

For this visit to Karelia we flew to Petrozavodsk, the largest town of the region, and zoomed across lakes in a hydrofoil to Kizhi. We found this whole expedition enthralling.

Day Trips from Moscow

As I sit back and recall those three years I spent in Moscow in the sixties, three pictures spring vividly to mind. They are of day trips undertaken at various times. One was to the great monastery at Rostov-Yaroslav, an excellent oil painting of which hangs on my wall. Grey clouds are drifting across the skies and the winter snows are melting in the great spring thaw. Our view of it was just like that on our first visit, but on our second visit the sun shone and it was later in the year and wild flowers bloomed on the banks of the river. The other two pictures are of day trips to the homes of two of the greatest giants of Russian culture. They were the homes of Tchaikovsky and of Tolstoy.

Klin, where Tchaikovsky took refuge when the stresses of his life weighed heavily upon him, is an unimpressive abode on the Moscow–Leningrad highway, a few miles beyond Zavidova, where the Soviets had set up the holiday compound for the foreign community in Moscow and which is situated on the banks of the mighty Volga. As I recollect, Tchaikovsky's studio/music room was the open hall at the top of the stairs with views of the wide open countryside from its windows. The master's grand piano was there, its top bestrewn with musical scores. Around the wall were glass-fronted low cupboards with more scores in manuscript form, and which also housed a number of musical instruments.

Klin's interest lies in the fact that this is where the great musician composed so many of his greatest works.

Yasnaya-Polyana was an estate of 2,000 acres and had two hundred serfs when Tolstoy inherited it at the age of 19 from his father. The history of Yasnaya-Polyana in the years of Tolstoy's ownership has been well documented. A visit to Tolstoy's home involved a very lengthy drive, some four hours' drive along a main but bumpy road, so it was a very exhausting expedition, but on both occasions that we went there, I found it very fascinating, quite especially on the second occasion, for I was then grappling with reading Tolstoy's *Recollections of a Childhood* in Russian with my Russian teacher, which details the first nine years of his life. It is written in a simple and straightforward style and visiting the home that he loved so passionately brought the book to life.

The country around and about, largely agricultural, but also partly forest land, is attractive and gently hilly. The white house itself, with a verandah, is set against the background of a wooded park in which we enjoyed a walk after a picnic lunch, before the long drive home.

I always regretted that we could not spare the time to

spend a night or two at the small hotel in the village. I would have liked to explore the grounds rather more.

Here end my reminiscences of Russia. There were moments of stress, but there were also many moments of enjoyment during the five years that I spent altogether in that country. They were certainly very educative and perhaps the most interesting years of my life for the many varied experiences that they offered.

Index

Achmanova, Madame 151, 161–3
Afghan Ambassador, Moscow 105–6
AJ (cousin) 260–5
Alps 25–6
Amalia (cook in Moscow) 58–9, 68–70, 71–2, 73, 106–7
Amberd, Armenia 231–2
Anan (panda in Moscow zoo) 176–7
Anglican Church 91–2
Anschluss (1938) 9, 12, 15
anti-Semitism, Nazi Germany 5–6, 8, 9, 12–14
Ararat, Mount 226, 232
Armenia 202, 223, 225–32
Astoria Hotel, Leningrad 65–6, 169, 186–9, 267–70
Attolico, Signor/Signora 16
Austria 6, 9–10, 15, 24, 25–6

Baku, Russia 45–9, 79–80
ballet 96–7, 142, 152–3, 197–8
Baltic States 270–1
Barbirolli, Lady 186–7, 190, 192
Barbirolli, Sir John 146, 163, 184–5, 186–7, 190, 192
Batrick, Mr (chef in British Embassy, Moscow) 122, 145
Batrick, Mrs (maid in British Embassy, Moscow) 122
Batumi, Georgia 221–3
BBC Orchestra 146, 163, 184–95
Bedford, Duke of 174–6

Belgium 12
Beneš, Edvard 10–11
Beria, Lavrenty 146, 148–9
Berlin 2–35
   arrival 1937 2–4
   evacuation of the British Embassy 21–2
   friendship with the Hardenbergs 32–5
   happy recollections of 24–5
   leaving 18–21
   post-war 23–4
   Potsdam Conference 42
Berlin Wall 50, 146, 149
Black Sea 80, 85–6, 212–25
Bled, Yugoslavia 27–8
Bohemia 17
Bolshoi Theatre 96–8, 126, 141, 160, 168, 197–8
Boulez, Pierre 185–7, 189
Bratsk, Siberia 210–11
Braun, Hanni 3
Brezhnev, Mrs 135, 142, 154
Brezhnev, Leonid 150–1, 165, 257–8
British Embassy, Moscow 118–20, 126–7
   dacha 151–2
   garden 179–81
   Queen's birthday 1966 179–82
Britten, Benjamin 178
Brown, George 135–7, 138

275

INDEX

Bukhara, Uzbekistan 238, 239, 240–1, 246–9, 250
Bulgaria 213
Burger, Frau 5–6
Burmese Embassy, Moscow 93–4
Byurakan, Armenia 231–2

Carswell, J. 254
Catherine the Great 169
Catholic Church, Armenia 227–31
Cecilia (child of diplomatic family in Moscow) 77
Cecilia (Intourist guide in Tbilisi) 81–5
Chamberlain, Neville 11–12, 15, 21, 34
Chi-Chi (panda in Moscow zoo) 176–7
Chinese Embassy, in Moscow 93
Churchill, Winston 36–42
Clive, [father]
    Belgium 1938 12
    British Minister in Teheran 44
    death 69, 74–5
    on Hitler 7
    holiday in Le Zoute 1939 20
    KH travelling through Russia 1930 47
    Munich 4
Clive, [mother] 74–5, 173
Clive, Peter 20
Clive, Robert 44–9, 120, 169–73
Cohen, Harriet 177
Cold War 146–7, 155
    Khrushchev 149
    Potsdam Conference 42
    Warsaw Pact 50
Congress Hall, Kremlin 126, 142
    operas in 168
    programme spring 1967 197–8
    visit of National Theatre 1967 166
Conservatoire of Music, Moscow 159–60, 178
'Cresta Run', Moscow 107–8
Cuban crisis 1962 150

Czechoslovakia 9, 10–12, 15, 17–18, 50

Dadya Maroz (Uncle Frost) 62, 109–11
Dalmatia 26–32
dance classes 100, 152–3
Daniel, Yuri 151
Danzig 15
Dolfuss, Engelbert 6, 7
du Pré, Jacqueline 159–60, 178, 184–5, 186
Dubrovnik, Yugoslavia 28–30, 201–2

Echmiadzin, Armenia 227–9
Elena (gardener at the British Embassy, Moscow) 179–80
Elfrieda (maid in Berlin) 19, 21
Elizabeth II, Queen 145, 179–82
Emma (maid in Moscow) 54–5, 68–70, 77, 107
England
    return to 1939 22–3
    visit April 1966 173

Fall, Brian 121, 179, 242, 250
Fall, Delmar 121
Fergana Valley, Uzbekistan 239, 250, 253–5
Finlay, Frank 164–5
Fonteyn, Margot 97
France 10–12
Fulham, Bishop of 196–7

Geckhard, Armenia 229–30
George V, King 119
Georgia
    holiday 1948 62, 78–85, 90
    holiday 1967 23–8, 215–25
Georgian Society 174
German Foreign Office 3–4
Germany 2–42
Gestapo 14
Gore-Booth, Sir Paul 133, 138
Gori 224–5

INDEX

Gorki Park, Moscow 77–8
Gothenburg, Sweden 75
Granitovaya Palace, Kremlin 135–6
Gromyko, Andrei 51, 74, 150
Gromyko, Lyudmila 135, 139, 154
Gross Glockner 25–6
Gur Emir, Samarkand 244–5

Hahn, Kurt 35
Hamlet (guide in Tbilisi) 235–6
Hanna (servant in Berlin) 19, 21
Hardenberg, Count and Countess of 32–5
Harper, Heather 185, 186, 190
Harrison, [daughter] 114, 173
Harrison, [mother-in-law] 16–17, 19–20, 21, 24–5
Harrison, Bruce
  arriving in Leningrad 1947 51–2
  arriving in Moscow 1947 53
  birth 23
  Christmas in Moscow 1947 60–2
  'Cresta Run' in Moscow 108
  learning piano in Moscow 113
  return to England 1949 113
  school in Moscow 77
  visit to Moscow 1967 197–8
Harrison, GW
  Afghan Ambassador 106
  arrest of general in Moscow 112
  arriving in Moscow 1947 53
  Baltic States trip 1968 270–1
  BBC Orchestra 1967 186–8
  Berlin 2, 20–1
  birth of daughter 114
  Bukhara 248
  buying the house in Sussex 16–17
  dinner at Hungarian Embassy, Moscow 92–3
  family's move to Perlovka 1948 73
  Georgia trip 1967 233, 237
  holiday 1938 25–32
  holiday in Georgia 1948 78–85
  journey to Teheran 1960 212
  leaving Berlin 1939 18, 19–20, 21–2
  Leningrad visit 1968 267–70
  Moscow Conference 35–6
  Novgorod 265
  Potsdam Conference 23–4, 42
  Queen's birthday 1966 180–1
  retirement 259–60
  return to Berlin after the war 23–4
  return to Moscow 1965 120–3
  Royal Shakespeare Company 1966 164
  Samarkand 245
  Second World War 23
  Siberia 206–9
  tour of Georgia and Armenia 1967 212–23
  trip to Uzbekistan 1966 238
  visit of Harold Wilson to Moscow 1966 139, 143–4
  visit of sister Sophie 1966 174, 176
  visiting the Diplomatic Dacha 1965 130–1
  Volga Germans 70
  Yalta Conference 36–42
  Zagorsk visit 1968 265
Harrison, John
  Berlin 2, 3, 7, 18, 24–5
  holiday in Le Zoute 1939 20–1
  holiday in Russia 1948 74–6
  school 113–14
  trips to Belgium 1938 12
  wedding 201
Harrison, Michael
  arriving in Leningrad 1947 51–2
  arriving in Moscow 1947 53
  birth 23
  Christmas in Moscow 1947 60–2
  'Cresta Run' in Moscow 108
  learning piano in Moscow 113
  return to England 1949 113
  visit to Moscow 1966 171–3
Harrison, Sophie 173–4, 176–8, 180
Hayter, Sir William 224
Heidelberg 5
Helsinki 76
Hemans, Simon 192, 202

277

INDEX

tour of Armenia and Georgia 1967 222–3, 224, 231, 236, 237
Henderson, Sir Nevile 7, 16
Henlein, Konrad 11
Hermitage, Leningrad 63–4, 188, 191–5
Himmler, Heinrich 14
Hitler, Adolf
  Anschluss 9–10
  Austria 6
  Danzig 15
  degenerate art 7–8
  invasion of Czechoslovakia 17–18
  Nüremberg rally 1937 4
  Putsch 1923 4
  Rhineland 6–7
  Sudeten lands 10–12
Hitler Youth (Hitlerjugend) 3, 5–6
Hopkins, Harry 38
Hulton, Rosemary 100
Hungarian Embassy, Moscow 92–3
Hungary, Russian invasion 146–7, 149

Ildica (wife of KH's cousin) 260–5
Imperial Hotel, Moscow 52–4
Inez (guide in Khiva) 251
International Women's Day 154
Iran 238
Irkutsk, Siberia 202–3, 205–9
Isabel (sister-in-law) 197–9
Isfahan, Iran 244, 247
Istanbul 212, 213

Kachaturian, Aram 158
Karelia 271–2
Kelly, Lady 70, 114, 183–4
Kelly, Sir David 114
Kerr, John 265
KGB 67
Khiva, Uzbekistan 238–9, 240, 249–53
Khrushchev, Nikita 149–50
Kiev 171–2
King's messenger 51, 59, 60–1, 62, 71

Kirkpatrick, Ivan 2
Kitzbühel, Austria 25
Klin 273
Kokand, Uzbekistan 250, 253, 255
Kolomenskoe, Russia 167–8
Kostaki, Mr 53–4, 121–2
Kosygin, Mrs 135, 139, 142, 145
Kosygin, Alexey 139, 142–3, 145, 150, 257–8
Kotor, Yugoslavia 28
Kremlin, Moscow
  British Embassy 118, 119, 120
  changes between 1949 and 1965 125–7
  Congress Hall 126, 142, 166, 168, 197–8
  Dadya Maroz (Uncle Frost) 109–11
  fiftieth anniversary of the Russian Revolution 257–8
  Granitovaya Palace 135–6
  KH and husband arrival in Moscow 1965 122
  November 7th celebrations 1947 102–3
  return to Moscow 1965 123
  visit of Harold Wilson to Moscow 1966 140–2, 143–4
  visit of Michael 1966 172–3
  visiting 1967 198–9
Kristal Nacht (1938) 9, 12–14
Kuskovo, Moscow 175–6
Kutaisi, Georgia 223, 224

Lake Baikal 202–5, 208
Le Zoute, Belgium 20–1
Leach, Hugh 251
Lee, Jenny 163–4
Lenin, Vladimir 199
Leningrad
  Hermitage tour 1967 188, 191–5
  Novgorod trip 1968 267–9
  visit 1947 51–2
  visit 1948 63–7
  visit 1966 168–9

visit of BBC Orchestra 1967
   186–91
visit with sister-in-law 1966 174
Livadia Palace, Yalta 215
London 113–14
Lubianka, Moscow 61, 67
Lupova, Madame 100

Masters, Rev. 197
Mat (brother-in-law) 197–9
Memel (Klaypeda) 15
Mischa (ballet teacher in Moscow) 153
Misha 47, 48
Molatov, Vyacheslav 37, 101, 104–5
Molotova, Madame 104–5
Moody, Mr (butler in British Embassy, Moscow) 122, 164
Moravia 17
Morris, Desmond 177
Moscow 49–51
   1947-1949 49–114
   1965-1968 95, 110, 117–274
   Afghan Ambassador 105–6
   arrest of British military attaché 1947 111–13
   arrival 1947 52–4
   British Embassy 118–20, 126–7
   changes between 1949 and 1965 123–7
   communications 167
   'Cresta Run' 107–8
   cultural activities 1947-1949 94–100
   cultural activities 1965-1968 155–60
   Dadya Maroz (Uncle Frost) 62, 109–11
   dance classes 152–3
   devaluation of the rouble 1947 57–60
   diplomatic calls 1965 128–31
   effect of Second World War 55–6
   encounters with Russians 153–63
   fiftieth anniversary of the Russian Revolution 256–8
   first month 1965 127–31
   first visit to 1930 45
   food shortages 1948 71–2
   leaving 1949 113–14
   leaving 1968 259–60
   leisure time 1965-1968 151–3
   living conditions 160–1
   milking cow 106–7
   move to Perlovka 1948 72–4
   November 7th celebrations 1947 101–5
   outdoor swimming pool 124–5
   Palace of Weddings 199–201
   politics 1965-1968 145–51
   rationing 56–7
   restrictions on travel 147–8
   return to 1948 (July) 75–6
   return to 1948 (Autumn) 77–8
   return to 1965 117–23
   Skatertnay Pereulok 54–5
   social life 1947-1949 91–4
   social life 1965-1968 127–31
   travel restrictions 152, 182
   visit of the BBC Orchestra 1967 184–6
   visit of George Brown 1966 135–7
   visit of Harold Wilson 1966 135, 136, 138–45
   visit of Michael Stewart 1965 133–5
   visit of National Theatre 1967 165–6
   visit of Royal Shakespeare Company 1966 163–5
   visiting the Diplomatic Dacha 1965 130–2, 133
   zoo 176–7
Moscow Conference 35–6
Moscow University 125
Mtskheta, Georgia 85, 233–5
Munich 4–5
Munich Agreement 1938 8–9, 10–12, 15, 34

279

INDEX

Mussolini, Benito 12, 16

Namenjan 253–4
National Socialism
  Anschluss 6, 9–10
  Heidelberg 4
  Kristal Nacht 12–14
  Munich Putsch 1923 4
  Rhineland 6–7
National Theatre 165–6
Nicholas II, Tsar 119
Nijni-Novgorod (Gorki), Russia 148
Nikolaeva, Tatiana 156–8
Novadevichi monastery, Russia 94–5, 111–12
Novgorod 265–7
Nüremberg rally 1937 4
Nureyev, Rudolf 97

Odessa 213–14
Ogden, John 177, 184–6, 189–91
Ogilvie-Forbes family 74–5, 76
Ogilvie-Forbes, Mary 74–5
Olivier, Sir Laurence 146, 163–4
opera 97–8, 197
Orient Hotel, Tbilisi 81
Ostankino, Moscow 175–6
Ovey, Sir Esmond 45, 46, 120

Palace of Weddings, Moscow 199–201
Passanaouri, Georgia 233, 236–7
Pavlovsk, Leningrad 270
Pérègne, Maurice 28–30
Perlovka, Russia 62, 72–4, 76, 151
Peter the Great 170, 172
Peterhof, Leningrad 169, 174, 191
Peterson, Lady 70, 79
  Anglican services 91–2
  arriving back in Moscow 1947 53–4
  Christmas 1947 59
  leaving Moscow 114
Peterson, Sir Maurice 53–4, 79, 101, 114

Plitvice, Yugoslavia 30–1
Plowright, Joan 146, 164–5
Podgorny 150
Poland 15, 18, 38, 41–2
Polish Embassy, Moscow 93
Potsdam Conference 23–4, 42
puppet theatre, Moscow 98–9

R, Miss (Governess in Moscow) 74–5, 77
Ragusa, Yugoslavia 28–30
Rhineland 6–7
Riga 271
Roberts, Frank 54
Roosevelt, FD 36–7, 39–41
Rostov-on-Don 237–8
Rostov-Yaroslav 272
Rostropovich, Mitislav 159–60, 178
Rothnie, Alan 121
Rothnie, Anne 121
Royal Shakespeare Company 146, 163–5
Royal Society for Asian Affairs 238–9

Sakarov, Andrei 148
Samarkand, Uzbekistan 238, 239–40, 241–6, 253
Schuschnigg, Kurt 6, 9–10
Second World War 18–23
  effect on Berlin 23–4
  effect on Russia 55–6
  end of 35–42
Semyonova, Marina 97
Shakhrisabz, Uzbekistan 243
Shostakovich, Dmitri 156–7
Siberia 132, 149, 168, 196–7, 202–11
Simoneski, Andrei 151
Skatertnay Pereulok, Moscow 54–60, 77, 78–9, 105–9
skiing 152, 162–3
Sochi, Georgia 80, 217–21
Soghdia, Uzbekistan 239
Sokolniki, Park, Moscow 78
Sonia (guide in Irkutsk) 206

INDEX

Soviet Union
  see also Leningrad; Moscow
  1947-1949 49–114
  1965-1968 95, 110, 117–274
  Dadya Maroz (Uncle Frost) 62, 109–11
  devaluation of the rouble 1947 57–60
  effect of Second World War 55–6
  first visit to 1930 44–9
  journey to 1947 51–2
  Moscow Conference 35–42
  November 7th celebrations 1947 101–5
  politics 1965-1968 145–51
  terror 1947-1949 67–70
Stalin, Joseph
  contact between Russians and foreigners 50
  death 146, 148–9
  denunciation by Khrushchev 149
  Gori, Georgia 225
  new building 125
  November 7th celebrations 1947 103–4
  Potsdam Conference 42
  puppet theatre 99
  Sochi 80
  social life in Moscow 1947-1949 91
  terror 1930s 72–3
  terror 1947-1949 67–70
  tomb 199
  Volga Germans 68
  Yalta Conference 36, 40–1
Steel, Catherine 2, 18, 24
Steel, Kit 2, 18
Stewart, Mrs 133–5, 140
Stewart, Michael 133–5, 136, 138
Stockholm, Sweden 75–6
Sudeten lands 9, 10–12, 15
Sukhumi, Georgia 222–3
Sussex, England 16–17, 19–20, 22–3
Suzdal, Russia 171–2, 182–4, 199
Svetlana (guide in Khiva) 251–3

Taiga, Siberia 210–11
Tallinn, Estonia 270–1
Tamerlane 239–40, 243–4, 246–7
Tanzanian mission, Moscow 129
Tbilisi, Georgia
  holiday 1948 62, 78–85, 90
  holiday 1967 223, 225–6, 233, 235–6
Tchaikovsky music competition 1966 177–8
Tchaikovsky, Pyotr 273
Teheran 44, 120, 212
Tereshkova, Valentina 154
Thomson, Lord 164–5
Tolstoy 273
Triatsin (chauffeur in Moscow) 182, 202
  Novgorod trip 1968 266
  tour of Armenia and Georgia 1967 225, 230, 231, 237–8
  tour of Baltic States 1968 271
  Zagorsk visit 261
Tshaltuba 223, 224
Tzaritzina, Moscow 61–2, 152
Tzarskoe Selo 169, 174, 191

Ugandan Mission, Moscow 128–9
Ulanova, Galina 97, 198
Ulug Beg 240, 245
United Nations 39
United States, Moscow Conference 35–42
Uzbekistan 238–55

Varna, Bulgaria 213
Versailles Peace Treaty (1918) 6–7, 15
Vishnevskaya, Galina 160
Vladimir, Russia 171–2, 182–4, 199
Volga Germans 67–70
Voronesh 85–90
Vorontsov Palace, Yalta 215–16
Vyshinski, Andrey 37

INDEX

Wallace, Mr (cook in British Embassy, Moscow) 122
Wannsee Yacht Club 19
Warsaw Pact 50
Wellington, Duke of 174–5
Whitelaw, Billie 164–5
Wilson, Sir Duncan 159
Wilson, Elizabeth 159–60, 178
Wilson, Harold 135, 136, 138–45, 168–9
Wilson, Mary 138, 139, 140, 142–4, 168–9
Windsor, Duchess of 20
Windsor, Duke of 20

Wood, Andrew 121–2

Yalta, holiday 1967 215–17
Yalta Conference 36–42
Yaroslav 169–71
Yasnaya-Polyana 273
Yerevan, Armenia 226–7, 231–2
Yugoslavia, holiday 1938 26–32

Zagorsk Monastery, Russia 94–5, 169–70, 171, 260–5
Zaleski, Mr and Mrs 93
Zavidova 130–2, 133, 151, 155

Index prepared by Indexing Specialists (UK) Ltd